ARMAGEDDON

V. BRENT DAVIS

CFI
SPRINGVILLE, UTAH

ISBN: 1-55517-765-4
v.1

Published by CFI,
an imprint of Cedar Fort, Inc.
925 N. Main, Springville, Utah, 84663
www.cedarfort.com

Distributed by:

CEDAR FORT

Cover design by Nicole Williams

Printed in the United States of America
10 9 8 7 6 5 4 3 2 1

Printed on acid-free paper.

ARMAGEDDON

B. Davis

Dedication

To Versal, Thelma, and LaVel.

CONTENTS

Acknowledgments

I am indebted to my parents, Versal L. and Thelma H. Davis, both deceased, who were staunch Latter-day Saints. As such, they encouraged me not only to study the scriptures but also to remain open-minded about all else as well.

Likewise, I profited greatly from long discussions with my older brother, Clint Davis, also deceased. A staunch member of the Church and a geologist, he and I spent long hours in the coal/methane fields of Wyoming discussing the "deep" things of the Church.

Similarly, my appreciation goes to my son-in-law, Mark Ritchie, professor of biology at Syracuse University, New York. A recent convert to the Church and a true scientist, he has a keen eye and inquisitive mind when studying scriptural and scientific events. His insight into such things during our discussions has helped me bolster and often realign my thinking about religion and science, although we do not necessarily agree on everything.

Of course, my wife, Inge S. Davis, also deserves substantial credit in this endeavor. As an intelligent and sharp critic of my ideas, she has helped me remain focused. She has encouraged my writing, even when it was obviously bad.

I am also indebted to Mark Dalby of Parker, Colorado. His website, ldslastdays.com, saved me hundreds of hours of research in preparing background for this book. He has provided a well-organized and comprehensive review of nearly every scripture and authoritative quote regarding the last days. By far, his website is *the* place to go for those who wish to further research my discussions throughout this book.

And finally, many thanks to the staff of Cedar Fort, who worked efficiently and expertly on my writing. They took off many of the rough edges, did a great deal of polishing, and proved that they often knew more about what I was writing than I did.

1

The Last Days—A Contemporary Overview

Think ye that humanity shall forever endure on the earth?
—Nostradamus

In most world religions throughout the last two millennia, and even before that, three fundamental themes or core beliefs have prevailed. The first, of course, is belief in a supreme being, who has prescribed for his followers a set of rules by which they should live. These rules have variously been known as commandments, scriptural dictates, and heavenly advice and have come through direct communication from the supreme being as revelations, personal inspiration, or simply human conscience.

The second is belief in an afterlife once we leave our earthly existence. Depending on the religion, this is usually expected to be a time of infinite duration, or eternity, and is characterized as a place of peace, plenty, and release from mortal cares. Except for the idea of reincarnation, which is believed to involve living on the earth more than once, and in more than one life form, we have come to know this afterlife as heaven, paradise, nirvana, and so forth.

The third belief is that at some time in the future, after we have lived in accordance with the rules dictated by the supreme being, an end will come. Then, mortality will cease to exist and all humanity will enter the afterlife. With our entrance into the third millennium after Christ, much of the Christian world has focused more and more on this third core belief—that the end of time is at hand and that we must prepare for what will soon transpire.

Although a large part of humanity adheres to one kind of religion or another, even agnostics and atheists have long agreed with believers that a distinct pattern is apparent in the history of humanity, one that should be instructive to us in our day. All great civilizations, from those of ancient Babylon to Macedonia, Egypt, Greece, and Rome, have risen and all, likewise, have fallen. They each rose to great power and then fell into comparative insignificance, each to be eventually replaced by the rise and fall of another power.

It is not our intent here to dissect the history of these bygone civilizations or to discuss what made them rise and fall. We are concerned with far greater things—the fall not only of individual nations but of humanity as a whole.

As noted above, most major world religions forecast the day when humanity may no longer exist on this earth. They may not agree on when or how this will be accomplished, but they do agree that this worldwide event will be far greater than the simple rise and fall of a single nation or world power.

Christians worldwide are increasingly speculating on, preparing for, and in many cases dreading the end of time prophesied in the Bible. One hears more and more religious and secular commentary on "the Millennium," the last days, Judgment Day, Armageddon, the Apocalypse, signs of the times, and the like. Admittedly, thousands of biblical scholars and theologians have written extensively on these subjects for centuries. Even our popular media is becoming saturated with these themes, although from a usually religiously dubious point of view. In other words, sensationalism sells. Witness the fact that armageddonbooks.com on the internet has available "750 prophecy offerings covering the full range of prophetic thought" and links to more than 275 prophecy-oriented websites. Similarly, the very successful *Left Behind* series of books by Tim LaHaye and Jerry Jenkins have topped 60 million in sales.

Our intent here, then, is to look at scriptural prophecy, old and new, and relate it to modern events and those still to come, incorporating as much knowledge as we can from history and the social and physical sciences.

Whether one regards the scriptures as a good set of rules by which to live one's life or as infallible word-for-word admonitions of God, their reference to the end of man's time on the earth is of concern to all, whether they are Christians or not.

The Bible—and the Old Testament in particular—provides us with a broad overview of relations between God and his people historically and especially of their repeated falling away from the Church and the ultimate consequences of doing so. The pattern we see in those scriptures is similar to what we can expect to see in our time—the last days—and the prophets have provided us with a remarkable amount of information concerning those coming events. This is also true of the Book of Mormon and latter-day scriptures, all of which corroborate what the biblical prophets foresaw and provide us with additional detail as well. All these scriptures combined show us a pattern of prophecies being fulfilled when God's wrath was poured out upon earlier peoples and nations who failed to follow his admonitions.

Familiar examples to most theologians and students of the scriptures are the destruction of ancient Babylon, the story of Noah's ark, the plagues and curses visited upon ancient Egypt to effect the release of the children of Israel from bondage (not to mention the destruction of the Egyptian army in the Red Sea), the destruction of Sodom and Gomorrah, the destruction of Jerusalem by the Babylonians and to LDS scholars, the destruction of the Jaredite and Nephite nations.

To set the stage for how such events in scriptural history may be of concern to us today, we should examine two of the above occurrences, one of which took place on a relatively local scale while the other entailed the destruction of nearly all humanity. They are stories we have heard since we were children, but they form part of a far larger picture that will be important in our discussion later on. So let's look at them a little more closely.

Sodom and Gomorrah

One bright spot in scriptural history is the account of the city of Enoch, also known as the city of Zion, which was taken up bodily into heaven because of the righteousness of its inhabitants (Moses 7:69). On the other hand, as recounted by Moses in Genesis, the Lord was displeased with the unrighteousness of the inhabitants of Sodom and Gomorrah. Despite Abraham's repeated pleas to the Lord that there might be a few righteous believers therein who could justify the cities' being spared their threatened destruction, only one family, that of Lot, remained steadfast in following God's commandments. Consequently, they were advised by the Lord to leave forthwith "into the mount" to avoid the results of his wrath.

What were the residents of Sodom and Gomorrah doing that so displeased God? Not much of anything that people nowadays aren't doing. They not only rejected his commandments but rejected his messengers as well. Prior to their destruction, for example, two angels—God's messengers who had taken up lodging with the family of Lot—were sought by the townspeople of Sodom, apparently to be humiliated by being sexually assaulted. It seems that the people's attempted persecution of God's messengers in this manner, however, was the last straw, for God ordered Lot and his family to leave the city immediately thereafter.

> The Lord rained upon Sodom and upon Gomorrah brimstone and fire from the Lord out of heaven; And he overthrew those cities, and all the plain, and all the inhabitants of the cities, and that which grew upon the ground. . . . And he [Abraham] looked toward Sodom and Gomorrah, and toward all the land of the plain, and beheld, and, lo, the smoke of the country went up as the smoke of a furnace. (Genesis 19:24–25, 28)

Moses' account of the fate of Sodom and Gomorrah is instructive in several respects.

First, the people were almost universally godless and paid little attention to God's laws, even to the point of persecuting his angelic messengers. A modern-day parallel would undoubtedly occur if a heavenly messenger or even Jesus Christ himself were to appear among us today. Our "enlightened" culture has become so steeped in technological marvels, video games, space flight, spectacular movies, and the like that a purported heavenly visitation would almost certainly meet with widespread cynicism and journalistic spin.

Although the destruction of Sodom and Gomorrah from on high was a localized event, as opposed to a destruction of all humanity, it was nevertheless complete. Note that not only were the two cities destroyed, but the surrounding plain upon which they were located was scorched as well. Even "that which grew upon the ground" was destroyed. In other words, all life was annihilated throughout the surrounding area.

We can now only speculate on how this destruction was accomplished. We have been raised to regard such occurrences as miracles. For example, the scriptures tell us that the destruction resulted from "brimstone and fire from the Lord out of heaven," and that "*he* overthrew those cities."

Many efforts have been made over the past two centuries by scholars, geologists, and historians to find the original locations of Sodom and Gomorrah and to explain what happened to them in order to determine if these events even took place at all. Were they simply folktales or legends, as many cynics contend? If one considers that to be the case, it is interesting to note that certain recent research indicates that the doomed cities did in fact exist. Traces of them may now be found under the southernmost portion of the Dead Sea. Even more interesting is the fact that that same area has a history of geological activity in biblical times, including earthquakes and volcanism.[1]

Noah's Ark

Because the account of Noah, his ark, and the watery destruction of nearly all humanity is well known to Christians and non-Christians alike, there is little point in discussing it here in detail. Suffice to say that this episode in world history took place many generations after Adam but before the destruction of Sodom and Gomorrah.

As was noted in the story of Sodom and Gomorrah, however, the condition of humanity at the time of Noah was abhorrent to God but on a much larger or universal scale:

> God saw that the wickedness of man was great in the earth, and that every imagination of the thoughts of his heart was only evil continually. And it repented the Lord that he had made man on the earth, and it grieved him at his heart. And the Lord said, I will destroy man whom I have created from the face of the earth; both man, and beast, and the creeping thing,

> and the fowls of the air; for it repententh me that I have made them. (Genesis 6:5–7)

God was dismayed at the violence he saw and the watery destruction he caused is well known in the Judeo-Christian tradition. After warning Noah to build an ark in preparation for the flood to come, he caused it to rain forty days and forty nights. As a result, all land disappeared under a vast, worldwide flood, which the scriptures tell us covered even the mountains. All life ceased to exist, with the exception of Noah, his family, and the creatures he had taken with him into the ark. The scriptures tell us further that the waters prevailed 150 days before dry land appeared again and that the family of Noah and the animals saved by the ark disembarked to begin the process of repopulating the earth.

Although the Bible makes it clear that the Flood was worldwide and that every living thing on the earth perished, modern cynics and scholars suspect that this deluge may have been much more limited in extent, if it occurred at all. Nevertheless, moviegoers may simply recall Kevin Costner's *Waterworld* to visualize how such a vast flood may have occurred.

That enormous event, which took place around 2400 B.C., did nevertheless apparently happen, as archaeologists and geologists in our day have found traces of what is believed to have been an enormous layer of mud in Middle Eastern excavations.[2] More important, however, whether one wants to accept the biblical account or not, is that God is fully prepared to put up with the waywardness of humanity for only so long. As with the great Flood and the cities of Sodom and Gomorrah, he will tolerate man's ungodly ways only until he runs out of patience and determines that there will be no further probation for his children.

There is, however, a major difference between God's former destruction of humanity and the destruction that is to occur in the last days. As will be seen in the following pages, man is absolutely no different today in straying from God's commandments than at any other time in history. But the destruction of the last days is to be the conclusion of all God's works here on the earth. Thereafter, there will be no more mortal existence or renewal of man's life here on the earth as we know it. Instead, the earth will be wiped clean permanently. That being the case, and because of the enormous number of people now on the earth—many more than ever before—the destruction of the last days will be more complete and violent than we might imagine.

A Broad View of That to Come

It is common knowledge among those who study the scriptures even superficially that they are often subject to many different interpretations, which is a topic we will be discussing shortly. Nevertheless, the hundreds of scriptures relating to the events of the last days and the Second Coming of the Messiah can't be ignored. The preponderance of such prophecies points to only one thing—that we are indeed in the last days and that the Second Coming of Christ will, in fact, occur soon. On this, both Judaism and Christianity agree, except that the former regard his impending coming as his first and only appearance on the earth.

Of course, there are many people who will ignore or laugh off such warnings as fables or vague mysteries. And then there will be many who will go to the other extreme and stockpile food, fuel, and weapons, preparing to stave off the inevitable panic and pandemonium they expect during the few years we have left.

Whichever is the case, the words of the prophets can't be ignored but must be seriously considered. For those who fail to do so, and who, in fact, find such "rantings" ludicrous, we must simply recall the words of another latter-day religious leader who said that the stupidity of an act or belief doesn't change because millions of people are doing it. This apt statement may well apply to many of the things we find in vogue in our modern world, things that are, nevertheless, contrary to the expressed scriptural wishes of God.

To reverse this statement, then, we can also say that even though millions of people fail to do the right thing, it is still the right thing! As the end approaches, it is well to keep in mind that the latter days may perhaps span some time as all the events prophesied in the scriptures won't happen all at once. Nevertheless, the scriptures have given us some clues as to what to expect beforehand. We must, at this point, keep in mind two things that will be discussed shortly.

First is that humanity, despite its perceived sophistication, has almost universally rejected God in both the Judaic and the Christian sense. And second, there is no handy timetable we can place next to our calendars to determine exactly what is going to happen or when it will occur. Doomsday cults, Jean Dixon, Nostradamus, and the supermarket tabloids notwithstanding, no one knows what God's timetable for the last days is. As Jesus said two thousand years ago, "But of that day and hour knoweth no man, no, not the angels of heaven, but my Father only" (Matthew 24:36).

That being the case, many of us turn occasionally to the scriptures to try to determine when and what the ultimate fate of humanity will be. Is it coming right away, or during the lifetimes of our children or grandchildren, or, hopefully, in a thousand years when we don't have to worry about it? Are the biblical prophecies describing, however vaguely, the end of the world to be believed, or are they merely fables written long ago by old senile religious fanatics? Are accounts of natural disasters, of which we hear so often nowadays, increasing in destructiveness and frequency, thus portending the last days, or are they simply a reflection of our inundation by an ever more efficient news media to sell more newspapers or television time? As millions of Christians and Jews and many religionists worldwide turn to the holy writ to try to make sense of such questions, let us consider what the Savior himself had to say.

Two thousand years ago, the disciples of Jesus asked about the last days and what man could expect:

> Tell us, when shall these things be? And what shall be the sign of thy coming, and of the end of the world? And Jesus answered and said unto them, Take heed that no man deceive you. For many shall come in my name, saying, I am Christ; and shall deceive many. And ye shall hear of wars and rumours of wars: see that ye be not troubled: for all these things must come to pass, but the end is not yet. For nation shall rise against nation, and kingdom against kingdom: and there shall be famines, and pestilences, and earthquakes, in divers places. . . .
>
> And then shall many be offended, and shall betray one another, and shall hate one another. . . . And many false prophets shall rise, and shall deceive many. And

> because iniquity shall abound, the love of many shall wax cold. . . . For then shall be great tribulation, such as was not since the beginning of the world to this time, no, nor ever shall be. And except those days should be shortened, there should no flesh be saved: but for the elect's sake those days shall be shortened.
>
> Then if any man shall say unto you, Lo, here is Christ, or there; believe it not. For there shall arise false Christs, and false prophets, and shall shew great signs and wonders; insomuch that, if it were possible, they shall deceive the very elect. . . .
>
> Immediately after the tribulation of those days shall the sun be darkened, and the moon shall not give her light, and the stars shall fall from heaven, and the powers of the heavens shall be shaken: And then shall appear the sign of the Son of man in heaven: . . . and they shall see the Son of man coming in the clouds of heaven with power and great glory. (Matthew 24:3–7, 10–12, 21–24, 29–30)

Jesus then went on to say that humanity won't be ready for his coming, comparing their unpreparedness to that of the people in Noah's day: "Before the flood they were eating and drinking . . . and knew not until the flood came, and took them all away" (Matthew 24:38–39).

There are dozens of similar references to the last days found throughout the holy scriptures, which we will examine shortly. See, for example, Isaiah 28:22; Ezekiel 38; Joel 2:30; Malachi 4:1; Matthew 13:40; and 2 Peter 3:10. And, of course, some of the most well-known and controversial scriptures relating to the last days are found in the book of Revelation, the last book of the Bible, which we will also examine.

Because Jesus, in his statement above, referred to many hallmarks of that which is to come, such as the emergence of false Christs and false prophets, wars, famines, pestilences, earthquakes, and the like, his prophecy is undoubtedly the clearest, most comprehensive, and most succinct concerning what we can expect to occur in the last days. His comments are more than generalities and describe events that will be easily recognizable when they occur.

Some who have studied these things will contend that many of these events have already occurred, are now occurring, or are about to occur in the near future. Others will say that such things have been commonplace as long as man has been on the earth, so what else is new? There have always been wars, rumors of wars, earthquakes, floods, volcanoes, and the like, any of which could herald the last days, as the scriptures tell us. Likewise, we certainly have plenty of preachers, most of whom could well fall under the designation of false prophets, trying to lead us astray. And they are very successful, given the number of gullible people who follow them, again as the scriptures foretold. Are they also a sign of the end?

The Nature of Prophecies

Like the instruction manuals that come with many of our modern appliances and gadgets, the scriptures are not always clear, at least not to us. This is because nearly all the prophets, from ancient times through the days of our own ancestors, spoke and wrote in a variety of foreign languages, some of which are now no longer in existence; or they phrased their prophecies according to assumptions, objects, and behaviors common to their own cultures and traditions. Don't forget, even Jesus and his apostles spoke and wrote in Aramaic or Greek, and Jesus' use of parables during his ministry is well known. Furthermore, these men were raised in a rigid Jewish culture with all its traditions and biases. And, as if that weren't enough, they lived in a world dominated by Rome, which also had a marked impact on their culture and times.

Much the same can be said of Old Testament prophets, all of whom were bound by Israelite tradition and the Mosaic law. Even our own immediate ancestors, the founders and followers of the restored Church in the 1800s, were members of a different society and culture than that in which we now live. Certainly most of them spoke English and grew up largely in the early United States of America (although the early Church admittedly attracted many foreigners from Europe), but they were an agrarian society and lacked the modern lifestyle we now enjoy with all its conveniences, including our educational institutions, our entertainment, and so forth. That is not to say that all these things have been for our betterment, as we shall later see, but our pioneer forefathers had no means to foresee how their society would change into that in which we now live. This fact is reflected in many of the prophecies we read in latter-day scriptures. For example, a cursory reading of the Doctrine and Covenants reveals many words and expressions that are little used today, or at least sound strange to our modern ears, as this verse illustrates:

> Stand, therefore, having your loins girt about with truth, having on the breastplate of righteousness, and your feet shod with the preparation of the gospel of peace, which I have sent mine angels to commit unto you. (D&C 27:16)

This by no means indicates that the messages in such scriptures are unimportant. It simply illustrates a manner of speech that to us is stilted and awkward, substantially different than that which we use today.

If we compare this, then, with the cultural and speech pattern differences found in the book of Revelation, we begin to see why there are so many different interpretations of various scriptures and prophecies. In reading the scriptures, we must therefore be constantly aware of the times and cultures in which they were spoken and written. Of course, many of them were also addressed to us in our day, so interpreting them correctly is that much more important.

As noted above, the ancient prophets, as well as Jesus, often resorted to parables to deliver their messages. This was a common practice in the Israelite or Jewish culture and is similar to our use of analogous speech today. We frequently use symbolism or draw parallels (or analogies) in order to make a point. In other words, we speak of something that applies to something else. A good example comes from Jesus himself:

> Therefore whosoever heareth these sayings of mine, and doeth them, I will liken him unto a wise man, which built his house upon a rock: And the rain descended, and the floods came, and the winds blew,

> and beat upon that house; and it fell not: for it was founded upon a rock.
>
> And every one that heareth these sayings of mine, and doeth them not, shall be likened unto a foolish man, which built his house upon the sand: And the rain descended, and the floods came, and the winds blew, and beat upon that house; and it fell: and great was the fall of it. (Matthew 7:24–27)

The point of this parable, or analogy, is the importance of hearing *and doing* the word of God. The person who does so, the wise man, can withstand the ways of the world, whereas the foolish man who does not will succumb to temptation and fall by the wayside.

In this same respect, God frequently hid his messages in the scriptures. Instead of speaking clearly, as we would prefer, he expects us, his children for whom the scriptures were intended, to study them and pray about them so that we can decipher their true meaning. This requires faith, diligence, and effort on our part, which is what God intended.

It is no wonder, then, that a large part of our culture today so totally misunderstands the words of God. To them, the scriptures are so much gobbledygook—confusing and contradictory to our common sense and modern understanding. Those today and in the past who have regarded the scriptures as such make no real effort to understand them and therefore fail to see their value. They lack the faith, diligence, and effort that God expects of his children. As the Apostle Paul said, "But the natural man receiveth not the things of the Spirit of God: for they are foolishness unto him: neither can he know them, because they are spiritually discerned" (1 Corinthians 2:14). Paul furthermore said of men in the last days that they would be "ever learning, and never able to come to the knowledge of the truth" (2 Timothy 3:7).

In reviewing prophecies, particularly those of the Bible and the Book of Mormon, it is also important to keep in mind that not all such prophecies were necessarily addressed to us. Some were, instead, addressed to a specific people or period of time, even as many scriptures in the modern Doctrine and Covenants were directed toward specific persons in the early days of the restored Church. Unfortunately, the biblical prophecies are not always clear in this respect.

Examples are the Old Testament prophecies regarding the building of the Temple of Solomon in Jerusalem, or the impending captivity and dispersion of the Israelites (or Jews). The temple in Jerusalem was destroyed and rebuilt more than once and is prophesied to be rebuilt again in the last days. Which prophecies apply to which rebuilding are sometimes difficult to ascertain. Likewise, the Israelites were captives in Egypt at the time of Moses and were later dispersed from the Holy Land and taken captive into Babylon.

In studying the scriptures, and particularly those prophesying of the last days, it is required that we study each scripture closely. First, what is it really saying? Second, to whom is it addressed? And third, we must examine its meaning carefully to determine how it applies to us—asking, for example, Is it talking to me or to the Church as a whole? Or is it intended for a totally separate group of people? In our discussion of scriptures relating to the latter days, which follows, this is the analytical reasoning we will use.

Fortunately, we also have the aid of latter-day prophets to help us along. Our latter-day church leaders have been able to provide a great deal of insight into what the (often confusing) ancient prophets were telling us. A good example is in interpreting the book of Revelation, a book aimed largely at the last days and which at the same time comprises some of the most misunderstood writing in the Bible. Latter-day insight and revelations from our modern prophets now shed a great deal of light on what John and the other ancient prophets were trying to tell us. For these reasons, we will later spend considerable time on what John the Revelator had to say.

One thing that is interesting, when studying the scriptures describing the last days, is that, although many of them are unclear to us, lacking specifics, others are remarkably clear in telling us what we can expect. A number of clearly described events must take place before the return of Christ to the earth. Not only have the prophets, old and new, given us much information, but some of those prophesied events will apparently occur in almost sequential order. This was implied by the words of Jesus earlier in this chapter when he spoke of wars, rumors of wars, and false christs, after which he said, "but the end is not yet" (Matthew 24:6). He then went on to prophesy that people would contend "nation . . . against nation, and kingdom against kingdom," and of "famines, and pestilences, and earthquakes in divers places" (Matthew 24:7). He then said that "*after* the tribulation of those days shall the sun be darkened, and the moon shall not give her light, and the stars shall fall from heaven, and the powers of the heavens shall be shaken" (Matthew 24:29). Only after all these events, he concluded, would he come.

Thus we can see that a series of events must occur up to and including the tribulation,[3] and then great events will happen in the heavens, and only then will he make his return. The only thing that Jesus failed to provide us with was a handy timetable or calendar of when all this will happen. However, much of this same sequential pattern can be found in other such prophecies of the last days, as stressed by Wilford Woodruff:

> He [Jesus] never will come until the revelations of God are fulfilled and a people are prepared for his coming. He will never come until the Jews are gathered home and have rebuilt their temple and city, and the Gentiles have gone up there to battle against them. He will never come until his Saints have built up Zion and have fulfilled the revelations which have been spoken concerning it. He will never come until the Gentiles throughout the whole Christian world have been warned by the inspired elders of Israel.[4]

Therefore, if we study such prophecies and pay attention to what is going on in the world around us, we should be able to connect the dots and see what is happening and what is going to happen. That will be our discussion in the pages to come.

Secular Prophets and Doomsday

Because the end of one's mortal life is of great concern to each of us, the end of man's time on the earth takes on added significance. For that reason, theologians and laymen alike have been studying doomsday scriptures for centuries. Also known as "signs of the times," such topics have resulted in literally hundreds of books that often agree little on what will happen before and during doomsday. Many conclude pessimistically that man will undoubtedly annihilate himself and that will be that—no heaven, no hell, no afterlife. On the other extreme, the optimists contend that humanity—most with little or no effort on their part—will be "caught up" to the returning Jesus—known as the "rapture" among certain Protestant denominations—and all will be well. To many of those caught up to meet Jesus, even judgment day, spoken of often in the scriptures, will be of little consequence.

Because of this universal interest in last days' events, a lucrative market has developed, especially in the last few decades, for would-be prophets, writers, religious leaders, journalists, philosophers, and even celebrities, to pontificate on the signs of the times. And much of this pontification borders on tabloid journalism and sensationalistic "religious" showmanship. Our modern tabloid media, including much otherwise respectable television programming, is often replete with even the most outlandish persons claiming prophetic powers. Anticipating just such spectacles, President Harold B. Lee issued the following words of warning several decades ago:

> There are among us many loose writings predicting the calamities which are about to overtake us. Some of these have been publicized as though they were necessary to wake up the world to the horrors about to overtake us. Many of these are from sources upon which there cannot be unquestioned reliance.[5]

With President Lee's words in mind, let us consider Thomas Malthus, who was not a prophet but a late-eighteenth-century economist. He proposed a number of gloomy ideas regarding the destiny of humanity, many of which are still parroted by modern day prognosticators. Summarized briefly, he contended that populations would always be limited by war, famine, and pestilence. In other words, as populations grew to unwieldy proportions, they would eventually again be reduced by war, famine, or disease.[6]

Despite these Malthusian limits, we now have a rapidly expanding human population, exponentially growing, which will soon surpass six billion individuals here on our little planet. Does this mean that the dire warnings of Malthus will be more applicable to us in the new millennium? With such warnings in mind, let us consider that we are rapidly approaching a point at which our planet can no longer support unbridled population growth. (Around eight billion human beings is the most the earth can support, given our present rates of resource use.) Our numbers will reach that figure probably between the years 2060 and 2095, despite recent population slowdowns in many countries.

In some respects, Malthus's contentions appear to have validity, which has provided fodder for modern sociologists, environmentalists, political movements, and doomsdayers. The best example of these neo-Malthusians is Paul Ehrlich, author of *The Population Bomb,* published in 1968, which instantly became a best seller and stirred up debate nationwide. Ehrlich, then a Stanford entomologist, contended that because of unbridled population growth, humanity, due to our earth's finite resources, was inevitably heading into an imminent period of mass starvation and misery. He said, "The battle to feed all of humanity is over. In the 1970s, the world will undergo famines—hundreds of millions of people are going to starve to death in spite of any crash programs embarked on now."[7]

Then, in 1970, Ehrlich postponed the date of the great die-off to between 1980 and 1989, when 65 million Americans and 4 billion people of other nations would die of starvation.[8] When that failed to happen, he pushed the date of the crisis still later by asserting, "One thing seems safe to predict: starvation and epidemic disease will raise the death rates over most of the planet near the beginning of the twenty-first century."[9]

Unfortunately for him, Ehrlich's dire predictions failed to materialize during the timetable he proposed. This was because he failed to take humanity's ingenuity into account. As our population has grown, we have simultaneously been able to increase our planet's food production at an even greater rate through improved agricultural methods, development of more productive food species, and better controls over weeds, plant diseases, and insects. As a result, malnutrition and starvation are decreasing worldwide and our fellow humans in even the less-developed countries are eating better now than ever before in history. Certainly, food shortages remain a chronic problem in many parts of the world, but they don't approach the apocalyptic disasters predicted by either Ehrlich or Malthus.

Nevertheless, dire Malthusian thought remains strong in certain sectors of our society. We find this in the literature of Lester Brown of the Worldwatch Institute; the Paddock Brothers, authors of *Famine 1975*; the Club of Rome, a group of politicians, businessmen, and high international bureaucrats; and others.[10]

Preceding Malthus, and of perhaps more renown today than in his own time, was Michel Nostradamus, whose gloomy prophecies about the last days seem now to be in vogue. His predictions are controversial and are framed in the form of quatrains (four lines of verse, similar to poetry).

Nostradamus was a sixteenth-century French physician and astrologer who wrote prodigiously (he wrote 942 quatrains). His quatrains, in French, were characterized by their obscure meanings, the result being that they are prone to wide interpretation. Consequently, his believers (of which there are still many) are able to find fulfillment of his prophecies only *after* the fact. On the other hand, his critics find them to be ludicrous gibberish. For example, one of his prophecies that, according to his disciples, was apparently fulfilled, was,

> The year 1999 seven months
> From the sky will come the great King of Terror
> To resuscitate the great king of the Mongols
> Before and after Mars reigns by good luck.

Nobody had a clue what this prophecy referred to until 1999 when John F. Kennedy Jr. and two others were killed in an airplane crash. Tragic as this incident was, Nostradamus's adherents immediately pointed to it as fulfillment of the above prophecy. Skeptics, however, could see no such fulfillment in his obfuscated writing, while still other Nostradamus believers felt that the same prophecy perhaps referred instead to a solar eclipse in the same year or the crash of a space probe to the earth, which didn't happen.

Still other believers contend that in others of his quatrains Nostradamus prophesied not only the 1986 explosion of the space shuttle *Challenger* but the invention of bombs, rockets, submarines, airplanes, the rise of Adolf Hitler, major wars, and other events of the last days. Skeptics again discount all this as they claim that anything can be read into Nostradamus' nebulous writings.[11]

America has its own prophets too and some of them are quite

recent. Perhaps one of the best known was Edward Cayce, a reputed forerunner of the recent New Age movement. Popularized by the media as "the American Prophet," Cayce was born in Kentucky in 1877 and went through a normal childhood, although he was characterized as accident-prone, having once got a nail stuck in his head.

Growing up, he became a photographer, married, moved around looking for success, and met with the usual difficulties in seeking his fortune. That is, until he became convinced of his mystical gifts and medical intuitions. After that, his psychic career took off with hundreds of claimed near-death and out-of-body experiences, many involving spirit or otherworldly personages.

His adherents claimed that, although he had had no medical training, he could diagnose ailments from great distances without ever seeing the patient. He developed a reputation for this "gift" as well as for his contacts with spirits and others who had passed on. His diagnoses were made while in a trance, during which he would receive medical advice from a spiritual "source," which was then passed on to the patient (often absent) or his physician, including needed prescriptions.

Cayce, his renown on the rise from widespread media attention, claimed to consort with a wide range of contemporary celebrities, including Thomas Edison, Woodrow Wilson, Charles Lindbergh, Ernest Hemingway, Amelia Earhart, and an equally great number of people who were no longer alive. After acquiring a wide following of believers, of whom there are many to this day, as well as a sizeable fortune by using his "gifts," Cayce passed on in the mid-1950s to join his spiritual counterparts.

His detractors, of course, were many. They felt that much of his success could be attributed, not to his "gifts" but to his penchant for self-promotion, the sycophantic hype accorded him by the sensation-oriented media, and his circle of celebrity friends. Many questioned his in-absentia diagnoses and their accompanying prescriptions, many of which required the use of somewhat outlandish cures, some of which would certainly not be prescribed by a normal physician. His actual success rate was anybody's guess.

Another more recent American "prophet"—a label that was attached to her by the media, not by herself—was Jean Dixon. Born in 1918, she was an astrologer and alleged psychic who was notorious for her hundreds of prophecies, one of which first vaulted her into national prominence by the ever-gullible media in 1956. That prophecy was a nebulous prediction about the assassination or death in office of President John F. Kennedy. In the crescendo of hype following such a famous and apparently accurate prediction, the same media overlooked the fact that Dixon had also predicted on two previous and separate occasions that Richard Nixon would win the presidency over John F. Kennedy.

Nevertheless, before long Dixon became a mainstay of publications that promoted sensational though not necessarily accurate, news, psychic reportings, and the like—essentially supermarket tabloids. At the same time, she became a celebrity herself, becoming known as the psychic to the stars. Throughout her long career (she died in 1997) Dixon prophesied regularly for such publications and her name became almost a household word throughout much of the country.

Even now there are many people who refer to her as a true prophet, although she herself never made any pretense of religious leanings in her psychic work. She also had many detractors, skeptics who relished pointing out the fact that the media provided her with an ideal stage on which to present only her successful work, ignoring the fact that among her hundreds of prophecies there were many that turned out to be unreliable, confusing, or outright wrong. Depending on whether a person was a Dixon supporter or skeptic, her success rate ranged anywhere from 2 to 100 percent.

There are, and have been, of course, literally hundreds of such psychics throughout the world, and there are many people who continue to prophesy today. Simply take a look at the weekly offerings of the supermarket tabloids. The accuracy of their prophecies probably ranges widely, and deceit is undoubtedly rampant when considering such psychic claims. Many psychics are well educated and excellent students of human nature, keenly observant of the world around them and well aware that history is often a good guide when looking at the future—all of which would enable one to predict the future with some accuracy. For example, a parent can quite often predict what a child is going to do, using the same sensibilities. Likewise, an intelligent, observant person can as easily look into the future and make some pretty good guesses about what is going to happen. Then, if one ignores the bad guesses, that person may appear to be a pretty good prophet. And finally, without a doubt, Satan plays a role in all of this, which we will discuss later.

Here we have been looking only at false prophets in the sense of secular psychics and doomsdayers, those who apparently have no religious agenda to promote. Do they really have a gift, or as has been postulated, do they just have extraordinarily well-developed extra sensory perception? That, however, is a question for another time and place. The prophets against whom we should be most on guard are the false prophets mentioned by Christ and the other biblical writers. Those prophets have only one goal: to turn God's children away from his word, especially in these latter days.

Notes

1. The search for Sodom and Gomorrah has spanned more than one and one-half centuries and is well described in Werner Keller, *The Bible as History* (New York: Bantam Books, 1974), 25–34.

2. Keller, 25–34.

3. T. R. Malthus, *An Essay on the Principle of Population*, ed. Geoffrey Gilbert (Oxford, New York: Oxford University Press, 1993), 61.

4. Wilford Woodruff, in *Journal of Discourses,* 18:111.

5. Harold B. Lee, "Admonitions for the Priesthood," *Ensign,* November 1972, 106.

6. Tribulation: severe afflictions, distress, deep sorrow (D&C 78:14; 109:51; 112:13; 122:5).

7. Paul Ehrlich, *The Population Bomb* (New York: Sierra Club Ballentine, 1968), i.

8. Paul Ehrlich, "Looking Backward from 2000 A.D.," *The Progressive,* April 1970, 23–25.

9. Paul and Anne Ehrlich, *The Population Explosion* (New York: Simon & Schuster, 1990), 193.

10. For both sides of this Malthusian issue, try reading *Earth Report 2000,* ed. Ronald Bailey (Blacklick, Ohio: McGraw-Hill, 2000) and Donella H. Meadows, Dennis L. Meadows, and Jorgen Randers, *Beyond the Limits* (Post Mills, Vt.: Chelsea Green Publishing, 1992).

11. The same seems true of supposed mysterious Bible codes that have sprung up in sensationalist media within the past few years. It seems that certain combinations of letters at key points in the holy text are alleged to have secret hidden meanings. Who inserted them and what their purpose is is not clear. Nevertheless, in a text as complex and large as the Bible, strange hidden

meanings and "codes" can be found or fabricated almost anywhere.

2

History Repeats Itself

History, as opposed to what most of us remember from our high school days, is much more than simply learning the names of kings and rulers, recalling great wars and conquests, and tracking the explorations of frontiers. Of course, those things are important but true history is far more than such isolated events. It is the record of societies, of civilizations, of cultural transformation, and of the common people who stood in the background of historical change. It deals with the traditions of peoples, their institutions, and the forces within their societies that generated the changes that appear in our history books—these are what is important.

Even today, we feel the same forces of historical metamorphosis as our economy fluctuates upward and downward, as our institutions debate over our legal system, as our political parties argue over what we the people want in our highest (and lowest) positions of government. We observe our scientific and medical institutions generating ever newer innovations that will some day enhance our health and standard of living, allowing the graduates of our educational institutions to enter the professional world with new ideas and motivations.

In other words, we are creating history every day. True, not much of it will ever appear in history books or be remembered fifty years from now, but cumulatively we as a people are generating the history of our country that will be remembered among future generations.

Apostasy Revisited

An in-depth look at humanity's history, no matter how far back we peer, reveals a distinct set of patterns that seem to change little from nation to nation or from century to century. The paradigm that emerges is that humanity changes little. The old truism we have all heard, if not from our history teachers then from someone else, still holds true: "Those who do not learn from history are bound to repeat it." And this is a lesson humanity has never mastered. Aside from the cyclic rise and fall of kingdoms and nations, which we have already discussed, there is a similar cycle to man's goodness and decadence.

The scriptures cite continuous examples of one apostasy after another: the evils of Sodom and Gomorrah, the apostate world destroyed by the great Flood, Moses descending from Mount Sinai to confront his idolatrous people, the Israelites' removal from the Holy Land, the apostasy after the ministries of Jesus and his apostles, and the apostasies of the Lamanites and Nephites.

Although the prophets and the scriptures repeatedly call God's children to repentance, his followers continue to weaken and fall away time after time. This, therefore, brings up the question, often debated among theologians, philosophers, and psychologists, of whether humanity is inherently good or evil. Do we have a good spirit ("a still, small voice" or a conscience) urging us to do good, despite our constantly being bombarded with evil influences, or is the opposite true—that we are by nature evil and that God is constantly urging us to overcome that evil?

Whichever the answer is, God must have a great deal of patience with us, as the apostasy of humanity as a whole seems to be our lot. Nevertheless, he has repeatedly provided us with the means—prophets, scriptures, and religious leaders—to turn back to him. Whether we are speaking of the apostasies in the scriptures or of the near universal apostasy in the world today, God keeps on trying, albeit with little visible success.

It seems to be a part of man's nature, confirmed by the scriptures, that humility and love for one another, which Jesus stressed so often, are hard for us to come by. The scriptures also point out—and we can see this from personal observation—that with affluence man tends to become proud, arrogant, and less tolerant of his fellow man:

> Lest when thou hast eaten and art full, and hast built goodly houses, and dwelt therein; And when thy

> herds and thy flocks multiply, and thy silver and thy gold is multiplied, and all that thou hast is multiplied; Then thy heart is lifted up, and thou forget the Lord thy God. (Deuteronomy 8:12–14)

This we see in all the cycles of man's apostasy and righteousness. Whether apostasy is instigated by their rulers or by the people themselves, humanity, as it prospers, begins to disregard the things of God, while those of lowly means tend to exhibit humility and righteousness. Perhaps that is why God gives us trials—to bring us to our knees. Of this, history and the scriptures cite dozens of examples. The Israelites, God's chosen people, after their forty-year trek through the wilderness with Moses, were given a bounteous land, their promised land. As a result, they prospered . . . and, predictably, began to fall away from their God-given heritage. Ultimately, apostasy became so widespread that they were removed from that land and taken into bondage.

Similarly, the followers of Lehi were led to the New World and given a chosen land of security and bounty. As the Book of Mormon reveals, the Lamanites fell away from God early and reverted to barbarism and savagery. The Nephites, likewise, fell away after centuries of prosperity.

When the Savior came into the world, he gave God's people a second chance, again in the Holy Land. And this illustrates man's penchant toward apostasy: the ministries of Jesus and his apostles lasted less than one hundred years, after which worldwide apostasy immediately ensued, including among Book of Mormon peoples. That last great apostasy endured nearly 1,800 years until the restoration of the Church 150 years ago. During that 1,800-year period, nations rose and fell, but humanity remained obstinately apostate. This was also a period of repeated wars, often in the name of nationalism, but in the name of God as well. It was the time of the Crusades, the Inquisition, and the wholesale slaughter or subjugation of what was left of the Lamanites. This was indeed a bleak period of rampant godlessness.

Even after the Dark Ages, this apostasy was reinforced by the Renaissance, a time when humanity, being "enlightened," began to progress. Education of the masses grew, the Industrial Age commenced, commerce began to flourish, freedom began to take root, medicine and human rights gained prominence, and man's standard of living improved. But did man turn to God with his newfound affluence? Not really. Certainly, Catholicism and religious revivals were a part of the Renaissance, but their prophets bore little resemblance to the teachings of Christ. As a matter of fact, Jesus encountered much the same thing among his own people. Speaking to the scribes and the Pharisees, he said, "This people draweth nigh unto me with their mouth, and honoureth me with their lips; but their heart is far from me. But in vain they do worship me, teaching for doctrines the commandments of men" (Matthew 15:8–9).

As Man Is

So how are we today, we who are living in an age of growing worldwide freedom and prosperity? We who are living at the end of a prolonged worldwide apostasy when God is apparently about to throw up his hands in despair and get rid of us? Have our bounty and worldly well-being resulted in our turning to God? Apparently not, according to Nephi 2,600 years ago,

> But, behold, in the last days, or in the days of the Gentiles—yea, behold all the nations of the Gentiles and also the Jews, both those who shall come upon this land and those who shall be upon other lands, yea, even upon all the lands of the earth, behold, they will be drunken with iniquity and all manner of abominations. (2 Nephi 27:1)

In the United States of America, we enjoy freedoms and luxuries such as the world has never known. We take them for granted and consider them almost as our right, seldom remembering that they are gifts of God. Consider what Nephi wrote so long ago, quoting his father, Lehi:

> Wherefore, this land is consecrated unto him whom he shall bring. And if it so be that they shall serve him according to the commandments which he hath given, it shall be a land of liberty unto them; wherefore, they

> shall never be brought down into captivity; if so, it shall be because of iniquity; for if iniquity shall abound cursed shall be the land for their sakes, but unto the righteous it shall be blessed forever. (2 Nephi 1:7)

Even earlier in the Americas, the Jaredites heard much the same thing: "Behold, this is a choice land, and whatsoever nation shall possess it shall be free from bondage, and from captivity, and from all other nations under heaven, if they will but serve the God of the land, who is Jesus Christ" (Ether 2:12; see also D&C 134). However, the liberty of this land is conditional. As the Apostle Paul wrote, "Now the Lord is that Spirit: and where the Spirit of the Lord is, there is liberty" (2 Corinthians 3:17).

It has been said that our current state of apostasy is as bad as, if not worse than, any in history. Can this be true? What *is* the spiritual state of humanity today?

To determine how near we, the human race, are to godliness (which is presumably our goal), we must review a few pertinent scriptures, both old and new. Most well-known to all Jews and Christians, of course, is the Exodus account of the Ten Commandments. Few would argue that by living in conformity with those ten dictates of God, humanity would not find things here on earth decidedly more peaceful and harmonious. However, in keeping with our rapidly advancing mass of knowledge, many of today's intellectual and cultural leaders now rationalize the Ten Commandments as largely irrelevant, antiquated, or at least open to question in modern society.

They question, for example, whether (relating to the first commandment) God exists or not. If he does, where is he and why doesn't he manifest himself to us? Many churches, likewise, have little or no inkling of who or what God is. One must simply review the ancient Nicene Creed, which is basic to Catholicism and much of Protestantism, to become confused about the true nature of God.[1] One notes also among certain churches references to "mother–father God," as if to make sure they are worshiping the correct one.

Even reverence toward God, as the scriptures repeatedly advise, is lacking among much of society at large. Judaism, for example, abiding by Old Testament dictates, stresses that even uttering the holy word "God" was forbidden ("Thou shalt not take the name of the Lord thy God in vain"). To do so is irreverent toward him. How does this conform to today's crude yet commonplace speech in which all sorts of profanity and vulgarity, including the name of God, are heard, and much of this from professed Christians? Consider, for example, the following scriptures:

> He that blasphemeth the name of the Lord, he shall surely be put to death, and all the congregation shall surely stone him. (Leviticus 24:16)

> But now ye also put off all these; anger, wrath, malice, blasphemy, filthy communication out of your mouth. (Colossians 3:8)

> And ye shall not swear by my name falsely, neither shalt thou profane the name of thy God: I am the Lord. (Leviticus 19:12)

Society quibbles over commandments as being black and white, when, as we all know (they contend), there are always shades of gray and we should allow for relativist concepts of right and wrong. They question, for example, what is wrong with lusting after another's spouse as long as nothing else happens. Or why can't there be different degrees of lying ("Thou shalt not bear false witness")? After all, there are little white lies, fibs, omissions of truth, prevarications, and the like, which may or may not cause harm to someone else. Isn't this reminiscent of a recent president of our country, an attorney, who, under legal oath, became notorious for "parsing" words?

Similarly, what is wrong with sports and other such activities on Sundays ("Thou shalt keep the Sabbath Day holy"), so long as we attend church occasionally? The Apostle Paul described the people who make such rationalizations—the learned as the wise—as "ever learning, and never able to come to the knowledge of the truth" (2 Timothy 3:7).

As with the Ten Commandments, the simplicity of Christ's guidance escapes most of us. His teachings lie at the core of successful and harmonious interpersonal relationships:

> Jesus said unto him [a lawyer], Thou shalt love the Lord thy God with all thy heart, and with all thy soul, and with all thy mind. This is the first and great commandment. And the second is like unto it, Thou shalt love thy neighbor as thyself. (Matthew 22:37–39)

It can't be stressed enough that throughout all of Christ's teachings, the theme of love between people and for God is repeatedly expressed. It should be noted equally strongly that it is precisely this godly concept that our modern world ignores. It not only ignores it but seems almost to push it aside. Not only don't we like many of our neighbors, but we also tend to dislike persons who look or act differently than we do, or persons of a different socioeconomic status, not to speak of the animosity and near-hatred we feel for those we consider our enemies.

In conjunction with Christ's theme of universal love, one can't omit the biblical concept of humility, which is so vital in our relationships with each other, as well as in our relationship to God. Note first and foremost that humility is the opposite of pride, something all humanity would do well to remember. As a matter of fact, the Old Testament states that "Before honour is humility" (Proverbs 15:33). A good example of such humility was that of Christ washing the feet of his apostles. How does this contrast with our modern preoccupations with politically correct self-esteem, greed, social status, and so forth? Even our children are taught that to be successful in life they must be assertive and competitive. Is this humility?

Satan

Another theme that is central to understanding and adhering to a godly life is belief in Satan. Now almost universally dismissed as a bogeyman or Christian myth, our modern society sees little need for the antithesis of God, Satan. As a matter of fact, many Christian churches either ignore the reality of Satan or officially deny his reality altogether.

Whether referred to as Satan, Lucifer, the devil, the serpent, or whatever, the scriptures are replete with references to this mysterious being who opposes God and his works. The Old Testament contains several such references, but those expressed in the New Testament leave little doubt as to his authenticity and goals. For example, referring to the last days, the Apostle Paul wrote of the anti-Christ and of the power he would possess during that time:

> Let no man deceive you by any means: for that day shall not come, except there come a falling away first, and that man of sin be revealed, the son of perdition; Who opposeth and exalteth himself above all that is called God, or that is worshipped; so that he as God sitteth in the temple of God, shewing himself that he is God. (2 Thessalonians 2:3–4)

Is it any wonder, then, that many people now regard God, the scriptures, and love for one another with skepticism? What better strategy could Satan employ against God and his works than to discredit him entirely, asserting that he doesn't even exist?

As the above verses make clear, such events must be seen as precursors to the last days. Many other indicators of this period of time and the influence of Satan are all around us, particularly in affluent Western cultures such as ours. We will return to the themes of Satan, his reality, and his strategy in our next chapter.

Adultery, Homosexuality, and Sexual Deviancy

"Thou shalt not commit adultery" (Exodus 20:14). "Thou shalt not covet thy neighbour's wife" (Exodus 20:17). "But I say unto you, That whosoever looketh on a woman to lust after her hath committed adultery with her already in his heart" (Matthew 5:28).

As simple as these admonitions appear, they are probably the least followed and most controversial dictates of God that we see in today's society. To the people of the Old Testament, adultery referred to the unlawful association of men and women, as well as to illicit activity of married persons. Even today, the dictionary defines it as "voluntary sexual intercourse between a married man (or married woman) and someone other than his wife (or her husband)."

The Old Testament condemns such acts, as does the New Testament. Adultery was then punishable by death: "And the man that committeth adultery with another man's wife, even he that committeth adultery with his neighbour's wife, the adulterer and the adulteress shall surely be put to death" (Leviticus 20.10, see also verses 11–21 for a variety of sexual sins).

In fact, Christ lumped those who commit adultery together with those who have evil thoughts and are fornicators and murderers (Mark 7:21; Matthew 15:19). And as fornication has also been condemned, it, likewise, is defined by modern dictionaries as "sexual intercourse other than between a man and his wife." For this reason, early Christians were taught, "Nevertheless, to avoid fornication, let every man have his own wife, and let every woman have her own husband" (1 Corinthians 7:2).

No one can deny that we now have a culture steeped in sexual activity of every kind, with virtually no restrictions whatsoever. Is this not opposite to the laws laid out in the scriptures? Much of our popular literature, media, arts, public figures, advertising, and so forth condone, if not promote, unmarried sexual activity in all its forms. Scarcely a popular magazine or book can be read, or television sitcom or movie viewed, without encountering illicit sexual activity and deviancy, either explicitly or in innuendo. Is it any wonder, then, that even our youth now regard illicit sexual activity and deviancy as acceptable?

Similarly, the term "sexual deviancy" has gone almost by the wayside as unbridled sexual practices have become commonplace everywhere one looks. It appears explicitly in legally protected pornographic materials (dubiously protected as freedom of speech, freedom of the press, or freedom of expression); in our schools, often under the guise of sex education or disease prevention; on the airwaves as entertainment; and even in our political system, where the sexual practices of high government officials are ignored or winked at jokingly with the phrase "everybody does it."

Open public references to oral sex, masturbation, condoms, sex organs, and the like are now considered as enlightened discourse or are used in humor, whereas until only a few decades ago the word "sex" was never uttered in public, and sex was considered a private matter.

Even many of today's churches are relaxing their stances on this issue, with open discussions on sexual topics such as unmarried male-female cohabitation (a glossy term for living together), methods of birth control, disease prevention, homosexuality, and the like. True, some of these discussions may have worthwhile objectives, but one must ask how many of them caution against *all* sexual activity except that between husband and wife?

It would seem that the increasing incidence of sexually transmitted diseases throughout our society and the rest of the world would seem to underline biblical warnings against sexual promiscuity, but apparently not. Instead, we have come to accept the fact that syphilis, gonorrhea, herpes, and other such diseases are here to stay but can (hopefully) be cured, or at least controlled, by modern miracle medicines. HIV infections and AIDS, on the other hand, have become major killers everywhere, and not exclusively of homosexuals.

Referred to above and similarly linked to the issue of adultery is our public's apparent acceptance of homosexuality as an unavoidable part of life. Because the scriptures condemn all forms of sex except between husband and wife, it should be apparent that sexual activity, married or not, between members of the same sex is also contrary to God's law. In addressing this issue, as well as that of adultery and sexual deviancy in general, the Apostle Paul said,

> Wherefore God also gave them [humanity] up to uncleanness through the lusts of their own hearts, to dishonor their own bodies between themselves:
>
> For this cause God gave them up unto vile affections: for even their women did change the natural use into that which is against nature: And likewise also the men, leaving the natural use of the woman, burned in their lust one toward another; men with men working that which is unseemly. (Romans 1:24, 26–27)

Centuries earlier God had warned, "Thou shalt not lie with mankind, as with a woman: it is abomination" (Leviticus 18:22), and "If a man also lie with mankind, as he lieth with a woman, both of them have committed an abomination" (Leviticus 20:13).

Contrary to dozens of biblical prohibitions against sexual deviancy, including adultery and homosexuality, we live in a culture in which such practices are socially and legally accommodated. Unwed motherhood is seldom condemned today; instead, it is now regarded only as a welfare problem. Homosexuality is not considered a deviancy, and is referred to simply as being "gay" or as an "alternative lifestyle." Efforts are made to prove that such proclivities are not a person's fault but that of his or her genetics or ancestry.

Today, we find many Christian churches not only condoning homosexuality but also encouraging it by making clergy positions available to openly practicing homosexuals. All this may be well intended in our efforts to be "fair" or "understanding" or "tolerant" or "accepting of diversity," but the fact remains that it is still contrary to God's laws. Sexual activity between other than husband and wife, as well as any sort of sexual deviancy, such as homosexuality, is thoroughly condemned throughout the scriptures. As a matter of fact, these are precisely some of the reasons cited in the Old Testament for God's destruction of Sodom and Gomorrah.

The only sexual practice that is seldom mentioned specifically in the Bible, yet which is condemned today, is pedophilia, which is sexual activity forced on a child by an adult. And even here we find contradictions in certain churches. When such activities are found to have occurred, particularly between members of the clergy and the (usually male) children under their charge, it has historically been quickly covered up and the offending clergyman discreetly transferred elsewhere or referred to "counseling." This practice has come under fire recently through lawsuits against the particular church and offending clergymen. Only thus have these situations, some of which have gone on for decades, come to light and the hypocrisy been exposed between the laws of God and the activities of the clergy.

Abortion

Relating to immorality, but equally as troubling, is our cultural acceptance of abortion. In the United States alone, over 1.3 million abortions are performed each year (over 3,500 per day), which is one in every five pregnancies. Just in the last three decades since abortions were legalized, over 40 million babies were not allowed the chance at life. Abortion providers continue to do a very good business.

The scriptures contain many references to the sanctity of life, with frequent condemnations of murder. Besides following the commandments of God, one of the greatest commandments ever given to humanity was to bear children. As was said to Adam and Eve, "Be fruitful, and multiply, and replenish the earth" (Genesis 1:28). This is why humanity was given the sex drive. Yet it has become a powerful and corrupting influence when practiced irresponsibly, as we see today. Not only has it led to sexual perversion, as discussed above, but it has also blinded many to the great potential it gives us. As the Apostle Paul said, "Know ye not that ye are the temple of God, and that the Spirit of God dwelleth in you? If any man defile the temple of God, him shall God destroy; for the temple of God is holy, which temple ye are" (1 Corinthians 3:16–17).

Given that we are referred to as a temple of God, how can we condone the destruction of that temple while it is still in the formative process?

Other scriptures refer frequently to the sanctity of man's life and the value of what takes place in a woman's womb. Yet we now feel that the destruction of a fetus is justified as a "personal choice." Can any conscientious practicing Christian seriously maintain that Jesus himself would condone the killing of a human life during any part of its nine months of creation?

Ever since the decision in *Roe v. Wade* over three decades ago, which gave legal sanction to the practice of abortion, this issue has become one of the most contentious in our country, as well as throughout much of the rest of the world. Indeed, it has become divisive on nearly every front in our society—social, political, and legal. More recently, it has been exacerbated by the revelation that even partial-birth abortions are relatively commonplace, in which late-term fetuses are killed during the birth process. Again, one must ask what Jesus would say to those participating in this barbaric practice.

Of course, many today contend that abortion entails a woman's "right to choose" or that she maintains the right to do whatever she wants with her own body. After all, they say, the fetus is not really a human-being-in-creation; it is simply a mass of tissue that can be disposed of for whatever reason. They quibble over when life in the womb begins or when a fetus is viable or becomes a child. They, including many Christians, seem to forget or ignore the fact that the fetus is a life being created in the image of God (Genesis 1:26). To destroy that sort of potential while in the process of creation appears to be absolutely antithetical to all the scriptures that stress the importance of life and humanity.

The Family, Feminism, and Divorce

While societies based on a matriarchal structure in which females assumed the dominant roles, they have been relatively few and far between and of little overall consequence on the world scene. A comprehensive study of the Bible, on the other hand, clearly demonstrates that Old and New Testament societal traditions were entirely those of a patriarchal society. All leadership roles, whether in the home, business, society, or religion, were strictly male-dominated. God himself was always referred to as masculine, and all religious leadership roles were assigned to males. Almost nowhere in the Bible can one find examples of females in the roles of priesthood, family leadership, or society. The few exceptions are references to prophetesses or to priestesses, the latter usually referring to those of pagan or gentile religions.

This patriarchal trend has also historically dominated in our Western cultures, although females have appeared in political and religious roles from time to time. They are, however, the exception, not the rule.

Notation of this rule of patriarchal dominance is not intended to convey the idea that men are superior to women in leadership roles. It points out only that religious and family leadership, as far as the Bible is concerned, has always been relegated to men (see for example Paul's comments concerning women in churches: 1 Corinthians 14:34–35). Obviously, the two sexes are different in many ways, men being better suited to some things and women to others.

Traditionally, and because we originated as a Bible-oriented culture, men have largely assumed leadership roles in government, religion, society, business, and the family, whereas women have mostly been regarded as homemakers and mothers. Since World War II, and especially since the turbulent post-Vietnam era, however, these distinctions have become blurred.

The rise of women's liberation has resulted in women demanding, and quite often receiving, entry into previously male-dominated positions such as political and business leadership as well as religious leadership. This is of particular concern because women have increasingly been moving from the role of homemakers and mothers into roles in the business world outside the home.

In response to this trend, one of our Church leaders made the observation a number of years ago that if women would return to their traditional roles as housewives and mothers, many of the problems besetting our society today would be greatly diminished, including crime, juvenile delinquency, drug abuse, marital breakups, out-of-wedlock births, and so forth. It can't be argued that a large part of such ailments in our society are a result of single-parent families, dysfunctional families, and families in which the wife is out of the home more than she is in it. These families often ignore the dozens of biblical references advising parents of their responsibilities toward properly raising their children.

Many will argue, nevertheless, that women nowadays are required to work outside the home in order to make ends meet. In many cases this may be true. However, in most cases, the wife finds it necessary to supplement the husband's income simply to maintain an artificially, almost extravagantly inflated lifestyle. Therefore, putting their offspring in a day care center or with a nanny while mother works seems the right thing to do. Unfortunately, such people seem to have lost the ability, or are unwilling, to consider the alternative: why not settle for a more modest lifestyle, at least until the kids are grown and gone? For example, do we really need such a large home in an exclusive neighborhood or a third (new) car? By making this choice, Mom could leave the business world and return to her proper role as homemaker and mother.

Admittedly, some mothers have no choice but to work outside the home, such as widows, divorced mothers, and the like. This is understandable, but it does not excuse those mothers who have children out of wedlock or simply want to have a baby, with or without a father around. After all, if Mom is working all day and sees her children only in the evenings, her children are being raised through the most crucial formative times of their lives by someone or something else, not by Mom.

For example, who is there when the child first learns to walk or talk, or is ill, or first learns to read, or has his or her first boyfriend or girlfriend, or encounters questions or problems with sex and drugs, and so forth? In such cases, the child is being raised not by Mom or Dad, but by the child's day care provider, nanny, peers, schoolteachers, or whomever. And the modern mantra of spending quality time with one's children has become too often a cop-out for those professional parents who have placed the proper upbringing of their children secondary to Mom's career.

This is not, it should be stressed, to excuse fathers, as heads of their families, from helping to properly raise their children. All sociologists and child psychologists will confirm that both the father's and the mother's roles in raising their children properly are vital. Likewise, when God gave fatherly advice to Abraham, he said, "For I know him, that he will command his children and his household after him, and they shall keep the way of the Lord, to do justice and judgment" (Genesis 18:19).

On the other hand, the father who abandons his proper role in the family will be harshly judged: "But if any provide not for his own, and specially for those of his own house, he hath denied the faith, and is worse than an infidel" (1 Timothy 5:8).

Linked to the problem of more and more parents not properly raising their children in the past few decades is a corresponding rise in levels of juvenile delinquency (with later criminal tendencies), out-of-wedlock births among teens, family breakups, drug abuse, and similar problems—all associated with children who are being raised without proper moral or ethical guidance. And this trend will only perpetuate itself from generation to generation.

Another problem associated with the rise of feminism—besides a generation of youth without adequate parental guidance—is that of dissolution of the family unit itself. In the past few decades, the divorce rate in this country has risen from 25 percent, which was then viewed as disturbing, to over 43 percent in 2002. This trend is alarming; it guarantees a further lack of proper parental guidance for the next generation. During their early years in particular, children need a home with stability and parental guidance and support. When Mom and Dad split up, both of these vital needs disappear, even if the new stepmother, stepfather, or live-in lover of the remaining parent is a good person.

An ordinance mentioned often throughout the Bible, and which was therefore of obvious importance to God, was that of marriage, in which a committed and covenanted union is made between a man and a woman, and which, by extension, included their children. To the Israelites, this was an absolutely binding contract that included the signing of a "marriage deed." The importance of this marital contract was also carried into New Testament times (Matthew 19:4–9; Mark 10:2–12). These same scriptures outline the vital aspects of fidelity in marriage between husband and wife (see also 1 Corinthians 7).

The New Testament makes it clear that the marital commitment, including a man's commitment to his family, is of utmost importance. As a matter of fact, it states that there are only two grounds on which a marriage may be terminated, either through the adultery of the husband or wife or through the death of a spouse. How does this contrast with the tenuous commitment of today's marriages, in which such unions may easily be dissolved for any number of often frivolous reasons, which reasons are often embellished with socially acceptable terms, such as "mental cruelty," "incompatibility," "they grew apart," or "they had little in common," and so forth? Marriage has therefore come to be accepted no longer as a lifelong commitment but more as a temporary arrangement. There used to be a stigma attached to divorce, but no longer. Now it is regarded as normal, and society hardly blinks.

Certainly, many marriages, which began with commitment and good intentions, can go wrong. This has always been the case, even in biblical times. But today, instead of working through the tough times together—which is a real part of living with someone else—many couples too easily feel that their differences or circumstances are too irreconcilable and take the convenient way out through divorce. This is sad, as a large part of our earthly learning experience revolves around being able to surmount difficult times with someone else and dealing with such trials patiently and harmoniously together. In other words, it is a means of determining whether we can overcome and learn from such things or if we are content to take the easy way out by abandoning our commitments to our spouses and children.

This is the crux of why God considers marriage so important. Nowhere in the scriptures can we find a single instance of inconsistency or vacillation by our Supreme Being. Can we trust a God who vacillates or doesn't honor commitments? Of course not. His messages to us invariably hinge on commitment to high standards and living by eternal rules of order, harmony, and love. Humanity is likewise expected to commit to high standards of order, harmony, and love, especially between a husband and wife. If a man and woman promise to love and honor one another in a lifelong (or eternal) commitment and then fail to do so, they thereby demonstrate that they can't meet the high standards that are so fundamental to God.

Furthermore, this demonstrates not only their own ungodly vacillation and lack of commitment but it also undermines the well-being of their children. This is the ultimate tragedy of divorce. How can we be concerned about the well-being of our own children when we can't even get along with our own spouse? By the same token, how can God or others trust us if we don't honor our commitments?

The unity of the family isn't unlike the unity of God with us (see Ephesians 5:22–32). He expects families to be strong unions of mutual commitment, exactly as he remains committed to us, but only if we honor our commitments to him and to our families. If children are raised in a home in which little marital unity prevails, they too will understandably grow to have little faith in the marital contract. Even more significantly, how can they be expected to "honor thy father and thy mother"?

And this is a key symptom of the apostasy in which we find ourselves. Our children, who are the next generation of adults and leaders, show increasingly little respect for *their* parents, authority (religious or otherwise), or anything that might crimp their self-centered and rebellious lifestyles. One must simply look around our cities or in our schools to see hundreds of youth, rebellious and showing little respect, defacing their bodies, using vile language, engaging in sex, and seemingly enjoying with their peers the fact that they can, with little consequence, snub the society around them. This is much more than simple youthful rebelliousness that we all experienced as we went through our adolescent years. It is instead an epidemic that infects our entire society as these children grow up with no values, morals, or social stability.

Instead of approaching marriage as a long-term commitment, which was the case until just a few decades ago, many now enter it cavalierly as a means of catering to sexual urges, to attain status, to conform to societal expectations, or even for financial reasons. Few seem to look at it anymore with religious sincerity, to be with their marital partner "for better or worse, through sickness and health, until death do us part." No, it seems now that many intend to stick it out only until the newness of it all wears off, until their spouses begin to show signs of age, until readily available sex slows down, or until financial prospects begin to dim. Then they find a socially and legally acceptable way—provided by our modern wealth of attorneys—to call it quits and go on to someone else who is younger and sexier or who has better economic prospects.

In the midst of divorce, the children are often forgotten or their pain is belittled. But would God or Jesus Christ approve of such an attitude any more than of those who marry and divorce with ease, especially when leaving the wreckage of their offspring behind?

The Apostle Paul, who was apparently a bachelor, indicated in some of his writings that it was probably better to remain single (and thus celibate) than to enter into a marriage without commitment (1 Corinthians 7:1–9).

An inescapable conclusion based on our culture's deteriorating attitude toward family and raising the next generation is that we are headed for disaster. We have had numerous decades of experience to see that the gradual dissolution of the family unit, with its consequential negative impact on the stability and moral upbringing of our children, is causing a steady and increasingly rapid erosion in our society, the family being only thing that gives our traditional way of life positive meaning, direction, and coherence. If we continue in the direction in which we are now heading, we must look at eventual and inevitable societal and moral collapse. It isn't difficult to assess the profound impact this disintegrating trend is having on our culture, communities, government, and attitudes toward one another.

Most important, however, as God said, speaking of the family of Eli, "For I have told him that I will judge his house for ever for the iniquity which he knoweth; because his sons made themselves vile, and he restrained them not" (1 Samuel 3:13).

Political and Legal Leadership

Jesus Christ undoubtedly had more impact on the history of humanity than any other person, with the possible exception of Adam, the biblical father of the human race. Because of Jesus, his philosophy, and teachings, the entire world has been changed, and continues to be changed. Although he was never a world political leader or the head of an economic empire, his impact on humanity throughout history has been enormous, continuing even to our own day. His philosophy is still evident in many of our modern governmental and social institutions, as well as in our personal and family lives.

Of course, this doesn't mean that everyone has always accepted him and his teachings, but his influence can be detected even among non-Christians. It is in our laws, our schools, and especially in the moral and personal codes to which our Western culture subscribes. It is in our traditions and customs. Furthermore, his influence is also felt by other competing religions and their followers, as well as by his detractors, and even his enemies.

For example, his philosophy of love, honesty, morality, and care for the poor and downtrodden is a fundamental part of our laws, culture, and governmental institutions. Even the Christmas and Easter holidays are in commemoration of him. Nevertheless, we see more and more within those same institutions a concerted effort to do away with Christ's influence and that of religion in general.

Although not ignored by the scriptures, the political leadership and government of our country are not given the same strict moral standards as are individuals. As a matter of fact, Jesus stated that we are obligated to support such institutions even when we find them repugnant to our personal feelings and values: "Render therefore unto Caesar the things which are Caesar's; and unto God the things that are God's" (Matthew 22:21; see also the Twelfth Article of Faith).

Fortunately, our founding fathers, who were admittedly not of a single mind in regard to religious beliefs, went to great lengths to protect our religious freedoms from government, as evidenced in our Bill of Rights.

Nevertheless, it is disturbing to see a continual, albeit gradual erosion of these protections over the past few decades. We have seen, for example, the elimination of prayer from our schools, the prohibition of religious displays from public buildings, the protection of abortion rights, and so forth. It has recently been said that our government has taken it upon itself to protect us *from* religion instead of protecting our freedom *of* religion.

Furthermore, corruption in government, although not exclusive to current times, has become almost rampant during the past few decades, especially since the Vietnam era. As a result, public distrust of and cynicism toward government is undermining the structure upon which our country is based. Is it any wonder why many now question the legitimate role and function of our political system when corporate and special interest money on a massive scale appears to distort our electoral process by shunting the individual voter aside?

Likewise, we see huge amounts of tax dollars squandered on questionable programs, pork barrel politics, give-away programs, and the like. And we see government at every level encroaching ever further into our private lives. Public resentment is increased by IRS enforcement of a tax system that many have come to regard as overbearing and unfair. Couple this with politicians' quickly forgotten promises and outright deception, and our political system is in jeopardy of losing sight of the lofty goals and protections that our founding fathers felt were so important.

Many may still recall such recent events as the removal from office of high political leaders involved in bribery, misuse of political power, deceit, criminal acts, lying, immorality, and other abuses of their office. During the last few decades alone, for example, we have seen two of our presidents subject to impeachment proceedings, something that has happened only once before in the history of our country. Unfortunately, and as a reflection of the moral and ethical bankruptcy of those who elect and support such leaders, the public has now reached the point in which such acts are accepted and even encouraged.

It would appear, then, that instead of demanding leadership of the highest quality, we are willing to accept leaders who attain only the lowest common denominator of those who vote for them. As we are a country of declining standards and morality, we seem to be happy with leaders of questionable character, integrity, honesty, and morals. What does this say about us as a country and about our future? As the Apostle Paul said, "Where the spirit of the Lord is, there is liberty" (2 Corinthians 3:17).

Our liberty *is,* in fact, in jeopardy as we turn our backs more and more on God and rely more and more on the whims and foibles of men. We must keep in mind as well that if many of our freedoms are being suppressed by an increasingly corrupt government, and virtues such as honor, ethics, integrity, and morality are considered antiquated, the legal system within our country is also partially responsible, for it is the mechanism by which the government asserts control over us. Amulek encountered the same thing among his people, the Nephites: "And now behold, I say unto you, that the foundation of the destruction of this people is beginning to be laid by the unrighteousness of your lawyers and your judges" (Alma 10:27).

No one would dispute the fact that laws are necessary to maintain an orderly society, but in a free society, such as ours, such laws should reflect the will of the people. This is frequently not the case today. And we must not forget that every law that is enacted deprives someone of a portion of his or her freedom.

As with our political leadership, we have seen a slow but steady erosion in our legal system away from biblical standards. For example, our courts have found that pornography and filthy language must be protected under freedom of the press, freedom of speech, and freedom of expression. Freedom of choice has resulted in a woman's "right" to an abortion. Suppression of religious expression, symbols, and displays has resulted, as noted previously, in the exclusion of prayers from schools and the removal of religious displays from public places. Isn't it curious, then, that Congress, the law-making body of our country, opens its sessions with prayer, and our government officials take their oaths of office on a Bible, and we continue to allow reference to God on our coinage and in the Pledge of Allegiance (although the latter too is now under attack)?

At the same time, we see our courts dispensing plea bargains and "justice" to the highest bidder. It is well known that if one has a skilled, high-priced attorney, one can expect greater "justice" in court than can a destitute person. Our courts are not necessarily courts of justice, they are courts of law, laws created by men that don't necessarily reflect the laws of God.

The Apostle Paul summarized the purpose of laws, which stands in stark contrast to how law is commonly administered today: "But we know that the law is good, if a man use it lawfully; Knowing this, that the law is not made for a righteous man, but for the lawless and disobedient" (1 Timothy 1:8–9).

It is difficult to reconcile this notion with the modern-day prosecution of someone who desires to pray in school or erect a nativity scene in a town square, especially when we often see the release of criminals on legal technicalities, political misdeeds swept under the rug, career criminals walking the streets, and babies killed before birth.

The most telling indicator of the apostate morass into which our country is sinking is not only that the bulk of our people ignore the laws of God but that our own government is institutionalizing our spiritual corruption and depravity. By condoning and legalizing abortion, homosexuality, corruption, and so forth, our learned leaders and judges, no matter what their motives and best intentions might be, are encoding our abandonment of God, one issue or law at a time. The current pressure to legalize homosexual marriage in various states is a glaring example of this trend. Another is the lawsuits under way of late against the Boy Scouts of America for their sworn bias in favor of religious standards.

Role Models, Ideals, and Goals

In biblical times, those who followed God's teachings undoubtedly aspired to follow the examples of their spiritual leaders: "Christ also suffered for us, leaving us an example, that ye should follow his steps" (1 Peter 2:21).

Even in our own times, at least until recently, children were encouraged to follow the example of respected leaders and to become like them. Popular role models were church leaders, parents, and leaders of our country. Boys and girls were told to set their goals high, to become like the president, like George Washington, like their parents, and like their forefathers. Now, however, such significant figures have been displaced as role models by rappers, punk rockers, Madonna, the Spice Girls, Mike Tyson, Michael Jackson, movie and television stars, and the like, few of whom can be noted for their high moral character or spiritual achievements. Many of them, as a matter of fact, send destructive messages to our youth through their speech, dress, music, and personal conduct.

Furthermore, a significant portion of those in the entertainment industry have gained and maintain their popularity through vile language, disgusting conduct, and denunciation of social and moral standards. Judging by the fact that they are surrounded by thousands of screaming, adoring fans, they cater to what the public wants. One must simply view today's television programming aimed at our young people—with its unkempt, partially nude, painted, and sweaty entertainers shouting vile lyrics to harsh and strident music—to recognize this fact. It is noteworthy that of all the most popular weekly television programs now on the air, the only characters who attend church are the Simpsons, and they are hardly a model family. Few of even our current political and social leaders can now be counted on as good role models.

We must also keep in mind that role models, like goals, can be either good or bad. How often do we hear parents counseling children nowadays to become like the president or other political, business, and societal leaders? The same question may be asked about using many of our nation's spiritual leaders as role models. As a matter of fact, how many parents who spend "quality time" with their children even discuss with them such things as setting high goals, striving for high standards, and choosing proper role models? If a parent fails to do so, he or she fails his or her children: "Train up a child in the way he should go: and when he is old, he will not depart from it" (Proverbs 22:6).

This may well be a major reason why we now see a generation of children who have little or no self-esteem or who feel little or no sense of personal responsibility. They have parents, often divorced, who have been so involved in their own pursuits and self-fulfillment that they spend little time, "quality" or otherwise, with their children. How else can one account for the thousands of youth today who are in trouble with the law, who live on the streets, abuse drugs, father illegitimate children, and resent authority as well as personal responsibility?

Drugs, Gangs, and Crime

Until the last half of the previous century, drug abuse and juvenile gangs were a rarity, and crime, although it has always existed, didn't reach the epidemic levels we see today. It is a disturbing trend when we see literally thousands of our youth—the next generation—abusing drugs and then turning to crime to support their drug habits. Even most of the gang activities that have come to plague our cities are a consequence of a widespread demand for drugs. And they now affect even smaller towns and rural communities. Truly, drugs have become one of the most insidious social problems our country has ever faced and are another sign of our apostate condition.

Several decades ago, one could walk the streets of our cities in safety; our parks were places for children to play; even our schools were safe. This is no longer the case. A person today must be continually on guard, not only in public places but in their homes as well. Many neighborhoods, in fact, have become so drug- and gang-infested that they are little more than battlegrounds. Police and government efforts to halt such problems have been largely ineffective as the appetite for drugs seems unrelenting.

Dozens of programs have been tried to curtail these intertwined problems, such as the DARE program, the "war on drugs," special drug treatment clinics, and the like. To date, nothing seems to work. Incarceration of drug offenders has proven to be no solution, and for every drug dealer who is locked up, another takes his place. The personal and social problems caused by this epidemic are painfully obvious in broken homes, crime, violence, and deaths. In all this chaos, how is there room for spirituality and love for one another?

Perhaps equally as frightening is the increasing acceptance of violence in our society, and among our youth in particular. Guns and killing are too often regarded as an acceptable means of settling disputes, even at the cost of innocent lives. Whether this stems from the explicit portrayal of violence in our popular media or is a consequence of the Vietnam War, video games, poor parenting, or whatever, it indicates that the cohesiveness of our society is very fragile indeed. How far this is from Jesus' admonition to "love one another, as I have loved you" (John 15:12), or "Therefore all things whatsoever ye would that men should do to you, do ye even so to them" (Matthew 7:12)?

Instead of promoting this sort of biblical thinking, our popular media, especially television and movies, have hardened us and our youth with explicit dramatizations of killing and mayhem that have served only to make violence and murder appear an acceptable means of resolving social problems. One need look no further than our film industry as it produces dozens of popular action movies, starring Bruce Willis, Sylvester Stallone, and Arnold Schwarzenegger, heroes who gun down the bad guys one after another. And as if blood and mayhem aren't enough, the film industry even threatens lawsuits against those who want to clean up their sound tracks in an effort to remove the filthy dialogue found in the majority of its films.

Similarly, video games are a vice loved by both children and adults. But if one pays attention, many of these, as in our movies, portray explicitly every kind of violence imaginable, from machine-gunning hordes of bad guys or the enemy to karate-chopping enemies, pummeling them into submission, or blowing them up. Even our toy industry has gotten on the bandwagon with replicas of knives, Uzis, and AK-47s, many of which are so realistic that many states and communities have outlawed them in order to avoid them being used in robberies. And finally, one would do well to remember that in this country some forty children die each year as a result of guns in schools.

Not only should we be concerned with violence and crime among our youth, but we should also be concerned with the increasing prevalence of what we regard as nonviolent crime in our society. This is sometimes referred to as "victimless crime." As we have become more and more obsessed with money and the worldly things it brings, we are seeing more and more cases of corporate corruption, tax cheating, welfare fraud, insurance fraud, Medicare fraud, outrageous lawsuits, and the like—all aimed at obtaining unearned wealth.

All cases noted above, whether attributable to the youth of our society or to their elders, dramatize the fact that we are fast becoming a society of low ethics, morality, integrity, and character. We are becoming willing, and almost enthusiastic, to replace such spiritual traits with those of selfish personal gain.

Our System of Education

Traditionally, the children of our country have received their learning and training for life at the local level, from parents and schools. Except in the case of institutions of higher learning, schools have for two centuries served our local communities well, and the education children received there reflected the needs and values of parents and local educators. Through this system we have produced generations of children who have come to create and build the greatest free society the world has ever known. As in the Old Testament days of Daniel, "God gave them knowledge and skill in all learning and wisdom" (Daniel 1:17).

Recently, however, some feel that our original system of education has become outmoded and needs to be replaced by new methods and controlled more and more by the federal government, largely out of the hands of parents and local educators.

Undoubtedly, the old, locally based system would have benefited from certain improvements, but instead we now see several disturbing trends becoming evident as control of our schools is taken away from parents and local communities. For example, such virtues as morality, integrity, and even patriotism, which many of us were taught in our youth, have largely been replaced with social programs that emphasize such things as self-esteem, social skills, and moral relativism. Not that these programs are necessarily bad, but they have tended to replace programs that have traditionally been deemed fundamental to a good education, such as basic learning ("the three Rs," if you will), character building, patriotism, personal responsibility, and so forth. No more can teachers discuss sexual morality, biblical concepts, or such simple black-and-white concepts as right and wrong. In other words, our schools are rapidly becoming amoral institutions.

While thousands of good teachers in our education system might like to teach such things, they themselves are now bound by powerful atheistic forces, immense teachers' unions (specifically the National Education Association and the National Federation of Teachers), and the federal government. These are interlinked politically and are far removed from the local level. As a result, local school administrators and teachers are virtually powerless in determining what our children will learn and how they are taught.

Even more detrimental is our university system (with the exception of private religious institutions), in which many faculty seemingly relish deriding such values as morality, religion, and good character. To them, relativism is what really counts, undermining such "archaic" concepts as right and wrong.[2] It is sad that these teachers, who are among our most gifted and brilliant citizens, use their vast potential to teach our youth everything except that which has eternal value—spiritual and biblical standards. As Isaiah stated so long ago, "Woe unto them that call evil good, and good evil" (Isaiah 5:20). They have instead become what the Apostle Peter called "false teachers . . . who privily shall bring in damnable heresies, even denying the Lord that bought them" (2 Peter 2:1).

The Apostle Paul further warned about the learned: "Beware lest any man spoil you through philosophy and vain deceit, after the tradition of men, after the rudiments of the world, and not after Christ" (Colossians 2:8); "Professing themselves to be wise, they became fools" (Romans 1:22); "Ever learning, and never able to come to the knowledge of the truth" (2 Timothy 3:7).

We have, then, an atheistic school system that, when coupled with (oftentimes) poor parenting, produces children who have no foundation in such important traits as morality, ethics, and good character. Even worse, many of them don't even receive a good foundation in such basic educational skills as reading, writing, and arithmetic. Consequently, today's students in this country are beginning to fall academically below those of other nations. Is it any wonder, then, that we now see many families who prefer to homeschool their children or send them to private schools?

The declining character of our nation, which has largely turned its back on God and spiritual values, is reflected in our education system. While it has the potential of continuing to lead the world in progressive and valuable character-building programs, it is faltering instead into an atheistic morass of bureaucracy and unions, with declining hope for our children. It is only when this trend is reversed that the words of Jesus will have meaning: "And ye shall know the truth, and the truth shall make you free" (John 8:32).

Science and Technology

We are living in a time when our knowledge is expanding at a pace we can scarcely appreciate. As a result, we enjoy many things that people throughout history could hardly comprehend. For example, our standard of living has been greatly enhanced through modern medicines, instant worldwide communications, automation, rapid transportation, and a myriad of labor-saving and entertainment devices. Most of these advances have, without argument, been beneficial, providing us with a longer life and more enjoyable lifestyle, and also providing us with a greatly increased amount of leisure time.

If all such benefits were put to productive use, one could scarcely fault us for taking advantage of them. However, as humanity's knowledge and inventiveness have increased, this hasn't always been the case. Many are becoming concerned, for example, with certain trends in the rapidly expanding fields of automation and communications.

Consider that every citizen in this country, as well as almost anywhere in the world, has a portion of his or her life recorded in a database somewhere. His or her birth and school records, religious and political affiliations, spending habits, place of residence, military service, family members, employment and financial history, property ownership, tax records, vehicle and gun ownership, and so forth are all recorded not only in business and computer files, but in government databanks everywhere. Imagine, then, what could happen to us as a citizenry and as individuals, if this information were consolidated and put to improper use. Thus have many feared control and suppression of the populace by our own government if our political system were to go awry.

An example of misuse of our technological system, although it may seem innocuous, is the hordes of spam (often pornographic) with which internet users must contend every day. Likewise, telephone boiler-room operations systematically call homes every evening with offers of cruises, "you're a winner," and any number of get-rich-quick schemes.

Likewise, we have long resisted a system of personal identification in this country, but we can easily be tracked down by our social security numbers, especially now that the Internal Revenue Service requires reporting such information even on our minor children. In other words, our long-cherished concept of privacy no longer exists for anyone having access to a computer and the knowledge of how to get into these databanks. A sure sign of this threat is the growing crime of identity theft in which unscrupulous computer users gain access to our bank accounts and credit card information, plus whatever else they may be able to use, thus enriching themselves at our expense. Even sensitive or classified government databanks are proving vulnerable to such tampering by hackers.

Equally disquieting is science's new and expanding knowledge in such areas as medicine, genetics, and biology. For example, organ transplants have become a new and promising field in medicine, the benefits of which are well recognized. Nevertheless, we have seen emerging a lucrative new market in human organs for money, the source of the organs sometimes being questionable.[3] Also, scientists are now looking into using animals to grow organs for transplantation into humans, which highlights even more obvious ethical and moral questions, despite their benefits to humanity.

Cloning is the most recent conquest of these scientists, and now they are further delving into such problematic areas as the cloning of humans (in spite of various governments' efforts to stave off such research) and creating genetically engineered living organisms comprised not only of animals' DNA but of humans' as well. These researchers, and the medical community that supports them, regard such developments as a further step in creating advanced medical products and another source of transplant organs for eventual use in human beings. Even fetal tissue has been used in such research, with the laudable goal of finding the ultimate cure for several dreaded diseases such as cancer, Alzheimer's disease, and so forth. The use of fetal tissue, or stem cells, is resisted by our government but probably to no avail, as researchers are already seeking ways to circumvent what they consider religion-oriented intrusion into their domain.

Ostensibly, such advances will come to greatly benefit humanity, and we will then see even further increases in our life spans as well as an improved quality of life. However, the room for abuse is too great to overlook. When science begins to create organisms that are part animal and part human, where is the line drawn between what man can do and what God intended for the life he created here on earth? This appears to approach invasion of God's domain, a place where man should seriously reconsider how far he should go. It is a much greater step than abortion, in which human life is destroyed prior to birth. It is instead tampering with human life in areas that could result in great damage to the human race itself, no matter what the good intentions of the scientific and medical communities may be.

Similarly, we have seen throughout our history the unfortunate tendency of man to turn his increasing knowledge away from those inventions that are beneficial to humanity and instead to those that have one purpose only—to destroy humanity. We often cloak these advances in terms that mask their true intent, calling them weapons of defense. No matter what they are called, they are weapons intended primarily for human destruction.

Long ago, tribes turned their spears, knives, clubs, and arrows from killing wild game for food into weapons to be used against other tribes. Then came explosives and firearms, all of which were much more efficient. Not only could they be used to provide food, but they were much better at killing other human beings. And finally, we have become so sophisticated in the last century that we can now kill not only all human beings living on the earth but probably all other life as well. We have chemical, biological, and nuclear weapons, any of which can easily do God's job of ridding the earth of all humanity entirely.

With the recent collapse of the Soviet Union and the corresponding end of the Cold War, we naively feel that such threats have become things of the past. We fail to remember, however, that most of the weapons that were produced during the Cold War are still in existence somewhere, despite much-acclaimed programs to destroy weapons stockpiles (amounting only to the disposal of a small percentage of all such weapons still in existence). And with the collapse of Eastern European communist governments, and the consequent instability of that region, those weapons are becoming increasingly difficult to control.

That, coupled with the current threat of international terrorism, means that we can now expect it to be only a matter of time until one or more of these weapons of mass destruction will be used somewhere in the world. For example, no one can presently account for all of the chemical, biological, and nuclear weapons that were once stockpiled in the former Soviet Union, many of which are easily transportable. We are not even sure what other countries, or which unstable (frequently hostile) governments, such as Iran, North Korea, and others may now be producing and preparing in order to use these types of weapons against their neighbors or against us.

If that were to happen, even if on a limited scale, the worldwide repercussions would be obvious. The world is no safer now than it has ever been. As a matter of fact, because of the development and accessibility of such destructive potential, the time is ripe for it to be used. Perhaps this will be humanity's legacy for relying too much on itself and its intellect, rather than on God.

False Gods, Prophets, and Churches

Although this is a topic also included in chapter 4, it is nevertheless appropriate to address it here as representative of the way humanity has fallen away from spirituality and reliance on scripture. While God says, "Thou shalt have no other gods before me" (Exodus 20:3), Christians today, believing they are worshiping the God of the Bible, can be found to worship and follow an entire assortment of gods and deities.

From the profusion of conflicting Christian and Jewish beliefs, it is virtually impossible to determine who, in fact, the God of the Bible is. For instance, many regard him as a great spirit of some kind, surrounded by mystery and incomprehensibility. Others regard him as an equally incomprehensible amalgamation of God, Jesus Christ, and the Holy Ghost all rolled into one, which we as mortals can't possibly understand (as purported in the Nicene Creed, cited earlier). There are even those who have professed to be God incarnate himself, living here on the earth and drawing many believers to them. That is, until they (the self-proclaimed "Gods") die or are otherwise found to indulge in commonplace human vices.[4] Other denominations believe God to be an alien from another galaxy, and still others, as in some of the New Age religions, don't seem to be particularly concerned about who or what he is.

It is obvious, then, that many, including a large part of Christianity, are not sure whom they are worshiping. This lack of understanding has resulted in much of modern-day humanity following what they perceive—or hope—to be deities, though not necessarily the God who created this world and all humanity. This is not necessarily the fault of laymen within the various churches, but more often the fault of their long traditions and leadership, which have strayed over time from a real understanding of God.

One can't say that these leaders have intentionally distorted scriptural teachings or their own church's dogma, but changes have nevertheless crept in over decades, if not centuries, confusing the true intent, or content, of God's and Jesus' teachings. As a result, Jesus himself would doubtlessly fail to recognize most of today's churches, or they him. This is yet another symptom of the great apostasy.

Subtler in straying from following the true God is man's propensity to place worldly things ahead of religious values or of God, replacing him, as it were, with substitutes. Examples are our preoccupation with wealth, prestige, power, social status, and the like. Most of our adult days are spent trying to gain such things. As a result, worldly motives have come to play a more influential role in many lives than have religious values, even among devout Christians.

Few can dispute that we live in a world in which a new car, a higher-paying position, winning the lottery, a bigger and more expensive house in a more exclusive neighborhood, and so forth play much larger roles in our lives than does going to church or following uncomfortable religious dictates. Have these things, then, not become gods to us? When our whole lives are consumed by the pursuit of such distractions, to the near exclusion of everything religious, can we then contend that we have "no other gods before him" as we are commanded in the Bible?

Since many of our efforts revolve in one way or another around worldly wealth, it is hardly any wonder that the Apostle Paul warned, "The love of money is the root of all evil" (1 Timothy 6:10).

The scriptures are replete with references to the destructive temptation to follow money, the adulation of our fellow man, and other worldly pursuits. It is obvious, however, that none of these will be of much use to us in the life hereafter.

As indicated earlier, there are, and have been, those who prey on others by claiming to be God or Jesus Christ, or a prophet of one kind or another. The last days, as we are often warned in the scriptures, will produce many such characters: "For false Christs and false prophets shall rise, and shall shew signs and wonders, to seduce, if it were possible, even the elect" (Mark 13:22).

Note that Jesus mentioned here not only that such false persons would arise, but that they would also have the ability to perform signs and wonders. How many ministers and churches in our day do we see wherein apparent wonders are performed, such as healings, speaking in tongues, prophecies, and the like? Not only are many of them eventually exposed as false, but many also rely on the gullibility of their followers who fail to remember that even Satan has the ability to do such things (see 2 Thessalonians 2). More telling is the fact that many of these fraudulent persons become remarkably wealthy at the expense of their converts.

The past few decades have produced many such religions and religious leaders of questionable authenticity. We should never forget the fate of those who died in the Jamestown debacle in 1978, the dozens of doomsday cults who still live in survivalist isolation awaiting the end of humanity, those who followed their Heaven's Gate leader in suicide to board the Hale-Bopp comet in 1997, the gullible followers of the Baghwan Shree Rajnish in Oregon (who made him rich in the 1980s), the doomed followers of David Koresh at Waco in 1993, and the thousands who believed in and donated profusely to such now-discredited television evangelists as Jimmy Swaggart and Jim Baker.

As stated before, the scriptures warn us again and again about predatory preachers and prophets who, in the last days, will prey on humanity (see 2 Peter 2:1; Matthew 7:15; 24:24). Jesus and his apostles must have foreseen that religion in our day would be big business.

Only several short decades ago, Christian churches and sects numbered only 250 or so. Today that number has climbed to over 1,200 with the proliferation of New Age religions. To a non-Christian, it would seem incomprehensible that there could possibly be so many different interpretations of God, the Bible, and the teachings of Jesus Christ, each contending that theirs is the only true church, although some contend that any church affiliation is okay and that there is no exclusive, true church. After all, founding one's church nowadays is relatively easy to do.

This large-scale fragmentation in Christianity is indicative of only one thing: "Grievous wolves [shall] enter in among you, not sparing the flock. Also of your own selves shall men arise, speaking perverse things, to draw away disciples after them" (Acts 20:29–30). Furthermore, to reiterate the words of Jesus, "Many false prophets shall rise, and shall deceive many" (Matthew 24:11).

It should be telling that there are some churches today who make no pretense about who they are or what they believe in, especially those who epitomize today's apostasy. Among them are those assorted churches devoted to Satan and to witchcraft. We will devote more attention to them and to false prophets in the following chapters.

Decreasing Resources and Environmental Degradation

The biblical account of the creation in Genesis 1:26–30 states that man was to have dominion over the earth and over all living things, which blessing would provide for all his needs. Yet today we hear frequent and increasing worries about overpopulation, decreasing resources, and the destruction of the resources we have. We discussed some of these concerns earlier.

Despite the ever-increasing human population on this planet, the earth still maintains the potential to provide us with everything we need for centuries to come—if our resources are managed wisely.

The fact that we hear of malnutrition and starvation in so many parts of the world today is more a problem of politics and distribution than of production. This is borne out when we hear that in such places as Africa, the Balkan countries, North Korea, and others, widespread starvation is not a matter of the unavailability of food, but rather of war exacerbated by corrupt, inefficient, and indifferent governments that won't or can't provide for their people, even when food is available. In fact, one-fourth to one-half of all food aid that is shipped to the above countries never reaches its destination due to poor storage and shipping conditions under which it either spoils, is consumed by vermin, or is stolen for the black market.

Another culprit, when we hear of shortages in needed resources, may well be in our own ever-increasing standard of living. As other countries rush to achieve the same standard of living as ours, the shortage of resources becomes even more acute. It must be pointed out, therefore, that much of what we regard as shortages are not actually in resources required for basic living, such as food, water, and shelter, but rather in what may better be deemed as luxuries, such as bigger, more modern homes, more and larger automobiles that require more fuel (not to mention roads), appliances of every description, entertainment devices, exotic clothing, jewelry, and the like. It is certainly nice to have such conveniences and luxuries, but they are an enormous drain on the finite resources we have on the earth.

Compounding the problem of finite and decreasing resources is the fact that we have managed to destroy, and continue to do so, many of the resources we have long taken for granted. For example, we frequently hear of polluted oceans and rivers, polluted soil, loss of topsoil from some of our most productive farming areas, mountains of trash accumulating, destruction of forests and rainforests, and polluted air in our cities.

Even ancient biblical prophets discussed pollution, although to them the term "pollution" usually referred to the defiling of biblical cultures with heathen or gentile beliefs and practices (see Leviticus 18:25; Numbers 35:3; Ezekiel 32:2).

Despite our recent efforts to curb abuses to the environment and to better use our resources, our treatment of our God-given home—earth—continues to be deplorable. As noted before in the Genesis account of the Creation, we were given dominion over an earth filled with everything we would need. But now questions loom as to how well we have been able to handle our environmental responsibilities.

The Great Apostasy

In summary, then, despite the wealth of spiritual guidance available to us through the scriptures, church leadership, and even modern-day prophets and continuing divine revelation, we see all around us every reason to believe that humanity has, in fact, slid down into the greatest apostasy the earth has ever seen. All around us we see a culture, especially among our youth, in which the things of God are increasingly ignored in favor of the things of the world. God himself is jokingly referred to as either nonexistent or a thing of the past. Satan, likewise, is widely regarded as a fictitious being.

The proliferation of churches, especially of Christian churches, indicates that no one can agree on who God is or what he wants of us. Our families are disintegrating; we have a generation of youth growing up with no morals, values, or other spiritual guidelines. We no longer have respect for life (as evidenced by the legality of abortions and our murder rate). Sexual practices and perversion of every sort are becoming more and more commonplace, as people ignore the warnings of the Old Testament prophets, of Jesus and his apostles, and of modern-day prophets regarding adultery, homosexuality, and fornication. Finally, humanity's preoccupation with wealth, status, and power over others has pushed true religious pursuits aside.

In other words, the overwhelming bulk of humanity has become so immersed in the things of this world that spiritual things are no longer of consequence. Humility, love, morality, the family, good character, and nearly all the virtues of godliness are now regarded as antiquated, are snickered at, or are shrugged off as being of little importance. As Isaiah prophesied, "Behold, darkness shall cover the earth, and gross darkness the people" (Isaiah 60:2).

The Apostle Paul also described our present apostate world in detail:

> This know also, that in the last days perilous times shall come. For men shall be lovers of their own selves, covetous, boasters, proud, blasphemers, disobedient to parents, unthankful, unholy,
>
> Without natural affection, trucebreakers, false accusers, incontinent, fierce, despisers of those that are good, traitors, heady, highminded, lovers of pleasures more than lovers of God; having a form of godliness, but denying the power thereof: from such turn away.
>
> For of this sort are they which creep into houses, and lead captive silly women laden with sins, led away with divers lusts, ever learning, and never able to come to the knowledge of the truth.
>
> Yea, and all that live godly in Christ Jesus shall suffer persecution. But evil men and seducers shall wax worse and worse, deceiving, and being deceived. (2 Timothy 3:1–7, 12–13)

One must simply look at the degradation of Christianity's most holy day, Christmas, to see the signs of apostasy. Even among those who profess to be devout followers of Jesus, we see more and more distractions and commercialism and less and less religious significance in this commemoration of Christ's birth. For example, how many of our more popular Christmas carols fail to mention Jesus at all? The overwhelming importance of his birth, life, and ministry is being replaced by Santa Claus, reindeer, Christmas trees, the commercialism of gift giving (especially expensive toys, jewelry, and the like), and overly large meals complete with an abundance of alcoholic beverages. True, these traditions have come down to us as Christian practices, but they now nearly eclipse the true meaning of the Christmas holiday, which should be a time of thanksgiving and somber reflection.

Even Easter, which supposedly commemorates the significance of Christ's resurrection, is falling prey to similar distractions, with Easter bunnies, colored eggs, picnics, and the like, which have little to do with our Savior having risen from the dead. Furthermore, as mentioned earlier, how many ministers and Christian churches themselves can truly contend that they follow precisely the precepts taught by Jesus? Or do they exhibit some of these same apostate symptoms as well?

Notes

1. Adopted by Catholicism in the fourth century A.D., the Nicene Creed reads as follows: "We believe in one God the Father Almighty, Maker of heaven and earth, and of all things visible and invisible. And in one Lord Jesus Christ, the only-begotten Son of God, begotten of the Father before all worlds, God of God, Light of Light, Very God of Very God, begotten, not made, being of one substance with the Father by whom all things were made; who for us men, and for our salvation, came down from heaven, and was incarnate by the Holy Spirit of the Virgin Mary, and was made man, and was crucified also for us under Pontius Pilate. He suffered and was buried, and the third day he rose again according to the Scriptures, and ascended into heaven, and sitteth on the right hand of the Father. And he shall come again with glory to judge both the quick and the dead, whose kingdom shall have no end.

"And we believe in the Holy Spirit, the Lord and Giver of Life, who proceedeth from the Father and the Son, who with the Father and the Son together is worshipped and glorified, who spoke by the prophets. And we believe one holy catholic and apostolic Church. We acknowledge one baptism for the remission of sins. And we look for the resurrection of the dead, and the life of the world to come. Amen."

2. A recent book that clearly describes such liberal bias in our institutions of higher learning is *Brainwashed: How Universities Indoctrinate America's Youth,* by Ben Shapiro.

3. China, for instance, was recently discovered to have been marketing organs harvested from those executed in prison.

4. A classic example of such a "God" incarnate was George Baker, also known as Father Divine. A black cult leader born in Savannah, Georgia, in 1875, he was worshiped as God by his (apparently) tens of thousands of followers. The movement declined rapidly after his death in 1965.

3

Satan, the Prince of Darkness

I will give unto you a pattern in all things, that ye may not be deceived; for Satan is abroad in the land, and he goeth forth deceiving the nations.

—D&C 52:14

It is interesting to note that when one sits through fast-and-testimony meetings, one regularly hears testimonies about the reality of God and Jesus Christ, that they live. One also hears about the blessings of the gospel. These are key ingredients of our faith. They are the foundation of our eternal lives and of the plan of salvation.

But as noted in the last chapter, we are in the final stages of the greatest apostasy the world has ever known. We have also noted that the history of humanity is little more than a series of apostasies interspersed with short periods of righteousness, those brief moments when prophets prevailed and the word of God held sway. And for that reason, the question was posed earlier of whether the nature of man is inherently good or evil.

Another question to be posed, then, is that if we testify of the reality of God and our Savior, shouldn't we also have a testimony of the reality of Satan?

The Reality of Satan

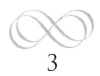

Christianity and Judaism have traditionally referred to Satan under various names such as Lucifer, the Prince or Angel of Darkness, the beast, the tempter, the serpent, the Prince of Demons, the adversary, the Prince of the World, a fallen angel, Beelzebub (which in Hebrew means "Lord of the Flies"), and the devil.[1] But as with other religious entities we have discussed, our modern culture has by and large relegated him to almost fictional status or to fable.

For example, many people nowadays deny his existence entirely or consider him only a "boogeyman," one who caters to our lower earthly natures (as on T-shirts and bumper stickers which proclaim, "The devil made me do it!"). This is also unfortunately the attitude of many modern denominations. As a matter of fact, only 27 percent of Americans believe in the reality of the devil (17 percent among Catholics). Bizarre depictions of Satan are no doubt true in part, but we should beware of regarding this "mythical" person too whimsically.

The scriptures definitely don't regard him lightly, as he is mentioned hundreds of times in both the Old and the New Testaments. He is mentioned many times by Jesus himself; the most notable interaction in the scriptures is Christ's personal confrontation with Satan in the wilderness during his temptation, as is so clearly described in Matthew 4:1–11. In other words, if we can regard God, Jesus Christ, and the Holy Ghost as real beings, then we must regard Satan as a real being as well. And we must consider him and his influence as playing a real and significant part in our existence. That being the case, the scriptures are replete not only with general references to him but specific ones as well.

Keeping that in mind, it seems logical that if God and his heavenly associates try to help us along, then something or someone else may well attempt to block our progress. Think about it, if only God's influence worked on us, we, all of us, would probably already be perfect, would we not? As this is obviously not the case, and we have a tough time improving our spiritual natures, something must be causing us to resist God. This resisting influence may be attributed to "human nature," whatever that is, or simply to the assertion that we are innately bad. These are the sorts of terms used by modern society to acknowledge that it doesn't have a clue as to why we humans aren't automatically endowed with goodness and higher ideals.

Atheists, philosophers, and many of those who deny the existence of a supreme being often contend that humanity alone has the ability to create and practice moral codes that mirror those enunciated by Jesus and the prophets of Judeo-Christianity. This is, of course, in part true, as many great thinkers over millennia have, without reference to the Bible, recognized, practiced, and preached the values of harmonious living, charity, honor, and personal integrity. As a matter of fact, several of the founding fathers of this country were atheists or nonpracticing Christians.[2] It is then surprising that they were capable of establishing a nation that has proved to be one of the most enlightened and blessed in history.

The fact, however, is that despite such enlightened thinkers, humanity as a whole, when left to its own devices, tends to deviate from such lofty values and becomes "worldly" or "base," to use biblical terms. For example, our history is rife with accounts of wars, depravity, human subjugation, and all sorts of ugliness when man is left to himself to determine by what ethical and moral codes he will live. True, many of these degrading characteristics are adopted and perpetuated by individual leaders and governments, as was the case in the recent history of Naziism, communism, the bloody Pol Pot regime of Cambodia several decades ago, and more recently in Sadam Hussein's Iraq. But entire nations have nevertheless followed them, often with enthusiasm, despite small isolated voices who recognized that doing so was wrong.

The Bible too is full of such accounts, in which tens of thousands followed despicable leaders, even when they too knew it was wrong. Simply consider, for example, ancient Egypt at the time of Moses; the Roman Empire, in which all kinds of barbaric practices took place for their entertainment value; and the Japanese Empire of World War II, which enjoyed the wide popular support of its people, yet was well known for its deviousness and atrocities. And even in our own country, we had the Confederate States of America, who practiced human bondage.

Yes, many who lived in those countries during those times later recanted, saying they were unaware of or disagreed with what was going on, but many of them undoubtedly closed their eyes to the evil around them. The fact remains that if enough of them had stood up and said that what their leaders were doing was wrong, such barbaric and corrupt governments wouldn't have endured long.

These points are underlined by the fact that very few nations have arisen and lasted for long who were led by genuinely moral and uplifting persons or governments. On the contrary, such leaders are often regarded as weak and ineffective, sure prey for the unscrupulous and ruthless within their own countries or surrounding, less honorable countries.

A case in point in our recent history was that of the Carter administration during the 1970s. Widely regarded as a devout and honorable Christian and American, President Jimmy Carter was at the same time perceived by many (including those abroad) as weak and ineffective. As a matter of fact, if one studies history honestly, it becomes quickly apparent that few governments in the earth's history (ours being one of the rare exceptions) have arisen without resort to deceit, bloodshed, or force, often inflicted on their own populations. And this includes many who have done so in the name of God.

Even worse than the corruption and degradation of governments is the corruption and degradation of entire nations, in which such practices are adopted and championed by the people themselves and thus become a part of their culture and way of life. In other words, those ungodly practices become institutionalized. This was the case with the Book of Mormon Lamanites after their arrival in the Americas.

As unpleasant as it may seem, we are seeing in the last few decades a continual erosion, not only in this country, but in many others as well, of the godlike qualities that were so important to the writers of the Bible. We have, for example, seen the powerful resilience and growth of the Ku Klux Klan and the many skinhead and white supremacist organizations, whose ideals revolve around hatred, yet proclaim at the same time that they follow lofty goals in the name of God.

In the last chapter we noted that we see within our own country a society that, despite our claim to being a Christian nation, has corrupted itself and is now surrounded by all kinds of unchristian practices, many of which are deemed acceptable and are protected by law. They are becoming acceptable because we consider ourselves a liberated and enlightened society that doesn't want anyone to feel alienated because of his or her lifestyle, no matter how unchristian, degrading, or disgusting it may be. We even consider some of these things to be freedoms. Let's not forget, however, that

Jesus himself alienated a lot of people.

One must simply look at which television programs and literature have become enduringly popular in our "Christian" nation: Jerry Springer, Howard Stern, Larry Flint, Jay Leno, and the like; each of these personalities have become famous and wealthy by catering to the depravity and dregs of our society.

Yes, there is a very real force constantly at work, intent on undermining the influence of good in this world, especially that taught by God and Jesus Christ. With that in mind, the Bible tells us a little about the reality and history of Satan and his associates:

> There was war in heaven: Michael and his angels fought against the dragon; and the dragon fought and his angels. And prevailed not; neither was their place found any more in heaven. And the great dragon was cast out, that old serpent, called the Devil, and Satan, which deceiveth the whole world: he was cast out into the earth, and his angels were cast out with him. (Revelation 12:7–9)

It is apparent from John's account above that beginning in the premortal existence, Satan led a large-scale rebellion against God, joined by many spirits or "angels" (constituting one-third of God's children). They were "cast out into the earth" and are among us today. And their goal is clear:

> How art thou fallen from heaven, O Lucifer, son of the morning! How art thou cut down to the ground, which didst weaken the nations! For thou hast said in thine heart, I will ascend into heaven, I will exalt my throne above the stars of God: I will sit also upon the mount of the congregation, in the sides of the north: I will ascend above the heights of the clouds: I will be like the most High. (Isaiah 14:12–14)

It seems fairly clear from these latter verses that Satan has the ultimate goal of replacing God, or at least of competing with him for dominance over the earth and humanity. His reality is further confirmed many times by Christ and his apostles throughout the New Testament, as we will see below.

Satan and his followers, from what we can learn from the scriptures, are apparently spiritual beings without bodies, similar to the Holy Ghost. Yet they are undoubtedly intelligent and well organized with a single goal: to oppose God, undermine his works, and assume dominance over humanity. To do so, he and they are, and have been, working ceaselessly to lure as much of humanity as possible away from God and the teachings of Christ.

What we have, then, are two massive forces striving against each other with the eternal future of humanity at stake. This is not unlike two enormous nations of spiritual and mortal beings engaged in a global conflict over our eternal souls—God, Jesus Christ, and their Church, as opposed by Satan and billions of his followers.

And let us not forget that not only are God and Jesus surrounded by angels, but Satan is as well, as the above verses make clear.

Lucifer, the Master Adversary

Of course, Satan has many weapons at his disposal, the most powerful of which is to convince humanity that he doesn't exist. With this strategy he has been remarkably successful, as a majority of humanity has no inkling that such a powerful force for evil exists, or else it refuses to recognize it for what it is. To avoid detection, Satan employs numerous strategies, few of which announce him as an adversary of God. No, he is far more subtle. Instead of personally appearing to humanity and announcing, "I am Satan, and I am here to lead you away from God," he works surreptitiously through us and our leaders. He realizes that without the physical evidence of his existence, strategies, and goals, most of humanity will have no clue that he exists. This is much the same as the fact that a great part of humanity rejects the idea that God exists because we haven't seen him lately.

Another weapon Satan utilizes, and which he constantly favors, is his ability to mimic God and other heavenly beings. To do so, he uses many of the same powers as God, as he is not a mortal and has been studying us and accumulating knowledge for thousands if not millions of years. He therefore knows us almost as well as God does and knows how to exploit our mortal weaknesses. He is able to move about freely, as do God and other heavenly beings, and can influence us both directly, by physical means as discussed below, and also indirectly, by simply subverting our thoughts or by placing temptations in our paths.

Not only can he influence our thoughts, but he and his followers can also appear as angels and do miraculous things. This is confirmed by the Apostle Paul in at least two instances:

> For such are false apostles, deceitful workers, transforming themselves into the apostles of Christ. And no marvel; for Satan himself is transformed into an angel of light. Therefore it is no great thing if his ministers also be transformed as the ministers of righteousness; whose end shall be according to their works. (2 Corinthians 11:13–15)

> Even him, whose coming is after the working of Satan with all power and signs and lying wonders. (2 Thessalonians 2:9)

In the Book of Mormon Korihor told Alma, "But behold, the devil hath deceived me: for he appeared unto me in the form of an angel" (Alma 30:53).

Furthermore, John the Revelator, again looking into the future, prophesied that Satan would also have remarkable healing powers (as do many modern faith healers) and would exercise persuasiveness over humanity (Revelation 13). A further example of Satan's accomplices performing wonders were the wise men and sorcerers of the Pharaoh who, as did Moses and Aaron, turned their rods into serpents (Exodus 7:10–12).

Note in the verses above that among Satan's disciples are those who are "transformed as the ministers of righteousness" in another instance of his deceits. This may well be a partial answer as to why we have so many competing denominations that call themselves Christian. On the other hand, in our day churches exist that unabashedly worship Satan. The Church of Satan, for example, has been operating openly in California for decades. Obviously, Satan would also readily encourage confusion among the followers of Jesus Christ through ministers and clergy who, though they may be well intentioned and devoutly convinced they are called of God and doing his work, are in fact preaching doctrines that are at variance with what God and Jesus Christ intended.

This could well be the case today in which we see and hear hundreds of preachers, behind pulpits and on radio and television shows, who expound all sorts of strange doctrines, many of which sound only slightly like that of Jesus Christ.

Even more deceptive are those who seem to be devout members of the ministry but who, smoothly and with great personal charisma, preach nice-sounding generalities, platitudes, and warm-fuzzy doctrines, yet who misconstrue or ignore the scriptures and omit those portions of doctrine (baptism, the priesthood, humility, avoidance of greed) that are difficult or inconvenient to them and their congregations or churches. To them, Jesus would certainly say, "This people draweth nigh unto me with their mouth, and honoureth me with their lips; but their heart is far from me. But in vain they do worship me, teaching for doctrines the commandments of men" (Matthew 15:8–9; see also Galatians 1:7–11).

The doctrine Jesus Christ preached was not one of smooth generalities and platitudes but of self-denial, personal responsibility, integrity, avoidance of worldly pleasures, love, and humility, all of which are at odds with the values of our modern society.

In addition to distorting the thinking of men, Satan also effectively uses the tactic of distorting God's word, the scriptures, for his own ends. This he tried to do in his well-known confrontation with and temptation of Jesus, to which we have already referred. Satan certainly knows the Bible better than we do. After all, he was one of its main characters from the beginning. And he knows how to use it against us through sophistry and semantics, abilities that many of our academics, clergy, lawyers, and politicians routinely practice.[3]

It is furthermore not inconceivable that Satan played a great part in making the Bible a confusing and difficult book to read. This is illustrated by the fact that Jesus spent much of his ministry arguing with the Jewish hierarchy of his time over how the Old Testament scriptures were to be read and understood.

Another powerful yet effective weapon Satan uses, and which is naturally terrifying to us, is his ability and that of his followers to possess the bodies of mortal beings:

> And when he [Jesus] came out of the ship, immediately there met him out of the tombs a man with an unclean spirit, Who had his dwelling among the tombs; and no man could bind him, no, not with chains: Because that he had been often bound with fetters and chains, and the chains had been plucked asunder by him, and the fetters broken in pieces: neither could any man tame him. And always, night and day, he was in the mountains, and in the tombs, crying, and cutting himself with stones.
>
> But when he saw Jesus afar off, he ran and worshiped him, And cried with a loud voice, and said, What have I to do with thee, Jesus thou Son of the most high God? I adjure thee by God, that thou torment me not. For he said unto him, Come out of the man, thou unclean spirit. And he asked him, What is thy name? And he answered, saying, My name is Legion: for we are many. And he besought him much that he would not send them away out of the country.
>
> Now there was there nigh unto the mountains a great herd of swine feeding. And all the devils besought him, saying, Send us unto the swine, that we may enter into them. And forthwith Jesus gave them leave. And the unclean spirits went out, and entered into the swine: and the herd ran violently down a steep place into the sea, (they were about two thousand;) and were choked in the sea. (Mark 5:2–13; see also Matthew 9:32–33; 12:22; Mark 1:23–26)

Note that the "unclean spirit" acknowledged that "we are many" (two thousand) and that when cast out they entered into the bodies of swine. This is the stuff of modern horror movies and novels, of which there are many, but most of which are fiction.

Before dismissing such scriptural accounts as nonsense or fiction, however, nearly everyone would admit that there are persons in our society or in the world whom we can characterize as evil. These are those who are sociopaths, schizophrenics, pedophiles, serial killers, and the like, who despite all efforts at rehabilitation are incurable. They seemingly have no concept of good or of love or of any of the uplifting traits that place us above animals. They have often been referred to, for lack of a better description, as lunatics, the criminally insane, social deviants, and so on, not unlike the demon-possessed man mentioned above.

Isn't it possible, then, that their ailments aren't necessarily the result of psychosis or a bad childhood, as many modern psychologists and psychiatrists contend, but rather of satanic influences or evil spirits? Of course this possibility is frightening and certainly at odds with modern clinical thinking, but it does account for many of the so-called mental ailments our abundance of psychologists and psychiatrists find bafflingly untreatable.

Undoubtedly, two of the greatest devices Satan uses against us, particularly in our modern era—although they have also been used effectively throughout humanity's history—are money (greed) and sex. Regarding the former, money is a means of gaining power and prestige, often at the expense of others. After all, money is the basis of our entire free enterprise or capitalist system. This was well demonstrated a decade or so ago in the movie *Wall Street,* in which Michael Douglas, portraying a ruthless Wall Street tycoon, declared that, "Greed is good!" And that is one reason Christ preached against being obsessed with worldly wealth. Besides, power and prestige are antithetical to humility, which he also considered so important.

As Jesus pointed out, worldly possessions and personal power won't accompany us in the life hereafter. It is no wonder, then, that Satan continually tries to instill into so many of us the idea that worldly riches and power are so important. Just look around and note how much of our society is focused on newer, more luxurious homes, investment portfolios, expensive automobiles, get-rich-quick schemes, plush vacations, and the like. Furthermore, we shouldn't lose sight of the fact that envy also plays a significant role in all this as well. For example, we envy others who have more of such things than we do, or on the other hand, we feel smug that we have more than someone else. The Christian concepts of humility, charity, and brotherly love are thus drowned out in our rush to get ahead and live the good life.

Equally as important as the love of money and the power it brings is Satan's use of sex to undermine God's plan for us. And his use of it is no longer subtle, but pervasive, blatant, and pernicious. Our sex drives were instilled in us for two purposes only: to perpetuate the human race and to provide extreme physical and personal pleasure between husband and wife. As such, sex was intended, as we have noted previously, as a private personal act that creates bonding and intimacy between two married people. The end result, then, is to produce children born into a tightly knit family raised with love and caring, so that they can become honorable children of God.

On the other end of the spectrum—a prime example of one of Satan's greatest triumphs—is abortion. Now legalized and thus sanctioned by our own government, clinics today routinely destroy tens of thousands of potential human beings each year merely as a means of birth control. Although this barbaric act[4] is now labeled with socially acceptable names such as "pro-choice" or "a woman's right to choose," it is virtually impossible to think that Jesus would not have condemned it. And our country's founding fathers certainly didn't ever intend our Constitution or Bill of Rights to include abortion as one of our freedoms, despite *Roe v. Wade*. We are not such an enlightened society if we think that sacrificing our unborn children in the name of personal convenience is much different than the ancient Israelites tossing their children into burning cauldrons as human sacrifices to the god Molech (Deuteronomy 18:10; 2 Chronicles 28:3).

Earlier, we dwelt at length on the enormous human potential that is lost with each abortion. Since one can't tell beforehand how a child will turn out, what would the loss to our humanity have been if the mothers of Jesus, Moses, George Washington, Abraham Lincoln, Martin Luther King Jr., the Prophet Joseph Smith, or any other of our great world leaders had practiced abortion? Far more important than his potential as a human being, however, is the fact that, as Bruce R. McConkie wrote, man comes forth in an embryonic state possessing "all the faculties and powers of a god."[5] With every abortion, therefore, Satan must howl with glee.

In addition, we can easily see around us how Satan has perverted and cheapened this private bonding experience of sex and physical intimacy between husband and wife. Our society no longer looks on marriage or the tightly knit family as important. Many mothers are now career women, abandoning the children they don't abort to day care centers. And extramarital sex is now regarded as normal. In other words, "everybody does it," even if it still constitutes fornication or adultery, both of which, as noted previously, the Bible condemns. Our laws and entertainment media have insured this with glamorous and explicit portrayals of easy divorces and abortions, as well as sports figures, politicians, and celebrities jumping in and out of bed with anyone and everyone.

Sex has even become a profitable spectacle in our theaters and on television screens. Note, for example, how many of our television sitcoms and movies feature graphic sex scenes between unmarried couples and gays, or use them as comedy themes accompanied by clever innuendo and titillation. Furthermore, X-rated channels on our televisions and pornographic publications, those devoted to explicit sex, are lucrative enterprises. Our society pays millions of dollars each year to see such stuff.[6] This is certainly a far cry from the privacy and intimacy that the sex act was originally intended to provide.

Worse yet, pornography of every type is now acceptable, legal (one of our "freedoms"), and rampant. Gay relationships and marriages are no longer frowned on but are "out of the closet" under the guise that we tolerate and even celebrate diversity. Even those sex practices that were once regarded as the most depraved are now close to being institutionalized in our laws and culture: bestiality, sodomy, group sex, pedophilia, incest, bondage, sadomasochism, and the like. For example, the American Association of Psychiatrists no longer regards pedophilia and homosexuality as abnormalities. Likewise, the American Library Association feels it has no right or obligation to prohibit minors from access to computer internet terminals on which kids can freely surf through porn websites. Don't forget that our public libraries are taxpayer-supported institutions.

And Satan is certainly smugly rejoicing in his great success: disintegrating families, breeding suspicion, causing broken vows, abortions, sexually transmitted diseases, and social instability, not to mention the casting aside of the constraints of God and burdens of religion.

Of course, when speaking of Satan, we can't ignore the related topics of hell and false prophets, both of which also receive much scriptural attention. The concepts of hell and damnation are old and greatly distorted subjects in all of Judeo-Christian theology and the Bible has difficulty describing them clearly.[7] Christian tradition has long held that hell is a place of burning and eternal, ceaseless torment that is reserved for those who defy God and the teachings of Jesus Christ.

Many scriptures do, in fact, relate hell to fire, burning, and torment (see Mark 9:43, 45, 47; James 3:6; Revelation 20:10, 14, 15) but don't provide further details. It is therefore unclear to the casual Bible reader if there actually is such a horrific place to which the enemies of God will go (a place perhaps reminiscent of Dante's *Inferno*), or if scriptural references to it are only symbolic. After all, it is difficult to conceive of a God who would allow this to happen to his children, even if they don't like him very much. Fortunately, latter-day scriptures enlighten us greatly on this topic and clarify the Bible's description of hell.

It is certainly more comforting and logical to think that the hell of the Bible, instead of being eternal burning and torment, will be a place where the evil among us will go, having failed their test of earthly mortality. If that is the case, their torment will be in the knowledge that they will always, eternally, realize that they failed to attain the exaltation and blessings they could have. They will leave this life to dwell at a much lower level than those who continue on to exaltation.

But how about those billions on this earth who never hear of God or Jesus Christ, or never have the opportunity to accept or reject the teachings of Jesus? The Bible fails entirely to address this reality (which is just fine with Satan), so we can only assume that such persons will still, at a later time in eternity, be able to begin or resume their progression, just the same as we do who have a head start now. This presumes that God, in his wisdom and fairness (and through temple ordinances for the dead), will give us all the same opportunities to progress, whether we have the chance to hear of him while on this earth or not.

In our discussion of Satan above, brief mention was made of false prophets who, under his influence, will try to reroute us away from following the teachings of Jesus. Christ was well aware of Satan's tactics in this respect and spoke often of them:

> Jesus answered and said unto them, Take heed that no man deceive you. For many shall come in my name, saying, I am Christ; and shall deceive many. Then if any man shall say unto you, Lo, here is Christ, or there; believe it not. For there shall arise false Christs, and false prophets, and shall shew great signs and wonders; insomuch that, if it were possible, they shall deceive the very elect. (Matthew 24:4–5, 23–24)

Such instances of Satan and his angels imitating Christ, performing miracles, and stirring up dissension among the followers of God is similar to incidents reported in the Old Testament. As a matter of fact, the ancient Israelites were apparently besieged by false prophets:

> The prophets prophesy falsely; and the priests bear rule by their means; and my people love to have it so: (Jeremiah 5:31)

> Therefore hearken not unto the words of the prophets that speak unto you, saying, Ye shall not serve the king of Babylon: for they prophesy a lie unto you. For I have not sent them, saith the Lord, yet they prophesy a lie in my name; that I might drive you out, and that ye might perish, ye, and the prophets that prophesy unto you. (Jeremiah 27:14–15)

> For thus saith the Lord of hosts, the God of Israel; Let not your prophets and your diviners, that be in the midst of you, deceive you. . . . For they prophesy falsely unto you in my name; I have not sent them, saith the Lord. (Jeremiah 29:8–9; see also Micah 3:11)

Doesn't this sound like many congregations today? The history of Satan, "the king of liars," utilizing falsehoods to achieve his ends, then, is nothing new, yet he has been remarkably successful with his deceptions. We hear often nowadays of persons portraying themselves as Christ, such as "Father Divine," or "God," whom we referred to earlier. Or the "Jesus" who recently tried to rob a garbage truck driver with a pair of scissors. Yet another "Jesus" is a penitentiary inmate suing the government for special treatment due to his special status. Many prominent ministers and preachers sway large followings of worshipers away from Christ rather than to him through questionable religious preaching and services.

As pious and devoted as they may seem, many modern men of the cloth are undoubtedly inspired more by Satan than by Jesus Christ. For example, how many do we actually hear preaching strongly against abortion or homosexuality, as we would expect? Aren't these practices that, although acceptable and condoned in our modern society and in many churches, Jesus Christ would undoubtedly have condemned?

To summarize briefly, Satan and his hordes of followers are as real as God, Jesus Christ, and ourselves. Furthermore, Satan, as a supremely intelligent and powerful being, plays a sinister adversarial role in attempting to sabotage God's plan of salvation. We should consequently by no means ignore or underestimate him. Perhaps we would do well to equate his role in our lives with that of "the evil empire" spoken of two decades ago by Ronald Reagan (although at that time he was referring to the Soviet Union, a political entity), or even with "the dark side" of George Lucas's *Star Wars,* which has become a well-known part of Hollywood history. There is, in fact, a dark side to be contended with while we are here on this earth, and the remainder of our eternity will depend on how we deal with it.

As noted above, in the great war that occurred in our premortal existence, Satan and a sizeable portion of God's children were banished from heaven to the earth, where they have remained to this day—and where they will continue to remain until Satan is bound at the beginning of Christ's millennial reign.

To adequately comprehend the size of his army of satanic angels, then, we are told in latter-day scriptures that those who were thus banished constituted one third of all God's spirit children (D&C 29:36–37). Since the present population of the earth is around six billion (not counting those who have historically lived and died since Adam), we can conservatively estimate that those banished followers of Satan number at least two billion. That enormous number of satanic angels, therefore, is now around us on this earth under Satan's command!

It would be our folly to underestimate Satan, the prince of this world. He has an intimate knowledge and understanding of God, of the plan of salvation, and of us, gained through thousands if not millions of years that began in the premortal existence. He therefore knows all about Jesus, the Bible, the prophets (both ancient and modern), and us as individuals. And he certainly knows much more than we individual mortals do about the implications of God's plan for us and the teachings of Jesus Christ. He is constantly using that knowledge and understanding against us, against God, and against the plan of salvation. As he knows full well that the end of his influence is approaching in these latter days, it is only logical that he is now greatly increasing his efforts and strategies in a final desperate act of rebellion against God.

To properly assess what we are up against, it would be a mistake to assume that Satan and his accomplices are carrying on their battle for humanity randomly or without strategy. On the contrary, Satan has been watching God's strategy here on the earth for a long time and has plenty of help in implementing a battle plan of his own.

For example, those who have worked in the corporate world or have served in the military will most certainly understand the term *chain of command.* Simply put, it is an organizational structure in which large-scale plans are formulated at the top (among the military chiefs of staff or a corporate board of directors), and orders for carrying out those plans are then given to the next lowest and subordinate echelons (the generals or managers). After that, more specific orders are passed on down through lower echelons (colonels and captains, or supervisors and foremen) until they reach the ones who must put them into action, who are the foot soldiers or lower level employees.

This is not unlike how governments work—from the executives at the top, to midlevel managers, to everyday employees. Furthermore, the Church of Jesus Christ of Latter-day Saints operates in much the same way. The Church is managed by the prophet, First

Presidency, and the Quorum of the Twelve Apostles. Church programs are formulated at this highest level (with direction from on high, of course), and their directions are given to stake presidencies, and from these to bishoprics all over the world. Under the bishoprics, the plans are implemented in the various ward quorums and auxiliaries.

Is there any reason to think that Satan wouldn't operate similarly? It doesn't seem logical that he is personally trying to mislead and deceive all six billion of us, does it? Among his top staff would be those spirits with the most enthusiasm and leadership abilities—his generals. Satan's orders would be passed on through the various levels of his organization until they reach his daily operatives, those satanic angels working on you and me. And don't forget, there are at least two billion of them to carry out his orders. Is it any wonder that apostasy is a trademark of humanity's history and that each of us must contend with difficulties and temptations on a daily basis?

Even worse is the fact that of those spirits who sided with Jesus Christ and God in the premortal existence, millions have since turned away from God their mortality here on the earth. For example, Josef Stalin, Adolf Hitler, Pol Pot, Sadam Hussein, and thousands upon thousands of other despicable people who opted for the course presented by Jesus during the premortal existence, just as we did have since chosen Satan as their leader. We commented earlier on the dregs of our society—mass murderers, abortionists, purveyors of pornography and smut, and the like—all of whom have turned their backs on Jesus Christ and God and have chosen to follow Satan here on the earth.

Many have become simply apathetic to religion and aren't concerned with either God or Satan. Similarly, many have become confused or are so wrapped up in the ways of the world that they have no concern about how they are going to spend the rest of eternity. Many have been led astray by religious leaders. And there are also many—tens of thousands—who have turned against God and actively seek to undermine the teachings of Christ. In other words, Satan and his two billion angels are now joined by tens of thousands of our fellow mortals against us!

Thus, Satan's campaigns and strategies have been very successful, for only a small minority of humanity throughout history has remained loyal to their allegiance to Jesus made in the premortal existence. And one strategy we have alluded to—Satan's reliance on false prophets and others to direct us away from the teachings of Jesus—will be dealt with at length in the following chapters. In short, we are referring to a great worldwide organization, created and administered by Satan and his associates, which the scriptures call "the great and abominable church." This church, whose sole goal is to lead man away from the intent and realities of Christ's teachings, has been another of his more effective tactics.

Many movies have been made, and books written, about Satan, both as a mythical figure and as a real enemy of man and God straight out of the scriptures. And while a few Americans believe in him as a real person, most don't, believing him to be myth or a religious construct whose entire purpose is to scare pious Christians into obedience to their respective churches.

Adding to this disbelief, Satan long ago created a perception of himself among men that he was a beast of some sort, with horns, a pointed tail, hooves, and such like. And that image of him has remained much the same through the centuries. Little wonder, then, that most people nowadays consider him only a mythical figure, just as they do the tooth fairy, Easter bunnies, and elves.

During the last few decades, however, popular depictions of Satan in books and on the screen have been somewhat more realistic than they were heretofore. In keeping with his various strategies, which we have already discussed, it is unlikely that he wants us to remember that he is much like us (minus the body, that is). Many now agree that instead of a beast, Satan is undoubtedly an ingenious, deceptive, and dangerous individual. As the following scripture suggests, many of these descriptions of Satan are undoubtedly true:

> Yea, he [Satan] saith unto them; Deceive and lie in wait to catch, that ye may destroy; behold, this is no harm. And thus he flattereth them, and telleth them that it is no sin to lie that he may catch a man in a lie, that he may destroy him. And thus he flattereth them, and leadeth them along until he draggeth their souls down to hell; and thus he causeth them to catch

> themselves in their own snare. And thus he goeth up and down, to and fro in the earth, seeking to destroy the souls of men. (D&C 10:25–27)

In the last days—our days—we can't afford to be complacent about Satan or the Church:

> For behold, at that day shall he [the devil] rage in the hearts of the children of men, and stir them up to anger against that which is good. And others will he pacify, and lull them away into carnal security, that they will say: All is well in Zion; yea, Zion prospereth, all is well—and thus the devil cheateth their souls, and leadeth them away carefully down to hell. And behold, others he flattereth away, and telleth them there is no hell; and he saith unto them: I am no devil, for there is none—and thus he whispereth in their ears, until he grasps them with his awful chains, from whence there is no deliverance. (2 Nephi 28:29–22)

Had Satan had his way in the premortal existence, our eternity would have been bleak, which is another reason we should respect him, know that he lives, and avoid joining him and his minions during our mortality:

> And our spirits must have become like unto him, and we become devils, angels to a devil, to be shut out from the presence of our God, and to remain with the father of lies, in misery, like unto himself; yea, to that being who beguiled our first parents, who transformeth himself nigh unto an angel of light, and stirreth up the children of men unto secret combinations of murder and all manner of secret works of darkness. (2 Nephi 9:8–9)

The Reality of Evil

Even those who deny the reality of Satan (as well as many of those who aren't particularly religious) must admit that much of humanity indeed has a dark side. And this dark side is difficult to explain despite decades of study by an army of psychiatrists, psychoanalysts, and sociologists. For some reason many of us here on this earth have a sick propensity not only to sin, as we all do, but to commit heinous crimes against our fellow man. We aren't talking about social deviants, burglars, shoplifters, embezzlers, and the like, but about those who seem to have no goodness in themselves whatsoever and who wreak havoc on humanity. The former are motivated by selfishness, greed, and power. The latter, on the other hand, appear to have no motives whatsoever for the crimes they commit and for that reason we are at a loss to understand them or to otherwise help them.

When we consider this latter group, we are speaking of serial killers, mass murderers, pedophiles, serial rapists, and the like. Theirs are crimes against humanity, and because there is no detectable reason why they do what they do, we must simply conclude that they are evil. They, for the most part, have no respect for human life, often not even for their own. As with the man who came to Jesus out of the tombs, cited previously, they often damage themselves and demonstrate few of the characteristics of civilized humanity. That being the case, the most likely culprit—which of course our modern psychiatrists and psychoanalysts refuse to consider—is Satan.

Such evil has existed throughout humanity's history and in many cases is difficult to deny. Sometimes, all evidence points toward Satan or satanism, yet in other cases it just happens and is difficult to recognize for the evil that it is. In the former case, one hears from time to time of what appear to be ritual sacrifices or killings of animals—cats, dogs, and even horses and cattle—but such ritual killings may extend even to human sacrifice. Likewise, one hears from time to time of cults who practice satanic worship and strange rituals, many of which include blood ordinances.

These sorts of dark practices take place from time to time throughout the United States, but happen in other places around the world as well. For example, in Canada there has been a rash of similar practices, particularly among teenagers who were willing to offer themselves or even their family members as blood sacrifices to their "religion." There has long been an epidemic of satanism and occult practices throughout both Canada and the United States. However, reports of them seem to reach the press only around Halloween.

On a broader scale, some of the greatest instances of man's inhumanity to man have been reported around the world, often reaching our history books. Many aren't cases in which satanism or occult practices can be established without doubt, but they can most assuredly be regarded as evil of the worst sort. Familiar examples are Charles Manson and his accomplices, all of whom are serving life sentences in the California prison system for three random and ritualistic murders in southern California; a series of school shootings by students throughout the United States during the past decade, including sixteen students killed by two fellow students at Columbine High School in Colorado; the mass suicides of the residents of Jonestown, Guyana, in 1978, at the behest of their cult leader, Jim Jones; the similar deaths of the residents of the Branch Davidian Compound in 1993 outside of Waco, Texas, who were following the orders of their cult leader, David Koresh, and chose to shoot it out with federal authorities; the Son of Sam killings in New York in 1976 and 1977; the Zodiac Killer who serially killed several people in southern California two decades ago; and the Green River Killer in Washington state who serially murdered forty-eight women before being caught just a year or two ago.

Although much publicity was given to the above cases, such things have been going on throughout human history. They are true examples of evil, but they aren't the worst. Far worse were mass murderers such as Adolf Hitler, "Der Führer" of Nazi Germany during World War II. Not only did his grandiose scheme of world domination and German supremacy cause the deaths of hundreds of thousands in the war, many millions died in Nazi concentration camps and death chambers, including over six million Jews. Hitler was a believer in occult practices, astrology, and witchcraft.

Manuel Noriega, the former Panamanian dictator, drug boss, and admirer of both Hitler and Cuban president Fidel Castro, was responsible for the deaths of thousands of his own countrymen. He too was involved in occult practices, including Palo Mayombe, which involves human sacrifice. He was captured by U.S. forces and imprisoned in early 1990.

Perhaps the worst of all was Josef Stalin, whose ruthless Soviet regime during and after World War II systematically murdered at least fifteen million, mostly his own countrymen.

Even Catholicism played a role in this tragic part of human history. For example, the Catholic Inquisition of the thirteenth century (in the name of God) systematically arrested, imprisoned, tortured, and executed thousands of accused heretics. Later Catholic expansion into the New World during the sixteenth and seventeenth centuries resulted in the deaths of tens of thousands of Native Americans who were killed under church or civil authority, which were usually one and the same. And then there were the Crusades, which lasted from the eleventh through the fifteenth century. Under the pretext of freeing the Holy Land from Islamic control, repeated waves of Catholic crusaders swept through Turkey, North Africa, the Holy Land, and the entire Middle East, killing thousands as they went.

In our day, Bosnia, under the ruthless leadership of Slobodan Milosevic, was the site of ethnic cleansing, reportedly yielding dozens of mass graves when the country was liberated in 1996. Similarly, Sadam Hussein and his ruthless Iraqi regime were responsible for dozens of mass graves filled with those who opposed his dictatorial power. He systematically tortured, imprisoned, and executed tens of thousands. His use of chemical weapons on his own countrymen, the Kurds, became a serious issue in turning world opinion against him.

Looming on the horizon is North Korea, which is still devoutly communist and is apparently willing to risk nuclear war and the mass starvation of its own people to maintain the power of its leader Kim Jong Il. Imprisonment and execution of political prisoners by the hundreds have been going on there for a decade.

Besides all the other chronic problems on the African continent, Uganda (the Sudan) fell into a civil war in 1983 between its major ethnic groups, the Tutsis and the Hutus. Somewhere between 500,000 and two million were killed before hostilities died down, although the country is still unstable.

Following the Vietnam War, under the Pol Pot regime of Cambodia, some two million Cambodians were imprisoned, tortured, and executed, so many that their bodies were used as dikes around hundreds of miles of rice paddies.

Closer to home, Fidel Castro, dictator of Cuba since the 1950s, has maintained his power to this day through imprisonment, torture, and execution of tens of thousands. To escape his tyranny, hundreds of Cubans risk death each year trying to get to the United States.

And right here at home, Timothy McVeigh, an anti-government sympathizer skinhead, blew up the Murrah Federal Building in Oklahoma City several years ago, killing 168 people, including children in a day care center.

Finally, leaving the past and looking into the future, random terrorist atrocities throughout the world are becoming commonplace. For the last several decades, thousands of innocent civilians have been murdered in such places as Ireland, the Middle East (particularly in Israel), Spain, Germany (the 1964 Olympic Games), Africa, and elsewhere.

However, the 2001 terrorist attack on the World Trade Center in New York City finally brought these mass murderers into sharp international focus. Whether perpetrated by al-Qaeda, Hamas, the PLO, Irish political groups, or solitary dictators (Uganda's Idi Ahmin), such attacks are usually provoked by political or religious fanaticism. The fact that they target innocent everyday bystanders with no ax to grind whatsoever, such as children, elderly people, businesspersons, worshipers at religious services, and tourists indicates that such atrocities are usually attributable to nothing more than hatred.

Doubtless, dozens of other examples could be cited, as mass murder, especially during war—as in the Korean War, the Vietnam War, and World War II, in which thousands of Allied POWs were systematically tortured and executed by Asians—has been going on as long as humanity has fought against humanity. This sort of enmity is obviously exactly what Satan desires and is the opposite of everything Jesus taught.

Although there has been a marked increase in serial killings in the United States during the past century, it is worthy of note that these accomplices of Satan have practiced their evil worldwide as well. Perhaps they have not created as much havoc among humanity as have the mass murderers above, they are nevertheless a further illustration of Satan's power over some.

We must simply recall such well-publicized serial killers as

Richard Speck, who, in 1966, killed eight student nurses in their dormitory; David Berkowitz, also known as the Son of Sam, who killed six and wounded seven in New York City in 1976–77; Ted Bundy, who killed dozens of women two decades ago; Andrew Cunanan, who killed five homosexual men in 1997; Jeffrey Dahmer, who killed at least fifteen boys and young men two decades ago (he was also a cannibal and used his victims' body parts as household decorations); Albert DeSalvo, also known as the Boston Strangler, who sexually assaulted and strangled twelve women in 1962–64; John Wayne Gacy Jr., who was a model citizen and Chicago businessman who molested and killed between twenty-eight and thirty-three boys two decades ago; Gary Leon Ridgeway, also known as the Green River Killer, who was recently captured and accused of the deaths of at least forty-eight women, mostly prostitutes, in the Pacific Northwest; Jack the Ripper, who killed five women in London in 1888, including his wife, whom he dismembered (he was also involved in satanism, black magic, and the occult); Ted Kaczynski, also known as the Unabomber, who was well educated and mailed letter bombs to his victims, killing three and injuring several others; Leonard Lake and Charles Ng, who kidnapped several women during the mid-1980s throughout California and the Pacific Northwest (their victims were brainwashed into becoming sex slaves and were then murdered); John Allen Muhammad and Lee Boyd Malvo, also known as the D.C. Snipers, who shot and killed ten and wounded three in the Washington, D.C., area in 2002; Charles Manson, who was an itinerant psychopath and attracted similar misfits to himself, plied them with drugs, and had them kill three apparently random victims in their southern California homes (his motto or trademark was helter-skelter, a slogan meant to incite warfare between the races); Tommy Lynn Sells, who confessed to twelve murders, mostly young girls, in Texas in 1999 (he used guns, knives, a bat, a shovel, an ice pick, and his bare hands); Michael Swango, who as an Ohio State University medical intern in the 1980s, allegedly killed forty-eight of his patients, calling them mercy killings; and the Zodiac Killer, who was never caught and has not been heard from since 1986 (he killed several people in southern California).

Serial killers have taken their toll in nearly every country in the world, not just in the United States. This abbreviated list, unsavory as it is, demonstrates the lengths to which Satan will go to achieve his ends. His sole intent is to turn us away from the teachings of Christ and against each other. And this diabolical intent will only intensify as the last days draw nearer.

> And now if ye are not the sheep of the good shepherd, of what fold are ye? Behold, I say to you, that the devil is your shepherd, and ye are of his fold; For I say unto you that whatsoever is good cometh from God. And whatsoever is evil cometh from the devil. Therefore, if a man bringeth forth good works, he hearkeneth unto the voice of the good shepherd, and he doth follow him; but whosoever bringeth forth evil works, the same becometh a child of the devil, for he hearkeneth unto his voice, and doth follow him. (Alma 5:39–41)

> Wherefore, a man being evil cannot do that which is good; . . . Wherefore all things which are good cometh of God; and that which is evil cometh of the devil; for the devil is an enemy unto God, and fighteth against him continually, and inviteth and enticeth to sin, and to do that which is evil continually. (Moroni 7:10–11)

Notes

1. The biblical term *devil* is used to represent several different words in Greek, such as slanderer, demon, and adversary. In Hebrew it meant the spoiler. Incidentally, he is certainly not endowed with horns and hoofs as has traditionally been depicted.

2. Many Christians, however, can hardly be called such. Attending church only occasionally or failing to consistently practice the tenets of one's religion in everyday life, as opposed to Sunday only, should indicate little religious conviction on the part of that person. How can one be labeled Christian if he practices only a small percentage of what Christ taught? We all undoubtedly know of many who deny Christianity yet lead better lives than do some of us who pay our religion lip service. Those in this latter category would do well to read Matthew 15:8–9 and James 2:17.

3. An excellent example is President Bill Clinton's absurd statement not so long ago that "oral sex is not sex."

4. It is a grisly act. Let there be no sanitized, socially acceptable pretense about it. Abortion means killing the fetus while in the womb with a saline solution or other chemicals and then sucking it out of the mother, often dismembered, into a sink or tray to be disposed of as garbage. Most parents who engage in this act are aware of these unsavory details but don't stick around to see what they have done. And make no mistake about it, even the new "morning after" pills are essentially the same thing (although they are certainly more private, inexpensive, less messy, and convenient—and thus more socially palatable). With these, the fertilized egg is aborted—an egg that at this point is a potential human being already beginning development. And this applies as well to a fertilized egg in a petri dish. Abortion, by whatever method, means that that baby, a child of God, is denied the opportunity to experience mortality, a fundamental part of the plan of salvation.

5. Bruce R. McConkie, *Mormon Doctrine,* 2d ed. (Salt Lake City: Bookcraft, 1966), 247.

6. Whenever sex is portrayed in such television programs, less than 30 percent is between a husband and wife.

7. The term *hell* originates with the Hebrew word *shoel,* signifying the abode of departed spirits. It is roughly equivalent to the Greek word *hades.*

4

THE SIGNS OF THE TIMES

As noted earlier, Jesus himself provided us with a fairly broad list of events that will occur before his Second Coming. We have also focused on numerous other scriptural references to such events, which references have traditionally come to be referred to as the signs of the times. And, as noted earlier, many such scriptures are symbolic, making them difficult to interpret, or they are general in nature, so much so that they could well apply to almost anything.

Let's now look at some of the events that have been prophesied to occur prior to Christ's Second Coming, and in doing so we'll try to appraise them realistically in terms of history (both man's history as well as that of the earth) and in terms of latter-day scripture. At the same time, we'll attempt to avoid religious dogma that fails to stand up to such an appraisal. In doing so, we'll also try not to attach dates to any of the prophesied events, but to simply determine, if we can, whether they have occurred; and if not, in what sequence we can logically, and scripturally, expect them to occur. To be more exact is folly, for "the day of the Lord will come as a thief in the night" (2 Peter 3:10).

President Joseph Fielding Smith, in 1966, however, provided us with a good synopsis of how near the Savior's Second Coming is:

> Many things have taken place during the past 136 years to impress faithful members of the Church with the fact that the coming of the Lord is near. The gospel has been restored. The Church has been fully organized. The priesthood has been conferred on man. . . . Israel has been and is being gathered to the land of Zion. The Jews are returning to Jerusalem. The

> gospel is being preached in all the world as a witness to every nation. Temples are being built, and ordinance work for the dead, as well as for the living, is performed in them. . . . Thus the work of the Lord is advancing, and all these things are signs of the near approach of the Lord.[1]

In examining the events that are to occur prior to Christ's Second Coming, it might be well to refer back to Jesus' own discussion with his apostles regarding his Second Coming, in which he referred to the Great Flood and Noah. Again, humanity's attitude toward God and the guidance of the scriptures hasn't changed drastically since those days:

> But as the days of Noe were, so shall also the coming of the Son of man be.
>
> For as in the days that were before the flood they were eating and drinking, marrying and giving in marriage, until the day that Noe entered into the ark,
>
> And knew not until the flood came, and took them all away; so shall also the coming of the Son of man be. (Matthew 24:37–39)

In other words, prior to Christ's Second Coming, it will be business as usual for those who ignore biblical prophecy.

There is no paucity of scriptures that prophesy of what we can expect in the last days. The Old Testament contains dozens of such references, although in many cases they may easily be interpreted as referring to the first coming of Christ as well as to his Second Coming. This has historically been the point of contention that caused the split between Judaism and Christianity centuries ago. Nonetheless, there are literally dozens of New Testament prophecies, latter-day prophecies, and commentary from our latter-day church leaders that tell us what to expect in the last days:

> And it shall come in a day when it shall be said that miracles are done away. . . . And it shall come in a day when the blood of the saints shall cry unto the

> Lord, because of secret combinations and the works of darkness. Yea, it shall come in a day when the power of God shall be denied, and churches become defiled and be lifted up in the pride of their hearts; yea, even in a day when leaders of churches and teachers shall rise in the pride of their hearts, even to the envying of them who belong to their churches. Yea, it shall come in a day when there shall be heard of fires, and tempests, and vapors of smoke in foreign lands; And there shall also be heard of wars, rumors of wars, and earthquakes in diverse places. Yea, it shall come in a day when there shall be great pollutions upon the face of the earth; there shall be murders, and robbing, and lying, and deceivings, and whoredoms, and all manner of abominations; when there shall be many who will say, Do this, or do that, and it mattereth not, for the Lord will uphold such at the last day. . . . Yea, it shall come in a day when there shall be churches built up that shall say: Come unto me, and for your money you shall be forgiven of your sins. (Mormon 8:26–32)

In these verses, Mormon, who at that time was fleeing for his life from the Lamanites, effectively described the last days, our own time, which we discussed in the last chapter.

Y2K

Although the prophets of the Bible didn't precisely predict this modern phenomenon, it is included here due its wide publicity a few years ago and as an example of the folly of trying too hastily to shout, "The end is in sight!"

For those who fail to recall the events of only a few years ago, two things occurred relatively simultaneously, neither of which was of monumental importance. But combined, they were pronounced by many as a sure sign of the end of times. The first applied to our reliance on computers. By and large, most computer users rely on IBM computers or those that are built to be essentially the same ("clones") and which use the same software. This is no affront to Mac users, but it is a fact. In any case, IBM personal computers began to appear in wide-scale use in the mid-1980s.

What nobody realized or worried about at that time was the fact that all IBM computers were built with an internal clock ticking away to conveniently help us to keep track of time without thinking about it. This was a great boon, not only for simply knowing what time of the day it was (or year, or month, or date), but it greatly facilitated properly assigning dates and times into any number of computerized functions, such as accounting (for example, due dates for invoices, or compiling month, end reports), opening and closing doors (as on bank vaults at 9 A.M.), lubricating the time-sensitive transactions of the stock market (which must operate efficiently and flawlessly at breakneck speed), coordinating military movements and governmental activities worldwide, and even setting off a timer when your microwave has completed warming your leftovers from yesterday.

In other words, not only has automation taken over many of our mundane everyday tasks, doing them more quickly and efficiently, but it also makes our power grids work, regulates the stoplights as you drive through town, punches the correct day and time on your time card, keeps track of your phone bill, and hundreds of other things we depend on every day. IBM-style computer chips are to be found in nearly all automated devices, each of which was then programmed to deal with dates only in the 1900s.

What IBM programmers failed to consider until around 1998 was the fact that their super machines had not been programmed to reckon into the future beyond 1999. The year 2000 was to be their undoing. Not to go into details about how all this came to be, it simply meant that as the year 2000 approached, automation experts became obsessed with the fact that at midnight, as 1999 became 2000, 90 percent of all computerized functions in the world would become confused, unable to figure out what the date 1/1/2000 was, and would simply shut down. This meant, as many widely feared, our electricity grids would leave us in the dark, banks wouldn't be able to open, traffic everywhere would come to a standstill, Wall Street would be in a panic, military and governmental functions would cease, international commerce would die, and failure of our automated coffeemakers and alarm clocks would render our daily existence unbearable.

Basically, the programmers were right. These things would have happened, except, man's innovation and problem solving came to the rescue. Aided by our free enterprise system, certain computer programmers saw that a fortune was to be made by solving the IBM Y2K problem, and solutions were forthcoming—and some of those programmers got rich. In a word, the great Y2K disaster was averted and humanity continues to exist.

At about the same time, as has happened on other occasions in the past, those who look intently at calendars and try to compute the date of Christ's Second Coming calculated that that event was certain to occur at the beginning of the third millennium A.D. In other words, the year 2000, roughly 2,000 years after the birth of Christ, was to be the beginning of the end. That, coupled with Y2K fears, was a sure sign to many that the end was at hand. All the great trials and tribulations predicted in the scriptures were definitely about to occur, undoubtedly set off by Y2K.

This didn't happen. Y2K went by and is now largely forgotten. And Christ didn't come. Of course, this doesn't mean that he won't come during our new millennium. On the contrary, he may very well do so, and again, when we are least prepared. As Joseph Fielding McConkie observed, when discussing the seven seals in the book of Revelation:

> In the Doctrine and Covenants we read: "In the beginning of the seventh thousand years will the Lord God sanctify the earth, and complete the salvation of man, and judge all things, and shall redeem all things, . . . and the sounding of the trumpet of the seven angels are the preparing and finishing of his work, in the beginning of the seventh thousand years—the preparing of the way before the time of his coming" (D&C 77:12; see Moses 7:62).
>
> Rather than welcome Christ at this time, we are told, we will begin the preparations for his coming. The revelation, which takes the form of questions and answers, then asks, "When are the things to be accomplished, which are written in the 9th chapter of Revelation?" which describes the wars and plagues

> to be poured out during the seventh seal. The Lord answered, "They are to be accomplished after the opening of the seventh seal, before the coming of Christ" (D&C 77:13). Again we are told that the coming of Christ and the beginning of the seventh seal are not synonymous. How close are we to the Second Coming? The question cannot be answered by turning to a calendar. It can only be answered in terms of the events that have been prophesied to take place before Christ's return.
>
> After the coming forth of the Book of Mormon and the restoration of the gospel, the most important event to precede the Second Coming is the declaration of the restored gospel throughout the nations of the earth (Matthew 1:31; Moses 7:62). John the Revelator promised that the message of the restored gospel would go to "every nation, and kindred, and tongue, and people" through the Book of Mormon (Revelation 14:6; D&C 13:37). . . . Nephi tells us that there will be congregations of the Saints "upon all the face of the earth" before Christ's return (1 Nephi 14:12) . . . and that they [will have the opportunity to receive] the fullness of temple blessings.
>
> This chain of thought suggests not only that the restored gospel must be freely taught among the Arab nations, for example. . . . It further requires that there be Latter-day Saint congregations throughout all Arab nations and that there be those in their congregations who have received the fullness of temple blessings. Some considerable time will be necessary for such promises to be fulfilled.[2]

It might be well to point out regarding Brother McConkie's assertion that the Arab nations must also receive the gospel and have the opportunity to do temple work before Christ's return also applies to Israel. In the case of the Jews, however, they are to receive the gospel only after the Gentile nations have received (or rejected) it. We will discuss this in more detail shortly.

As trivial as the apprehension about Y2K turned out to be, we must not lose sight of the fact that our modern world is extremely fragile. We continue to have dictatorial nations with grandiose schemes of world domination. We have weapons of mass destruction, many of which are hidden who knows where. We have international terrorists and fanatics who may have such weapons and can travel freely throughout the world with them.

A good example of such fragility is our growing reliance on international commerce. It has often been said that the world is growing smaller with our rapid modes of travel and instant worldwide communications. The world is also becoming more interconnected. In this country, we have a relatively stable economic system on which our daily needs, investments, retirements, medical care, and the like depend. Most Americans can't now recall the Great Depression or even many of the minor fluctuations in our economy that have since come and gone with only minor impact on most of us.

The past few years, as a matter of fact, have proven kind to the American people, with decreasing unemployment, low inflation, good wages, a higher, more comfortable standard of living, and an improving stock market. However, several factors have emerged over the past decade that should be of concern to us. First is the inescapable fact that the good times can't last forever. As our older generation from the first half of the 1900s can recall, this can (and probably will) change drastically.

Although economic experts assure us confidently that another severe depression can't now occur, as it did in the pre-World War II period, our world has experienced extensive transformations since that time. We have been going through several decades of deep political instability in which governmental corruption, campaign finance scandals, voter apathy and cynicism, and immorality and deceit by our political leaders are taking a decided toll on our traditional institutions. And since our economy is inextricably linked to our political soundness, our period of comfort and prosperity may well end before long.

In addition, we are, as a nation, economically tied to the rest of the world. Whenever the politics and economies of other countries experience good times and bad times, those ups and downs affect us as well. Several years ago, for example, our stock market and economy distinctly felt the effects of economic turmoil in many Asian countries as well as in Russia. As a result, our stock market experienced a period of severe ups and downs, which continued for months. If the economic conditions within those countries had become even worse, our stock market, with its international ties, would undoubtedly have suffered yet more. This could easily be the case again in the not far-distant future—an unsettling prospect as record numbers of Americans are now investing in the stock market with hopes of some day retiring on those investments.

Similarly, because we are a world trading power, not only is our stock market affected by other countries, but our trade economy is also affected. Due to the same problems in Asia and Russia that we noted above, many of our major international trading businesses suffered from declining sales to those areas of the world.

This is further exacerbated by the fact that much of our economy has undergone a transition during the past few decades from a manufacturing and exporting base to one aimed primarily at services. In other words, we are not the great industrial giant we once were, and we find ourselves becoming more and more dependent on the rest of the world to export to us the things we used to provide for ourselves and for everyone else. Consider, for example, that we are a huge importer of petroleum and electronic products, and that we now import much of our clothing, automobiles, and other significant items from elsewhere.

Add to this the fact that many of our larger industrial and manufacturing corporations, through recent international trade agreements (such as the North American Free Trade Agreement) and because of cheaper operating and labor costs elsewhere, have moved much of their manufacturing operations out of this country. This makes us even more dependent on the rest of the world, and consequently more susceptible to their whims and problems. Obviously, none of this bodes well for us as time goes on.

Wars and Rumors of Wars

> War is probably the most satanic and evil state of affairs that can or does exist on the earth. It is organized and systematic murder, with rapine, robbery, sexual

> immorality, and every other evil as a natural attendant. War is of the devil; it is born of lust (see James 4:1). If all men were righteous, there would be no war; and there will be none during the Millennium (see Isaiah 2:1–5) and in the eternal kingdom of God. Words are incapable of expressing the human depravity that has accompanied war in every age, but the era of time known as the last days is the one in which the most extensive and wicked of all wars have been and will be fought.
>
> Modern warfare began with the American Civil War, and it will continue to increase in severity and wickedness until the final great struggle at Armageddon when our Lord will return to cleanse the earth and usher in the millennial reign of peace.[3]

Brother McConkie does concede, however, that some wars are justified, as was the case in the Civil War and World Wars I and II. American engagement in the latter two was necessary in order to ensure worldwide freedom and the defense of our nation, which are also necessary requirements for the continued spread of the gospel. Even Alma expressed the same sentiment over two millennia ago:

> Now the Nephites were taught to defend themselves against their enemies, even to the shedding of blood if it were necessary; yea, and they were also taught never to give an offense, yea, and never to raise the sword except if it were against an enemy, except it were to preserve their lives. (Alma 48:14)

And most recently, President Gordon B. Hinckley stated,

> Modern revelation states that we are to "renounce war and proclaim peace" (D&C 98:16). . . . There are times and circumstances when nations are justified, in fact have an obligation, to fight for family, for liberty, and against tyranny, threat, and oppression.[4]

For some reason, most likely due to the unrelenting influence of Satan, men have always found justification to fight one another. The Old Testament is full of accounts of wars between peoples, some of them even instigated by God. Originally, many wars were fought over territory for food, but rulers soon expanded their reasons to include the need for more room not for food but for wealth and natural resources, for national pride, the settling of differences between rulers, for so-called just causes in the name of religion, and for any number of other reasons. Only recently in history have we come to include *national defense* in our sophisticated war lexicon, and now we even include preemptive wars as a reason to preclude anticipated wars, as in the recent U.S. invasion of Iraq.[5]

Perhaps for all these reasons, the scriptures contain so many references to the need for love, peace, humility, and harmony among men. As a matter of fact, the entire ministry of Jesus Christ was devoted to these virtues. But in the 2,000 years since his time, humanity has unfortunately learned little about how to avoid wars. This is perhaps the primary reason so many scriptures regarding the last days contain references to wars. The fact is that in the last days wars won't only continue but will increase in number and destructiveness. Seldom a year has gone by during the past two millennia, in fact, when there hasn't been some part of the world engaged in war, squabbling, or preparing for war.

Since the Peloponnesian War, around 450 B.C., there have been at least thirty-five major wars, including. The current United States War on Terror and the strife surrounding Israel. Twenty-one wars have taken place within the last century alone. According to the United Nations, there are today an average of fifty wars or smaller conflicts going on somewhere around the world at any given time. But we must not forget the greatest war of all, the war in the premortal existence when Satan and one-third of the hosts of heaven fought against the Lord for control over the destiny of humanity.

Commenting on ancient prophecy, our church leaders noted during the times of World Wars I and II:

> Peace has departed from the world. The devil has power today over his own dominion. This is made in the actions of men, in the distress among the nations,

> in the troubles that we see in all lands, including this land which was dedicated to liberty.[6]

> Our Heavenly Father has told us in great plainness that the world will be in distress, that there will be warfare from one end of the world to the other, that the wicked shall slay the wicked and that peace shall be taken from the earth.[7]

Our country alone, during its relatively short history, and with our repeated declarations of peaceful intent, has been engaged in numerous wars of one kind or another. With international affairs as tightly knit as they are by modern transportation and communications, our leaders have felt it necessary to become involved in conflicts all around the world, even when our national security isn't directly threatened. Furthermore, such organizations as the United Nations and the North Atlantic Treaty Organization, both of which have the proclaimed goals of peace and international security, and both of which are heavily underwritten by the United States, often seem unable to do anything to avoid wars and conflicts.

Of even more concern, however, is the fact that modern man now has destructive potential never heretofore imagined. As noted previously, we now have the ability with our modern weapons to destroy not only all humanity on the earth, but probably all other life as well.

In recent years, moreover, warfare and the potential for conflict have become simultaneously more subtle and confusing. Numerous rogue states exist, which when coupled with their support of terrorism and their influence in the international community, provide the tinder that could easily explode into World War III. For example, such nations as Libya (despite its peaceful overtures), Iran, other Arab states, and Iraq each are perpetual trouble spots that highlight an additional and even worse problem—religious conflicts.

The latest flash point in this respect is the growing militancy of the Islamic world against the West, terrorism being the best example. Imagine what would happen, then, if some extremist group were to destroy the remains of the Temple of David in Jerusalem, or, likewise, if some similar group were to bomb the Dome of the Rock nearby, one of Islam's holiest sites. The instant worldwide repercussions should be obvious.

It is a sad fact of history that religion has been one of the worst culprits in inciting wars, which obviously gives Satan great satisfaction. More wars have been fought in the name of religion than for any other reason. And this doesn't exclude wars fought in the name of God and Christianity. As noted above, the Old Testament records numerous wars fought over the Holy Land, which conflicts continue even today in the continuing disputes between the state of Israel and its surrounding Islamic neighbors.[8]

The scriptures even prophesy that the final battle of humanity will be fought there (Zechariah 14:2). This strife between the Muslim and the Judeo-Christian world will undoubtedly be the fuel to ignite that final battle. Note, for example, how many conflicts in our day can be traced to this traditional enmity—wars in the Holy Land, due to international terrorism, in much of the Middle East, in Pakistan, in Afghanistan, in Iraq, and elsewhere. In all of these, Muslims have been pitted against either Christians or Jews.

But even Christianity has some blame to share in historical and modern conflicts. Such shameful events as the Crusades, the Inquisition, and the continuing conflict in Ireland between Protestants and Catholics have resulted in hundreds of thousands of deaths, all in the name of God. Even today, in our own country we see political animosity between religious conservatives ("the religious right") and many on the political left. Is it any wonder, then, that given all of the above, Jesus prophesied, "And ye shall hear of wars and rumours of wars . . . For nation shall rise against nation, and kingdom against kingdom" (Matthew 24:6–7).

Perhaps one of the few good things that can be said about wars is that they sometimes further the Lord's work, as we have noted previously. For example, Orson Pratt labeled some wars as preparatory wars: "One purpose of the preparatory wars is to prepare nations for the preaching of the gospel."[9]

One of the best examples of Orson Pratt's "preparatory wars" was the Cold War, which ended in the '80s. When the traditional enmity between the United States and the Soviet Union ended and the states of Eastern Europe were freed, those former Soviet states opened up vast opportunities for missionary work. Those people, 122 million of them, who were virtually devoid of religious freedom for so long, are now turning to the restored Church by the hundreds.

But to reiterate Bruce R. McConkie's statement earlier, it can be fairly safely concluded that, as prophesied, wars (whether labeled as preparatory wars or simply those resulting from evils in the world) are in fact becoming more commonplace, devastating, and deadly. This was also the conclusion of Joseph Fielding Smith:

> Have we not had numerous rumors of wars? Have we not had wars, such wars as the world never saw before? Is there not today commotion among the nations, and are not their rulers troubled? Have not kingdoms been overturned and great changes been made among nations?[10]

Natural Calamities

Historians, geologists, and climatologists will confirm the fact that our earth has long undergone changes, including volcanic eruptions, earthquakes, continental shifts, climatological variations, and other assorted natural phenomena. These have all been part of what created the world as we now know it. All students learn in school, for instance, about weather systems, the structure of the earth, continental drift, ice ages, erosion, and what produces mountains, rivers, earthquakes, volcanoes, and the like.

This is all to say that the earth, which is in reality a complex system, is simultaneously dynamic and stable. We look at it from a short-term perspective, only of a few thousand years, about as long as man has been on our planet. All around us, however, changes are taking place, many of which go unnoticed because they are so commonplace and slow.

The wind blows and removes dirt and soil from one place, which it deposits somewhere else. As a result, traces of ancient civilizations and fossils are often buried under layers of soil. That is why paleontologists and archaeologists must often dig in order to pursue their studies. Similarly, rivers are slowly but steadily dredging out canyons while their sediment forms deltas along our seashores. Mountains are being either lifted up[11] or worn down. Continents are moving.[12]

Climates are changing. The Sahara Desert wasn't always a desert, and Antarctica was once tropical, as was the United States.

All of these changes, in turn, cause changes in the plant and animal life that inhabits the various parts of the earth's surface and oceans. Over the space of tens of thousands of years, the earth and its myriad ecosystems have changed dramatically. The world we perceive around us is nothing more than a short-term snapshot of those changes that are constantly underway.

Of course, many changes in our natural world occur relatively rapidly, and we can't help but be aware of them. Examples are earthquakes, storms, and volcanoes. Such events continue to illustrate the dynamic nature of the earth's many natural systems and the changes continually going on all around us.

The scriptures contain many references to enormous changes in the earth's natural systems that are to occur in the last days. Some are to take place over a period of time preparatory to the return of Jesus, while others—the most devastating—are to occur at or near his coming. Jesus referred to some of these, as have prophets, ancient and modern:

> For not many days hence and the earth shall tremble and reel to and fro as a drunken man; and the sun shall hide his face, and shall refuse to give light; and the moon shall be bathed in blood; and the stars shall become exceedingly angry, and shall cast themselves down. (D&C 88:87)

> And thus, with the sword and by bloodshed the inhabitants of the earth shall mourn; and with famine, and plague, and earthquake, and the thunder of heaven, and the fierce and vivid lightning also, shall the inhabitants of the earth be made to feel the wrath, and indignation, and chastening hand of an Almighty God, until the consumption decreed hath made a full end of all nations. (D&C 87:6)

The scriptures refer to darkness that will cover the earth. That particular event is mentioned many times but will probably not be like a simple solar eclipse, which humanity has experienced before. More than likely, it will be much like the absolute darkness that covered the land of the Nephites at the time of Christ's death:[13]

> And it came to pass that there was thick darkness upon all the face of the land, insomuch that the inhabitants thereof who had not fallen could feel the vapor of darkness; and there could be no light, because of the darkness, neither candles, neither torches; neither could there be fire kindled with their fine and exceedingly dry wood, so that there could not be any light at all;
>
> And there was not any light seen, neither fire, nor glimmer, neither the sun, nor the moon, nor the stars, for so great were the mists of darkness which were upon the face of the land. And it came to pass that it did last for the space of three days that there was no light seen. (3 Nephi 8:20–23)

Some say that calamities around the world, such as storms, earthquakes, volcanoes, and the like are accelerating in frequency and destructiveness, a sure sign that the last days are upon us. For example, M. Russell Ballard recently stated,

> And there shall be famines, and pestilences, and earthquakes, in divers places" (Matthew 24:7). Some of these things seem to be occurring with ever-increasing regularity.
>
> If we measured the natural disasters that have occurred in the world during the past ten years and plotted them year by year, we would see an acceleration. The earth is rumbling, and earthquakes are occurring in "divers places." Our human nature, being what it is, we don't normally pay much attention to these natural phenomena until they happen close to where we live. But when we contemplate what has happened during the past decade, not only with earthquakes but also with regard to hurricanes, floods, tornadoes,

> volcanic eruptions, and the like, we see an accelerating pattern.[14]

To properly assess the incidence and destructiveness of such natural calamities as they relate to the last days, let's discuss them one at a time.

Earthquakes

Many enormous storms, earthquakes, and volcanoes have occurred in the earth's recent history, but let us not forget that until the last several centuries few people were present, or they took place where few people lived, so that there exist few records of them. Don't forget that the earth's population, until the last several centuries, numbered only in the millions, not in the billions as it does today. The earth was much less densely populated a thousand years ago, and there was consequently a lot more unpopulated, empty space. As a matter of fact, our global population was less than two billion in 1900, whereas it is projected to surpass six billion within the next decade or so.

Geologists will readily acknowledge that earthquakes and volcanic eruptions, which were much more destructive than recent ones, have occurred often in our western states over the last several thousand years. However, little was recorded about them because they affected only the few Native Americans who were living there at the time. But more recently, one may ask, how about the widely reported earthquakes in Kobe, Japan, and in California, along the San Andreas Fault? In addition, our news services have provided us with dramatic recent coverage of earthquakes in Istanbul, Iran, in the Pacific Northwest, in Pakistan, in Afghanistan, and other places worldwide. These are well known as geologically active areas where massive earthquakes have regularly occurred for millennia.

In other words, current earthquakes and volcanoes around the world can't necessarily be construed to mean that they are signs of the end. We presently have a much larger population spread all over the earth, an efficient news media that reports such occurrences more dramatically and extensively, and geologists who study them more exhaustively than ever before. As a result, the public is now more keenly aware of such cataclysmic events than ever in the past.

Although composed predominantly of rock, the earth's crust (which is between five and thirty miles thick) on which we live is in a constant state of flux. It is constantly shifting up, down, and sideways as the result of pressures within the earth, as well as from the stresses of the continental plates that are also being driven by the same internal forces. This shifting of the earth's crust, measured in only fractions of inches per year in most places, is imperceptible to us, except when a large and sudden shift occurs, as in the earthquake and tsunami that occurred in southeast Asia in 2004.

Are there, in fact, more earthquakes lately than during the past 2,000 years? It is difficult to say. It should nevertheless be pointed out that fault lines, which are associated with earthquakes, crisscross every portion of the earth's surface like complex spider webs. They are simply areas where the earth's crust is fractured, where portions of the earth's surface are, or can be, moving slowly in different directions, as much as an inch or two each year.

With this slow movement, stresses within the crust build up and the surface may break loose and move quickly in one direction or the other. The result is vibrations throughout the surrounding area that we know as earthquakes. They may be minute shifts at varying depths beneath the ground, or they may be massive movements that cause major shifts beneath and at the surface, so great that landslides may result, cracks may appear, rivers may change their courses, or buildings may topple.

Furthermore, earthquakes are most concentrated in areas where the earth's crust is undergoing change, as at the edges of continental plates that are pushing slowly against one another, as discussed previously. These are generally mountainous areas, such as the Andes, our own Rocky Mountain and western coastal ranges, the mountain-islands of east and southeast Asia, which include Japan and the Philippines, the Himalayas, and so forth. It is precisely in these regions, geologists point out, that most earthquake and volcanic activity occur. Of more consequence now in the latter days is that more of the same is predicted in such regions.

Stories are commonplace about the San Andreas Fault, which is expected to shift before long,[15] causing another massive earthquake similar to the one that occurred in 1906. A similar fault, the Wasatch Fault, lies along the Wasatch Front in Salt Lake Valley and

Utah Valley, running directly through heavily settled portions of Salt Lake City. It too is expected to shift soon, resulting in an earthquake of fair size. The fault can be found to run through basements and foundations of existing homes throughout that area.

In fact, the Wasatch Fault is a classic example of the cyclic nature of earthquakes. It last slipped 1,284 years ago, and the intervals between earlier quakes at the same location range from 1,270 to 1,442 years apart. Obviously, another slippage, or earthquake, is due anytime. Its devastation is almost guaranteed. A quake of a magnitude of 7.5 on the Richter scale (a fairly large quake)[16] would kill an estimated 7,600 people in the Salt Lake Basin, injure 44,000 others, and cause $12 billion in damage.[17] Experts warn, furthermore, that no area within the Salt Lake Valley will be spared when the Wasatch Fault slips again.

Similar active faults, or earthquake and volcanic zones, have been mapped all along our West Coast as well as throughout coastal Alaska, Japan, the Philippines, and the western regions of Central and South America. These regions have been labeled the "ring of fire" by geologists because of the many active volcanoes (and earthquakes) that proliferate around the circumference of the Pacific Ocean.

In order to discuss earthquakes of the last days, it is first necessary to point out that the scriptures make a fairly firm distinction between earthquakes that are to occur in the last days and "the Great Earthquake," which is to occur as Jesus returns to the earth. The former we will discuss here and the latter in a later chapter when we discuss the return of the Savior.

Recent earthquakes, within the last century or two, have been well reported and studied by geologists. However, the scientific study of earthquakes is comparatively new. Until the eighteenth century, few factual descriptions of earthquakes were recorded, and the natural cause of earthquakes was then little understood.

The earliest earthquake for which we have descriptive information occurred in China in 1177 B.C. It was followed by several dozen large earthquakes during the next few thousand years. Earthquakes in Europe are mentioned as early as 580 B.C., but the earliest for which we have some descriptive information occurred in the mid-sixteenth century. The earliest known earthquakes in the Americas were in Mexico in the late fourteenth century and in Peru in 1471, but descriptions of their effects were not well documented.

The most widely felt earthquakes in the recorded history of North America were a series that occurred in 1811 and 1812 near New Madrid, Missouri. A great earthquake, whose magnitude is estimated to have been about 8.0, occurred on the morning of December 16, 1811. Another great earthquake occurred on January 23, 1812, and a third, the strongest yet, on February 7, 1812. Aftershocks were nearly continuous between these great earthquakes and continued for months afterwards. These earthquakes were felt by people as far away as Boston and Denver (750 and 400 miles away, respectively). Because the most intense effects were in a sparsely populated region, the destruction of human life and property was slight. If just one of these enormous earthquakes occurred in the same area today, millions of people and buildings and other structures worth billions of dollars would be affected.

The San Francisco earthquake of 1906 was one of the most destructive in the recorded history of North America. The earthquake and the fire that followed killed nearly seven hundred people and left the city in ruins. The Alaska earthquake of March 27, 1964, however, was of greater magnitude than the San Francisco one. It released perhaps twice as much energy and was felt over an area of almost 500,000 square miles. More than 114 people, some as far away as California, died as a result of this earthquake, but loss of life and property would have been far greater had Alaska been more densely populated.

Many earthquakes, in the eighteen centuries after Christ, killed hundreds of thousands each. However, few earthquakes ever reach a confirmed magnitude of 9.0 or greater. Only five that we know of have fallen into this category:

- January 1700 (9.0)—off the United States northwest Pacific coast (0 fatalities)
- November 1952 (9.0)—the Kamchatka Peninsula of the Soviet Union (0 fatalities)
- November 1957 (9.1)—the Andrean of Islands, Alaska (0 fatalities)
- May 1960 (9.5)—Chile (5,700 fatalities)
- March 1964 (9.2)—Prince William Sound, Alaska (125 fatalities)

No earthquake has approached these magnitudes since 1964. But are earthquakes increasing in number and destructiveness, as many contend when studying the writings about the last days? Joseph Fielding Smith hinted as much:

> The whole earth is in commotion. Earthquakes in divers places are reported every day. I took the liberty to call Dr. Melvin Cook and have him get for me some facts about how many earthquakes we have now. He quotes from a recent book (*Earthquakes and Earth Structure) by* John H. Hodgson (chief, Division of Seismology, Dominion Observatory, Ottawa) the following: "The way the numbers [of earthquakes] go up as the magnitude goes down makes it easy for us to accept the estimate that if all earthquakes down to zero magnitude could be detected, the number would be between one and ten million each year." Then he goes on to say that there are about 2,000 earthquakes each year with the magnitude between 5 and 6, and about 20,000 between 4 and 5. Therefore, it looks as if there are around 20,000 earthquakes a year that could be damaging if they occurred in populated areas.[18]

More recently, the U.S. Geological Survey declared 2003 the deadliest earthquake year in a decade: 43,819 people were killed, versus 1,711 in 2002. One must be careful in declaring this to be a sure sign of the end, however. Variables to be considered include the population densities in the areas where the earthquakes occurred—whether they occurred in poorly built cities or in more modern, earthquake resistant ones; the availability of emergency aid and medical treatments; and so forth. Obviously, if a majority of such earthquakes, even of moderate intensity, occurred in densely populated cities within many of the poorer countries of the world, the loss of life would have been much greater than in sparsely populated regions or in many more modern urban areas with stringent building codes.

Perhaps the best indicator of whether earthquakes are increasing in number and destructiveness over the last century would be to examine a summary of all major earthquakes (of magnitude 4.0 or greater) worldwide over that time period.

Table 4.1

Earthquake Magnitudes by Decade (1900–2003)

Decade	4.0–4.9	5.0–5.9	6.0–6.9	7.0–7.9	8.0–8.9	9.0 +	Fatalities
1900–09			1	4	4		155,500
1910–19			1	4			30,096
1920–29			6	5	4		546,033
1930–39			4	6	5		190,155
1940–49			1	6	4		118,835
1950–59		1	4	6	2	2	1,604
1960–69		4	3	4	2	2	46,609
1970–79		2	5	11	1		618,721
1980–89		7	14	9	2		48,373
1990–99	1	5	17	18	5		107,743
2000–03	5	21	14	20	2		25,999

Regarding the table above, a few comments are necessary. I have included all earthquakes of magnitude 4.0 or greater for which there are reliable records. As noted previously, many earthquakes occur daily somewhere in the world, the majority of which are small and of little consequence. Of the larger ones shown above, some resulted in great devastation and loss of life. Again, this is a reflection more of where they occurred than of their size. A careful study will show that many of these sizeable earthquakes in which tens of thousands of lives have been lost were in places of high population densities and where, due to economic conditions, homes and other structures were not soundly built with great earth tremors in mind. In addition, several earthquakes in coastal areas were accompanied by tsunamis, great tidal waves caused by seafloor earthquakes. Consequently, many of the fatalities shown were due to flooding and drowning rather than earth movement and collapsed buildings.

Note also that many smaller earthquakes, of magnitudes less than 6.0, don't begin to appear until the mid-1900s. This is a reflection of the fact that geologists and seismologists didn't acquire the technology necessary to measure these smaller earthquakes on a comprehensive, global basis until just a few decades ago. Larger earthquakes, greater than magnitude 5.9 (which are the most serious ones), have always been more readily detectable, but even more so during the past few decades as our global detection and recording capabilities have improved. This is a theme we will return to shortly.

It is also well to keep in mind that fatalities due to natural disasters, such as earthquakes, hurricanes, floods, and the like, have been decreasing substantially over the past century. This is a result of stricter building codes, greater public and official awareness of such dangers, improved emergency preparedness and aid, and better warning systems. Because of these improvements and because of generally rising economies in many underdeveloped countries around the world, fatalities should continue to decline from such calamities. Of course, tens of thousands may well still die from such catastrophic events, but the massive numbers in many cases shown above should definitely trend downward from what they have been historically, except for those resulting from unusually horrific natural disasters.

Which brings up the question we addressed earlier: Are earthquakes, in fact, increasing in frequency and destructiveness as the prophecies of the last days predict? A careful analysis of the above statistics yields contradictory conclusions.

Graph 4.1

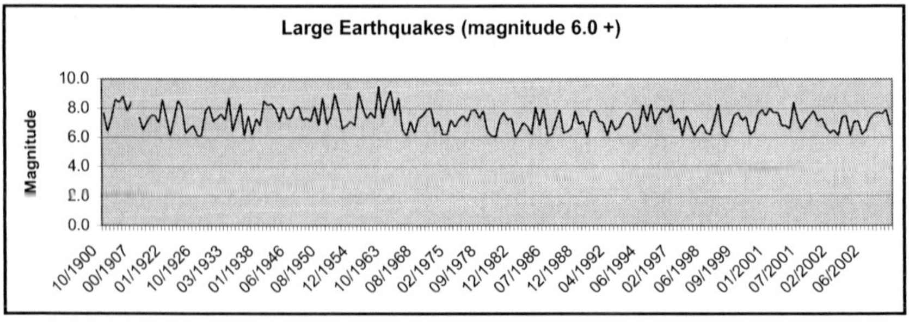

Looking only at the historical magnitude of large earthquakes (included in the graph above are those of magnitude 6.0 or greater), it would appear that they have remained relatively static in size for the last three decades. Although many above 8.0, and even above 9.0, occurred more frequently prior to 1970, none have exceeded 8.4 since then. It is interesting, however, to note that they surged upwardly significantly in the mid-1900s but since then tapered off. As a matter of fact, the past three decades appear to be relatively benign compared to those of the early and mid-1900s. Again, earthquake magnitude, and not the number of fatalities, is the best indicator of earthquake size.

The other prophetic factor to be considered, besides earthquake *magnitude*, is whether or not the total *number* of earthquakes is increasing. The graph below, which includes all earthquakes of which there are reliable records, indicates that the number of earthquakes each year has remained relatively static until just recently. The apparent recent surge in earthquake frequency may lend credence to prophecies that earthquakes will increase in the last days. Three comments, however, are in order.

Graph 4.2

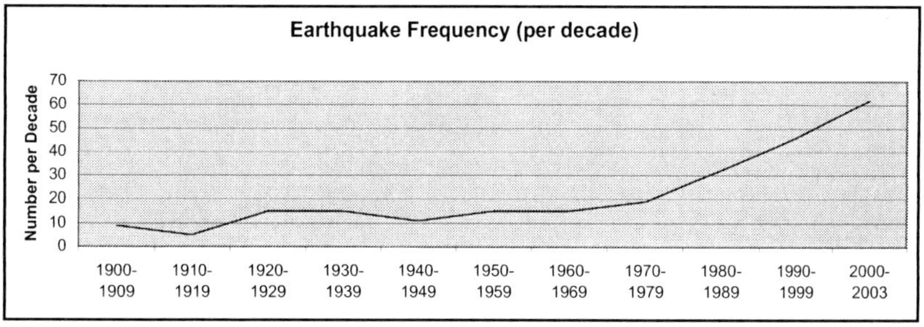

The first is that because large, destructive earthquakes seem to be on the wane of late, the bulk of the increase in numbers of earthquakes must consist of smaller ones. Secondly, we must wait a bit to see if this apparent upward trend continues or increases. (A brief spike upward may not mean much unless it continues.) And third, it may well be, and is probable, that comprehensive scientific detection, recording, and reporting on earthquakes around the world is improving. Dozens of earthquakes occur somewhere around the globe daily, and we may only recently have become capable of detecting, compiling, and reporting them all.

This was recently confirmed by earthquake experts at the California Institute of Technology, who stated that earthquake monitoring has greatly improved in the last few decades, which will account for the apparent increase in earthquake frequency. According to them, "due to increased detection and processing capability," many more earthquakes are now being recorded. These are primarily the smaller ones in the 4.0 and 5.0 range, which have always occurred, but previously "detection was so bad that no one noticed." This undoubtedly applies also to those between 5.0 and 7.0.

Note in Table 4–1 that earthquakes in the 4.0–5.9 range don't consistently appear until the 1960s. They undoubtedly also occurred much earlier but went undetected and unrecorded. As large earthquakes, those exceeding 6.0, are apparently not on the increase, the rapid rise in total earthquake frequency depicted in the graph above must have been attributable to smaller earthquakes that are just recently being detected.

In conclusion, then, it would appear that huge, destructive earthquakes have not been increasing lately even though the actual number of earthquakes, including smaller, insignificant ones, *may* be trending upward. As of now, we can't realistically claim that the prophecies are being fulfilled in this respect. Yes, earthquakes are occurring "in divers places," but they are no more destructive than in the past—not yet.

Volcanoes

Although volcanoes aren't mentioned specifically in the scriptures, except perhaps in references to fire and brimstone, many people include them among the calamities to occur during the last days. But as with earthquakes, volcanoes have been a significant part of the earth's history since its early formation, and much more so millions of years ago than recently. Similarly, many volcanoes have historically erupted (and continue to do so even now) largely unknown to most of us because they often do so in remote regions where few of us live. As a result, fatalities from volcanoes are relatively few when compared with those from earthquakes. Of course, we continue to hear of deaths due to volcanic eruptions from time to time and volcanoes are indeed fearsome and destructive spectacles wherever they occur.

Nevertheless, many of us live in volcanic regions without being aware of it, especially in our western states and even more so in Alaska and Hawaii. But because of end-of-the-world prophecies regarding fire, brimstone, and burning, of which there are many, and because of widespread media attention to these particularly spectacular natural disasters, we have become more aware of them now than ever before.

Are volcanic eruptions increasing in frequency and destructiveness, as many fear? What about Mount St. Helens in Washington state in 1980, or Popocateptl, near Mexico City, in 2002, or Pinatubo, in the Philippines, in 1993,[19] and the continuing eruptions of Hawaii's volcanoes? Many point to these, along with recent earthquakes, as sure signs of the end. This may or may not be the case, however, as many of these volcanoes have been cyclically erupting for tens of thousands of years.

In fact, there have been in excess of 8,000 volcanic eruptions over the past 10,000 years. The largest volcanic eruption in humanity's history with a VEI (Volcanic Explosivity Index) of 7 was that of Tambora in Indonesia in 1815. It exploded thirty-six cubic miles of ash into the air to an altitude of twenty-eight miles, which eventually spread around the earth. As a result, 92,000 persons around the world died, not from the eruption itself, but from starvation and disease as a result of worldwide cooling caused by the ash cloud encircling the earth. This atmospheric cooling effect is a theme we will return to later.

Today, about 550 volcanoes worldwide can be termed active, while twice that number may be dormant. At least fifty are active in North America alone.[20] And this doesn't include those on the ocean bottoms, of which there are a large number. About sixty volcanoes erupt each year, although the bulk of them are small eruptions, and there are usually as many as twenty in eruption somewhere in the world at any given time. A summary of the number of the world's major active volcanoes follows:

Africa and the Indian Ocean—7

Asia—67

Europe and the Atlantic Ocean—13

North America—47

Central America and the Caribbean—19

South America—18

Australia, New Zealand, and the Pacific Ocean—16

Antarctica—1

Recent eruptions or earthquakes, then, are often simply a continuation of the volcanoes' cyclic patterns.[21] Even Mount Etna in Sicily, south of Italy, has been erupting continuously since mid-2001, sending a hazy smoke plume southward as far as the Sahara Desert in North Africa, where it can be clearly seen in satellite photos. Similarly, Kilauea, in Hawaii, has been erupting almost continuously since 1983, and Pavlov, on the Alaskan coastline, erupts every five years on average.

A detailed and comprehensive record of known volcanic eruptions is available from the Smithsonian Museum of Natural History. Beginning in 9850 B.C., and continuing to our day, more than 225 significantly large (VEI 4 or greater) volcanic eruptions are known to have occurred around the world. This number doesn't, however, include those of less than 4 VEI, as few records are available concerning smaller eruptions. Let's not forget that not all volcanic eruptions are devastatingly explosive as is so often dramatically and spectacularly shown on television and in film. Many are simply upwellings of lava resulting in lava flows that aren't necessarily preceded or accompanied by massive explosions.

Here, we will focus only on those volcanic eruptions that have occurred in the last century with a VEI of 4 or greater.

Table 4.2

Volcano VEI by Decade (1900–2002)

Decade	4	5	6
1900–09	5	2	1
1910–19	9		1
1920–29	4		
1930–39	7	2	
1940–49	4		
1950–59	6	1	
1960–69	6	1	
1970–79	4		
1980–89	7	2	
1990–99	5	2	
2000–02	3		

As with earthquakes, some comments are necessary regarding the volcanic table above. For example, it must be reiterated that many volcanoes erupt cyclically over almost perfectly predictable time spans. Examples from the above are Vesuvius, which has erupted seven times since the time of Christ, Mount St. Helens, which has erupted six times since 1860 B.C., and Pinatubo, which has erupted twice since the 1300s.

Are there, however, more significantly large volcanic eruptions now than in the past? The above graph of volcanic eruptions of VEI 4 or larger indicates that this may not be the case.

Graph 4.3

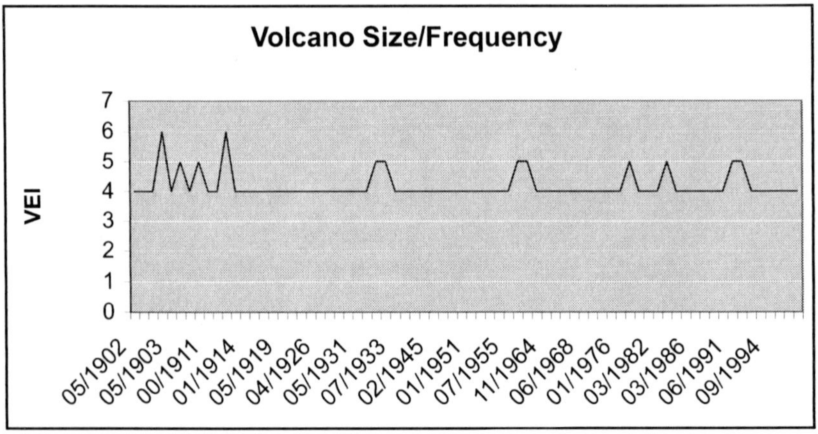

It is quite evident in the graph that, although a number of sizeable eruptions occurred throughout the early 1900s, less have done so since then. During the past 90 years, in fact, no volcanoes have erupted anywhere in the world with a VEI of over 5. Compared with eruptions in the past of 6 and even 7 VEI, the last several decades have been relatively quiet despite Mount St. Helens, Pinatubo, and Hawaii's volcanoes, all of which have received widespread media and public attention.

Furthermore, there doesn't appear to be a marked increase in the frequency of volcanic eruptions anywhere around the world. The number of volcanoes erupting each year remained fairly low throughout much of the 1800s and has shown fairly wide fluctuations each year since then. But there is no definite trend indicating any sort of increase in eruption frequency over the last century. Short of an occasional spike from time to time, there is a marked absence of any upward trend during the past couple of decades. It would appear, then, as we found with earthquakes, that there is little to show that prophecies surrounding these latter-day events have yet come to pass. Volcanic eruptions occur frequently, in various magnitudes, but don't seem to be increasing in either size or frequency.

Tornadoes

Consistent with prophecies describing the last days, many people are concerned about storms of various kinds and the devastation they wreak on humanity from time to time. To fit in with the great natural calamities that are to occur in the last days, tornadoes are probably some of the most fearsome natural events one can think of. We are just beginning to understand them, although weather watchers still have great difficulty forecasting precisely where a tornado will touch down or how violent it will be. They understand which weather systems are likely to spawn these violent windstorms, but beyond that there is still much to be learned.

This is all to say that tornadoes are often violent weather systems that are still basically unpredictable. As a result, few precautions can be taken against them except in terms of building better, tornado-resistant structures. In other words, resorting to an old-fashioned storm cellar is probably still the best defense against them.

Data regarding tornadoes is widely available, and in that data, as was the case with earthquakes, one will note that fatalities due to tornadoes fluctuate wildly, depending on whether they occur in heavily populated areas or in the open countryside. In addition, fatalities from these storms have been showing a general decline over the last few decades, undoubtedly due to stringent tornado-resistant building codes in tornado-prone areas and because of improved warning systems.

This brings up another important point regarding these particular storms. Although they occur from time to time in various places and countries,[22] the central United States is the world's hot spot for tornadoes. Without getting into climatological details, tornadoes generally proliferate in open country where warm moist air meets cooler, dry air. In other words, the open American plains provide an excellent meeting spot for warm, moist air moving northward from the Gulf of Mexico and cooler Canadian air moving southward. When these two air masses meet, turbulence results, which often spawns thunderstorms, hailstorms, and tornadoes.

Records are available of many larger tornadoes that have occurred in the United States since the mid-1800s. Until just recently, however, many tornado records were little more than compilations of newspaper accounts, which left much to be desired in terms of analytical accuracy. It is well to note that approximately 1,000 tornadoes per year touch down somewhere in the United States. Most are small, although they too cause damage and fatalities. Until lately, only the larger ones were recorded. Of these, F4s and F5s account for 67 percent of all tornado fatalities.

As was the case with earthquakes, accurate and comprehensive tornado records have been kept only since 1990 by the National Oceanic and Atmospheric Administration (NOAA) and the National Weather Service. Prior to that time, recording of smaller tornadoes (F3 and smaller) was spotty at best. We must therefore keep this in mind as we try to correlate tornado data with last-days prophecies.

Keep in mind also the fact that tornadoes are frequently spawned by hurricanes; they could then be called "spin-offs," if you will. In addition, the terms *tornado swarms* and *multiple vortices* are also now in use. These simply reflect the fact that large thunderstorm systems can generate multiple tornadoes. For example, as many as 147 separate tornadoes touched down from one huge thunderstorm system April 3–4, 1974, in Michigan, causing more than three hundred fatalities. Nearly all were rated F3 or above.

This can be a problem in record keeping, because tornadoes, or groups of them, often cross county and state lines. This means that the same tornado may be recorded separately in two separate places. A tornado swarm can likewise be difficult to accurately classify in terms of true F scales and locations.

As with earthquakes, which rely on the Richter Scale to determine how strong they are, scientists who study tornadoes have devised the "F" (Fujita) scale, which ranks tornadoes as F1, the smallest, through F5, the largest and most violent. The F scale, which first came into use in 1971, is determined primarily by wind speed within the tornado itself as well as by the destruction and size of its damage path on the ground. Larger tornadoes, for example—in the F4 category—may have a damage path a mile wide and fifty miles long. If this damage path were to go through the middle of a city (which several have historically done), it isn't difficult to imagine the death and destruction that would result.

To assess whether such violent windstorms are increasing in frequency and/or destructiveness (as many people who are concerned about the last days fear), the following provides a summary of all tornadoes in America for which we have accurate records during the past century.

Table 4.3

Tornadoes—Number per Decade by F Rating

Decade	1	2	3	4	5	Fatalities	Damage ($)
1900–09				4	1	543	1,250,000
1910–19				3		118	2,630,000
1920–29			1	2	2	1,021	85,230,000
1930–39			1	1	1	434	18,200,000
1940–49				1	1	281	7,700,000
1950–59			1	3	2	325	97,725,000
1960–69				4	4	548	87,000,000
1970–79				2	3	180	63,500,000
1980–89				1		4	1,300,000
1990–99	35	17	25	19	5	245	1.25 billion
2000–03	42	9	7	6		198	Incomplete data

This compilation of data is relatively complete, although there are sure to be some omissions wherein many tornadoes, especially smaller ones, went unrecorded. Smaller tornadoes—of F3 or less—comprise by far the bulk of all tornadoes, as can be seen during the last two decades in Table 4.3 above.

Are large, killer tornadoes increasing then, as prophecies of the last days predict?

Graph 4.4

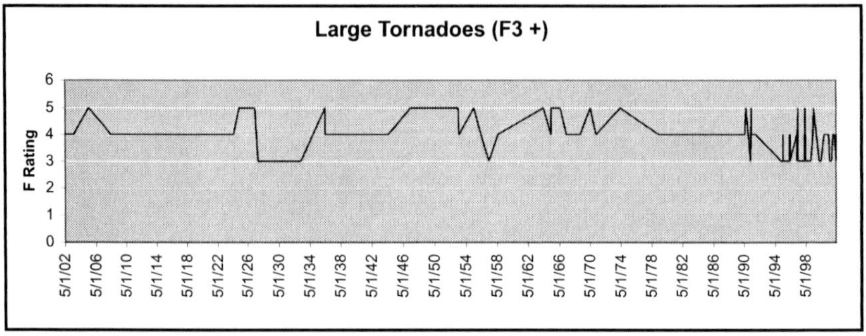

Not according to the graph above, which includes all tornadoes of F3 or greater. However, the overall trend recorded above is inconclusive.

Graph 4.5

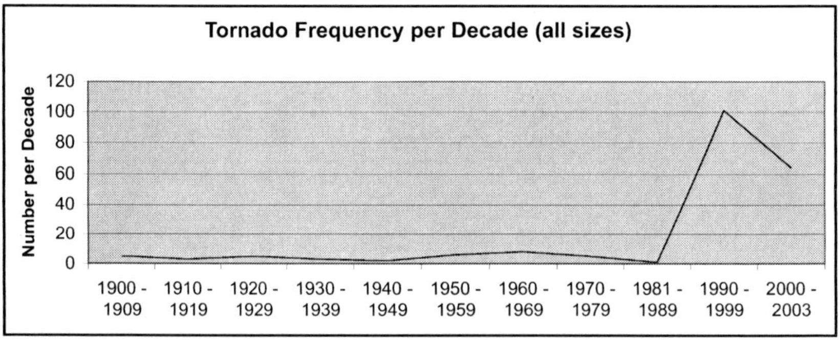

Average tornado size and frequency appears to have remained roughly the same until the last two decades, but the apparent upsurge in large tornadoes and overall frequency since 1990 may, in fact, be misleading. Note in Table 4.3 that smaller F1 through F4 tornadoes show an apparent marked increase since then.

However, instead of an actual increase, this data is more likely a reflection of two factors. The first is that weather watchers meticulously maintained long-term records over the years only for the larger, more significant tornadoes. As a result, many F3 and smaller tornadoes were ignored unless they caused substantial fatalities or destruction, or unless they received media attention. Many were undoubtedly not recorded at all if they occurred in sparsely populated countryside. Only within the past twenty years or so have tornadoes of size F3 or below also been comprehensively studied and recorded.

The second factor is that many thunderstorm systems spawn swarms of tornadoes, as noted previously. These swarms have certainly always occurred, generating dozens of smaller tornadoes as well as some large, killer ones. Weather watchers, until lately, had few means to record the masses of smaller tornadoes all at once. Consequently, most of them went unrecorded. Nowadays, through better monitoring technology, scientists can accurately record every tornado in a storm, even in sparsely populated areas, including those of size F3 or smaller.

The upsurge since 1990 in the graph above undoubtedly is comprised of swarms of F3 tornadoes. They too would have shown up in the left portion of the graph during earlier decades had they been recorded.

Hurricanes

Like tornadoes, hurricanes are fearsome storms that occur along many of our coastlines. As such, they too must be considered when discussing the signs of the times.

In the eastern hemisphere, hurricanes are referred to as typhoons, and they regularly cause concern and damage throughout the western Pacific, including the Philippines, Taiwan, Japan, and Oceania (including Hawaii). In the United States, however, most hurricanes, which develop in the Atlantic and Caribbean, are annual threats to our gulf states and the eastern seaboard. True, some strike the southwest United States coast on occasion, but they are much smaller and fewer, and are therefore of lesser significance.

Hurricanes are similar to tornadoes in that they are circular windstorms, but they are considerably larger and form over warm, open water. As a result, and due to their sometimes enormous size, their impact on our southern and eastern coastal areas makes them distinct and deadly threats. This is further exacerbated by the fact that they develop regularly far to our southeast during the warm months of each year. Hurricanes can be huge—as much as three hundred miles in diameter—and strike the United States mainland virtually every year. Fifteen hurricanes each year is normal, of which nearly half may be considered major.

As with tornadoes, which use the F scale to describe their destructiveness, hurricane watchers have resorted to the Saffir–Simpson Category to describe the destructiveness of hurricanes. These storms are ranked as category 1 for the smallest and up to category 5 for huge, killer hurricanes. And as with tornadoes, hurricane categories are determined by wind speeds within the hurricane as well as by the destruction they cause on the ground.

The table below summarizes hurricanes, by category, that have struck the United States mainland since 1900:

Table 4.4

United States Hurricane Strikes (1900–2004)

Decade	1	2	3	4	5
1900–09	5	5	4	2	
1910–19	8	3	5	3	
1920–29	6	4	3	2	
1930–39	4	5	5	1	1
1940–49	7	8	7	1	
1950–59	8	1	7	2	
1960–69	4	5	3	2	1
1970–79	6	2	4		
1980–89	9	1	5	1	
1990–99	3	6	4		1
2000–04	1	1	2	1	

It doesn't appear, from the data above, that hurricanes have been increasing in either size or frequency over the past few decades. In fact, major hurricanes have been less prevalent in the United States since the 1950s, whereas they occurred more frequently in the decades prior to that time. In general, as can be seen, they have been tapering off since 1960, with the exception of a nominal increase during the 1980s. On the other hand, the most recent, well-publicized hurricane to occur prior to the publication of this book—Hurricane Katrina, in 2005, a category 4—may pose an anomaly. However, its path led directly over the most vulnerable populated areas to hurricane damage in the United States, thus making its magnitude seem out of all proportion in relation recent hurricane weather patterns.

The larger question is whether or not hurricanes are increasing in total numbers, as one might expect in fulfillment of last-days prophecies.

Graph 4.6

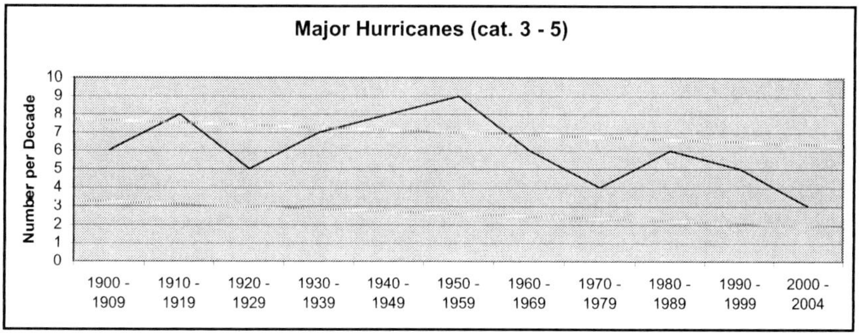

Graph 4.7

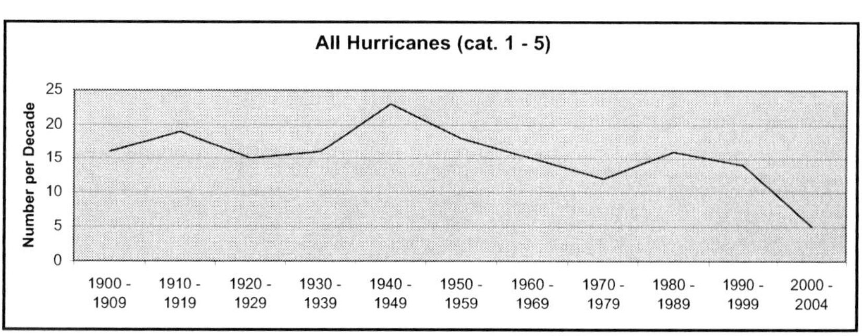

Again, we see little evidence of this in the graphs above. The possibility nevertheless exists that Hurricane Katrina has begun a new pattern of prophetic proportions related to hurricane size and destructiveness, and we will have to wait and see whether that will prove to be the case.

Floods and Tsunamis

Floods are commonplace occurrences every year somewhere on the earth and have been the cause of tens of thousands of fatalities and billions of dollars in property losses throughout history. We have discussed the great Flood at the time of Noah. Here, we will focus on others of historical significance. It should be noted at the outset, however, that floods occur for two broad yet interrelated reasons. First, many floods evolve from entirely natural phenomena, resulting from storms, tidal waves, and the like. These have always occurred and will continue to do so.

The second are floods resulting from man's near-sightedness, poor planning, or sheer stupidity. Examples of these are man's propensity to live along coastal areas and waterways. Although doing so is natural—as we have always relied on oceans, rivers, and streams for transportation routes, agricultural uses, and so forth—living in such places carries with it the distinct possibility of floods whenever water levels rise for whatever reason.

Building in a valley or river floodplain may seem practical and attractive, but all rivers and low places tend to flood at one time or another; that is how floodplains are formed. And throughout history, man has attempted to avert such floods or to divert waterways for better uses by constructing dams and levees. Although often this strategy is successful, it is also prone to failures, the Mississippi, Missouri, and Ohio River systems being good examples. Those waterways have historically been, and still are, the sites of massive floods when their complex systems of dams and levees have given way during unusually wet periods or hurricanes. We can't very well attribute such floods entirely to "acts of God."

Another example of man's poor planning in this respect is his tendency to live in lowlands, especially coastal lowlands. Floods in these places can often be expected, as in the case of Bangladesh and East Pakistan, located on opposite sides of the Indian Peninsula.

Both consist primarily of lowlands just a few feet above sea level. Every few years during the monsoon season, heavy rains are blown ashore from the Indian Ocean and deadly floods are the result. Similarly, Galveston Island on the Texas Gulf Coast was virtually destroyed by a hurricane in 1900. One of the worst natural disasters in United States history, the 12,000 fatalities during that storm were the result not of high winds, blowing debris, or collapsed buildings, but of the huge ocean surge that washed over the island. Galveston Island is a mere sand spit standing only a few feet above sea level.

With this in mind, it should be noted that thousands of luxurious beachfront homes have sprung up (many on hurricane platforms) all along the Gulf Coast and eastern seaboard since the Galveston disaster. They may be attractive places in which to live, but given the fact that a major hurricane strikes precisely those areas every few years, they are simply a disaster waiting to happen. Don't forget that, like Bangladesh, East Pakistan, and Galveston, much of the United States Gulf Coast and eastern seaboard (and Florida in particular) is only a few feet above sea level.

In addition, coastal areas in many parts of the world, especially throughout the Pacific region, are susceptible to tsunamis (or tidal waves, as they are popularly known). These massive walls of water, sometimes dozens of feet tall,[23] are caused by disturbances on the sea floor such as earthquakes, landslides, and the like.

When such a tremor occurs, the displaced mass of water near the quake's epicenter fans outward in a concentric circle at hundreds of miles per hour. A large undersea earthquake, such as some of those discussed earlier in this chapter, may send a tidal wave fanning outward for thousands of miles. An earthquake in the Aleutian Islands in the North Pacific, for example, generated a tidal wave striking Japan, Hawaii, Taiwan, the Philippines, and the entire west coasts of North and South America. Hilo, Hawaii, was nearly washed away by such a tidal wave sixty feet tall in the early 1900s, although it came from the south.

Few comprehensive records are available of floods and tidal waves in humanity's history despite the fact that they are frequent, tragic occurrences. Fatalities due to floods in particular have ranged into the hundreds of thousands, especially in countries like Bangladesh, India, Sri Lanka, Indonesia, and China, where entire cities have repeatedly been washed away. Examples of great floods include one in Holland, where 100,000 died due to a sea flood in 1228. It is well known that much of Holland lies below sea level and only its system of coastal dikes keep the North Sea out. In China, 3.7 million died in 1931 from disease, drowning, and starvation due to the flooding of the Yangtze River;[24] In East Pakistan, 200,000 died in 1970 as the result of a cyclone-driven tidal wave in the Bay of Bengal. And in Hanoi, North Vietnam, 100,000 were killed in 1971 during floods in the Red River Delta.

Although few prophecies predict floods per se in the last days, the Doctrine and Covenants tells us, "And also cometh the testimony of the voice of thunderings, and the voice of lightnings, and the voice of tempests, and the voice of the waves of the sea heaving themselves beyond their bounds" (D&C 88:90). It is apparent that these events haven't yet significantly come to pass, although it is always possible that the earthquake and tsunami to hit the coastal regions of Sri Lanka, Thailand, Malaysia, and Indonesia in 2005 may have begun a new trend.

Disease and Pestilence

> A desolating scourge shall go forth among the inhabitants of the earth, and shall continue to be poured out from time to time, if they repent not, until the earth is empty, and the inhabitants thereof are consumed away and utterly destroyed by the brightness of my coming. (D&C 5:19)

> I do think that one form or another of chastisement shall follow, with its seasons for repentance, for the preaching of the gospel, and crying to the nations of the earth, "Will you now listen unto the Lord," and if they shall not listen, then another affliction will come, until men shall either repent, or they shall perish. For these are the last days, the days preceding the coming of the Redeemer, and he will not come when the wicked stand and flourish.[25]

When the scriptures thus speak of afflictions, disease, and pestilence, we must consider these in two respects: those that will affect humanity directly and those that will affect the food and water supplies upon which we all depend. It is a fact that many of the pestilences and diseases that have historically taken their toll on humanity have been either conquered or, for the most part, controlled during the last century. Our history books, for example, are full of great plagues that at various times resulted in millions of deaths but that no longer do:

- 429 B.C.—A key factor in the downfall of the Athenian state was an outbreak of disease, either scarlet fever, bubonic plague, typhus, or smallpox.
- 1190 A.D.—Plagues and famine reduced armies of the Crusades from 100,000 soldiers to 5,000.
- 1566—Typhus destroyed the 80,000-man German army prior to its attack on Hungary.
- 1741—Austria surrendered Prague to the French after losing 30,000 soldiers to typhus.
- 1853 and 1856—During the Crimean War, 2,000 soldiers died in combat while 50,000 died of disease.
- 1878—During the Turko-Russian War, 80,000 soldiers died of disease, whereas one-fourth that number died in combat.
- 1917–23—Typhus killed at least 3 million in European Russia at the end of World War I.

These massive epidemics don't, of course, include the 25 million who died of the black death in Europe during the 1500s[26] or the tens of thousands of Native Americans who died of various European diseases—most commonly smallpox and influenza—from the days of the Spanish conquistadors to the settling of the American West. As a matter of fact, these imported diseases killed far more Native Americans during that period than did all the weapons of the invading Europeans or the United States Cavalry.

Despite the fact that modern science and technology have rendered most of these diseases meaningless in our modern, Western world, they are still commonplace in many third world countries. But even there, due to improving economies, sanitation, food supplies, and importation of Western medical advances, deadly diseases are becoming less and less the worldwide killers they once were. Cholera, scarlet fever, diphtheria, hepatitis, influenza, tuberculosis, pertussis (whooping cough), and malaria continue to decline throughout the world.

Thus, the world's population increase we have seen over the past century (which has been of such concern to neo-Malthusians) hasn't actually occurred from skyrocketing birthrates but from increased life expectancy worldwide. Nevertheless, some 17 million continue to die each year from infectious and parasitic diseases, most of these in developing countries.

No diseases now plaguing the earth, such the Ebola virus and hantavirus (which have received much media attention), or any of those mentioned above, now come anywhere near becoming the devastating mass killers that humanity regularly experienced just a few centuries ago. Even cancer, heart disease, and the like are no longer the guaranteed killers they were just fifty years ago. The most significant epidemic that affects many Americans nowadays is incongruously our own lifestyle, of which obesity, poor diet, and lack of exercise are the most obvious symptoms. Medical journals and the press are now full of concern that our lifestyle is killing us nearly as fast as any single disease.

The scriptures are full of prophecies about the afflictions and pestilences that are to be unleashed upon humanity if we don't repent prior to the Second Coming of the Messiah. However, it is unclear whether many of these repeated plagues are to be unleashed on us in our present day (or soon) or if they are to befall us just immediately before the Savior's return—at or near the battle of Armageddon, for example. Or, we could now be in an interim period just awaiting the next great plague, as it is obvious that the last great apostasy is well underway and that humanity doesn't appear inclined to repent any time soon.

It may well be that we already have the means at hand to release these promised plagues on ourselves. Weapons of mass destruction have long been developed and used by many nations for centuries. For example, the early settlers of the American West, in a show of apparent beneficence, were known to have distributed blankets to Native Americans that were contaminated with smallpox. More recently, mustard gas was used by the Germans in World War I against American and British troops.

Even more deadly, the United States use of nuclear weapons on Japan to end World War II introduced a new generation of weapons of mass destruction. During that war and since, numerous countries have developed even deadlier nuclear weapons, as well as a whole array of chemical and biological weapons. The idea that threats from these weapons have decreased with the end of the Cold War is naïve, to say the least. The bulk of such stockpiles continue to exist in various places despite worldwide condemnation of their use and widely proclaimed destruction of such arsenals.

Sadam Hussein used nerve agents against his own countrymen in Kurdish Iraq, and terrorists in Japan ineptly tried to use sarin gas, a nerve agent, several years ago in the Tokyo subway system. Even anthrax was sent through the United States postal system following the terrorist attacks on New York's World Trade Centers in 2001.

This brings up a troubling development in the possible—or rather probable—use of weapons of mass destruction. It is all but certain that terrorist organizations, of which there are dozens throughout the world, either now have, or soon will have, access to weapons of mass destruction. Today, small scattered hate groups such as al-Qaeda are mobile, well disguised, and travel freely wherever they want. Consequently, they are difficult to detect and track down despite the best efforts of international police agencies.

It has also been recently demonstrated that a nuclear weapon, even a mildly radioactive replica, can be smuggled from the Middle East through Europe into the United States with relative ease. It would therefore be a simple matter for a small terrorist cell to do the same with almost any sort of small nuclear, biological, or chemical weapon. Our borders are porous despite the best efforts of the United States Customs Service. The bottom line is that with the proliferation of terrorist groups throughout the world who have access to weapons of mass destruction, waves of disease and pestilence of which the scriptures speak could easily become a reality.

With regard to our crops and water supplies, they too are equally vulnerable. A terrorist group or rogue nation would have little difficulty dispersing chemical or biological agents into the water supplies of many of our metropolitan areas, as well as into many of our food supplies. Certainly, much of our imports of fruits and vegetables are monitored as they come into the United States, but many aren't. Our enemies are assuredly aware of this and constantly study our weak points.

As far as our domestic food supplies are concerned, we leave ourselves vulnerable with our modern agricultural techniques despite the fact that they are responsible for alleviating hunger problems throughout the world. Whereas farms at one time produced a variety of crops, we now have giant agribusinesses that practice monoculture—raising a single variety or strain of crop on mega-acreages. Notice, for example, the tens of thousands of acres in our country's midsection that are devoted to only a single strain of wheat or corn.

This situation, understandably, is simply a matter of efficiency and economics, and it has proven eminently successful. That practice could, however, result in widespread devastation of our food supply if a disease or insect showed up with a hearty appetite for that one specific strain of wheat or corn. The result wouldn't be dissimilar to the great potato famine of Ireland in 1845. Fortunately, we have enough of a diversified agricultural base in this country that we would doubtfully see widespread starvation, but the results would nevertheless be frightening.

We can thus see that the prospects of disease and pestilence are real, as the scriptures prophesy. We should therefore not be too smug in our affluence and realize instead that disease and pestilence are likely to strike us sooner or later, as well as harm many other nations, given the precarious state of the world today. We may not be suffering now, but the ingredients are all at hand to prove the prophecies true.

Famines

The scriptures, especially those of the Old Testament, are replete with references to famines, some of which were ordered by God to humble his rebellious and unrepentant people, the Israelites:

> Your strength shall be spent in vain: for your land shall not yield her increase, neither shall the trees of the land yield their fruits. And when I have broken the staff of your bread, ten women shall bake your bread in one oven, and they shall deliver you your bread again by weight: and ye shall eat, and not be satisfied.
>
> And if ye will not for all this hearken unto me, but walk contrary unto me;
>
> Then I will walk contrary unto you also in fury; and I, even I, will chastise you seven times for your sins. And ye shall eat the flesh of your sons, and the flesh of your daughters shall ye eat. (Leviticus 26:20, 26–29)

Famine has been a part of man's history since the time of Adam. But it needs to be noted that famines result from two broad yet interrelated reasons. First, many famines evolve from natural causes, resulting from adverse weather conditions, insect plagues, crop disease, and the like. Other famines are man-caused, such as those due to political strife, war, and inadequate storage and distribution.[27] The first of these causes—natural famines—have been the most prevalent throughout much of our history. The second, however—man-caused famines—have become the rule during the last few centuries.

To understand how ugly and disastrous large-scale famines can be (as few of us in this country miss many meals), let's review some famines described in the scriptures and in our history books:

- Abraham, as righteous as he was, suffered from famine. When Canaan's rains failed, he had to go to Egypt for food (see Genesis 12:10).

- Joseph, the great-grandson of Abraham, encountered a seven-year famine while in Egypt (see Genesis 41:53–57).

- Famine occurred in the days of King David (see 2 Samuel 21:1).

- During the famine of 1065 A.D. in Egypt, a single cake of

bread sold for $14, eggs for $10 per dozen, and a bushel of grain for $20. During that time, hungry and desperate Egyptians resorted to cannibalism.

- Prior to the Black Death in England, in 1314, food became so scarce that people ate dogs, cats, horses, and even human babies.

- The Irish Potato Famine in 1845 was so severe that the death toll reached between 200,000 and 300,000. Like numbers immigrated to England and America to escape this calamity.

- China experienced severe famines in 1906 and 1911 due to the flooding of the Yangtze River. The death toll reached into the millions.

Tens of millions more people died as a result of the great Chinese famine of 1958–61, the Soviet famines of 1921 and 1932–33, and the all-too-frequent recent famines in African countries such as Ethiopia, Uganda, Somalia, and others. These latter are familiar to us through vivid television coverage of sick and starving black children, images that have affected us all, yet which never seem to disappear.

Despite our revolution in agriculture during the past few decades, and the fact that much of the world, the Western nations in particular, have enough to eat, the precarious state now existing between nations is a fair guarantee that our good life can't last forever. All nations are increasingly bound together politically and economically, mostly through trade, which means that another major war or economic catastrophe could easily disrupt our worldwide food supply.

Certainly, we in the United States could easily provide enough food for ourselves, but such an event would almost certainly disrupt our economy in terms of reduced exports, with a consequent loss of jobs. Our political and economic system is both stable and at the same time fragile. We live in a country that is largely governed by the will of the people. Yet, were things to go drastically wrong, especially if the country were not unified, human nature—selfishness, greed, and profiteering—undoubtedly would rear its ugly head. Even though in World War II the people of this nation were unified behind the war effort, we still saw rationing and sharp price increases on many goods, including food items. Farmers fared well, as they had sufficient food and were exempt from military service, and "victory gardens" became a national priority.

We live in precarious times in other ways as well. We, in our affluence relative to the rest of the world, think little of shopping each week at any number of well-stocked superstores. We fill our shopping carts at Albertsons or Safeway with all sorts of items, including many that aren't necessities but are in reality junk food and luxuries. We then put them in our pantries without giving them a further thought. Few of us realize, however, that such stores maintain supplies of inventory on hand to meet normal consumer demand for only a few days at a time. These stores rely on timely shipments of their food and commodities from chains of distribution centers scattered throughout the country.

Visualize, then, what would happen if a sizeable disruption in our transportation system were to occur. Stores' shelves would empty within a few days at most. Similarly, for those who have experienced a hurricane or similar crisis (for which there is usually adequate advance warning), stores run out of food items within a few hours, especially canned goods, bread, eggs, bottled water, milk; camping supplies such as candles, lanterns, flashlights and batteries, camp stoves; and emergency essentials such as generators. Gasoline stations and lumberyards are also overwhelmed and are soon empty.

In other words, we are a nation that is ill prepared for a large-scale crisis of this sort. This is part of the reasoning behind our Church authorities' repeated admonitions to maintain long-term and short-term supplies of food and living essentials for our families. This is prudence and common sense and is a theme to which we will return shortly.

The Great and Abominable Church

Found primarily in the Book of Mormon and in latter-day revelation, this great evil organization—the Great and Abominable Church—is mentioned often in regard to the latter days. As such, its rise (and eventual fall) must be included in the signs of the times. Traditionally, many Latter-day Saints have interpreted the Great and Abominable Church to be Catholicism. But the fact remains that Catholicism is only a small part of the abomination of which the prophets have warned. Nephi enunciated an accurate description of this great church of the devil:

> And he [the angel] said unto me: Behold there are save two churches only; the one is the church of the Lamb of God, and the other is the church of the devil; wherefore, whoso belongeth not to the church of the Lamb of God belongeth to that great church, which is the mother of abominations; and she is the whore of all the earth. (1 Nephi 14:10)

The above situation was the reason behind why Joseph Smith was instructed during his first vision that he should join no church—they were all abominations:

> I was answered [by Jesus] that I must join none of them [the then-existing churches of the world], for they were all wrong; and the Personage who addressed me said that all their creeds were an abomination in his sight; that those professors were all corrupt; that: "they draw near to me with their lips, but their hearts are far from me, they teach for doctrines the commandments of men, having a form of godliness, but they deny the power thereof." (Joseph Smith–History 1:19)

We have already discussed the fact that the final great apostasy is well under way and has been so for nearly 2,000 years. Satan, the master strategist, has effectively employed during that time the lure of a plethora of false religions, enticing billions into believing that they are following the dictates of Christ when in fact few of those religions bear any resemblance to the teachings of the Savior. Worse yet, humanity has become such a slave to apathy and the pursuit of the good life that few seem to care or question the teachings of their churches; or they discard religion entirely.

In that respect, prophecy has assuredly been fulfilled. The Great and Abominable Church is now well established and thriving:

> And it came to pass that I looked and beheld the whore of all the earth, and she sat upon many waters; and she had dominion over all the earth, among all nations, kindreds, tongues, and people. . . . And it came to pass that I beheld that the wrath of God was poured out upon that great and abominable church, insomuch that there were wars and rumors of wars among all the nations and kindreds of the earth. (1 Nephi 14:11, 15)

This latter verse is particularly important because we have seen since the time of Christ great wars not only between non-Christian nations, but between Christian nations as well. Examples are the repeated wars among European nations (nearly all of which nations are predominantly Christian), our own Revolutionary and Civil Wars, and World Wars I and II. The continuing bitter strife between Catholics and Protestants in Ireland is a further example. One must then wonder, as the central theme of Jesus' ministry was love and peace, why it is that Christian nations came to hate each other so much. This too is a fulfillment of prophecy and a good example of Satan's corrupting influence on religion.

True, many such wars were instigated by national leaders who were absolutely corrupt and placed their own power and aggrandizement over sincere religious interests. As a matter of fact, many of them used religion as a tool to achieve their political goals. Prime examples were Adolf Hitler and Benito Mussolini, Axis leaders during World War II. Italy, of course, was predominantly Catholic during World War II,[28] while much of Germanic Europe was either Catholic or Protestant. One must then ask whether those millions of Catholics and Protestants ever questioned why they were fighting against other Christians of the allied powers, when Jesus had proclaimed to all alike, "Thou shalt love one another," and "Thou shalt love thy enemy" (John 13:34; Matthew 5:44).

Even within Catholicism itself, wars have been waged between Catholic nations and over who was the rightful heir to the papacy, or over the right of the papacy to rule other nations. A particularly tragic example of war between Christians—and the fulfillment of much of Nephi's prophecy—occurred immediately before and during the Thirty Years' War in Europe, when the Catholic church tried, through intimidation and force, to maintain its hold against Protestant breakaways. The violence and corruption that ensued, however, wasn't all one-sided.

Due to Catholic pressure to suppress French Protestantism (Calvinism), crowds of Protestants attacked and killed Catholics, smashed statues and stained glass windows, and defiled sacred vestments, vessels, and Eucharistic elements. Catholics, in turn, attacked and killed Protestants. Hundreds of French Calvinists (called Huguenots) were tortured, maimed, and murdered. This violence persisted from 1559 to 1589. The upheaval that took place in France has been described as the greatest bloodshed in France's history aside from the French Revolution.

Such religious violence was duplicated in the Netherlands. In Antwerp on six successive summer evenings, Protestant crowds armed with axes and sledgehammers went after things they claimed reflected false doctrine. They smashed Antwerp's Cathedral of Notre Dame. They smashed altars, paintings, books, and tombs, and destroyed ecclesiastical vestments. They destroyed manuscripts, ornaments, stained glass windows, and sculptures. They sacked over thirty churches and burned libraries. Finally, with the help of 20,000 troops from Spain, the Catholic church, in 1568, reestablished its control over the Netherlands after executing 1,500 Protestant dissidents.

Twenty years later, King Philip of Spain beheaded Mary Stuart, Queen of Scots, a Roman Catholic, in a power play over the throne of England. Upon hearing of Mary's execution, Pope Sixtus V promised to pay Philip one million gold ducats if his troops invaded England. In 1588, an armada of 30,000 men and 130 ships sailed for an attack on England. The English navy, however, was victorious, and only sixty-five Spanish ships returned to Spain.

The Thirty Years' War itself began in 1618 when Spanish armies, intending to secure the rule of the Catholic church, attacked Prague. This attack included mass executions, confiscation of Protestant properties, the forced conversion of Protestants to Catholicism, and a mobile inquisition to weed out heretics who refused loyalty to Catholicism. At least 250 "witches" were put to death, while over 1,500 Protestant leaders were burned at the stake. The persecutions were, according to Catholic authorities, done with love to save the "wicked."

As religious wars spread, Denmark and Norway, who were intent on defending Protestantism, invaded Germany in 1625. France became involved as well when it marched into Germany on the side of Catholicism. As a result, the entire European continent became embroiled in the largest war it had ever known—all in the name of Christianity.

This great war finally ended in 1648. The settlement that ended hostilities spoke of a Christian peace. Nothing, however, had really been gained; Calvinism, Lutheranism, and Catholicism were all recognized as legitimate faiths. Perhaps, then, the best description that can be attached to the Great and Abominable Church is that of Jesus when he said,

> Not every one that saith unto me, Lord, Lord, shall enter into the kingdom of heaven; but he that doeth the will of my Father which is in heaven. Many will say to me in that day, Lord, Lord, have we not prophesied in thy name? And in thy name have cast out devils? And in thy name done many wonderful works? And then will I profess unto them, I never knew you: depart from me, ye that work iniquity. (Matthew 7:21–23)

The Restoration of the Gospel

> And I saw another angel fly in the midst of heaven, having the everlasting gospel to preach unto them that dwell on the earth, and to every nation, and kindred, and tongue, and people. (Revelation 14:6)

> Behold, I will send my messenger, and he shall prepare the way before me: and the Lord, whom ye seek, shall suddenly come to his temple. (Malachi 3:1)

Curiously unknown today among nearly all of humanity, the

restoration of the gospel toward the end of the last great apostasy is one of the greatest of the signs of the times. Despite all the learned scholars who have ever existed on the earth during the last two millennia—especially those who are theologians or have otherwise intensively studied the scriptures—virtually no major church in the world today, aside from the restored Church of Jesus Christ, believes in such a restoration. Somehow these churches seem to ignore the words of Isaiah:

> It shall come to pass in the last days, that the mountain of the Lord's house shall be established in the top of the mountains, and shall be exalted above the hills; and all nations shall flow unto it. (Isaiah 2:2)

> And he shall set up an ensign for the nations, and shall assemble the outcasts of Israel,[29] and gather together the dispersed of Judah from the four corners of the earth. (Isaiah 11:12)

Over a century and a half ago, on April 6, 1830,[30] this long promised restoration of the true and complete gospel of Jesus Christ commenced with the formal organization of the Church of Jesus Christ of Latter-day Saints. All Latter-day Saints are familiar with the story of Joseph Smith and of how the fullness of the gospel was restored through him. The complete organization of the Church, including the restoration of the priesthood, was accomplished largely unknown to the rest of the world. This was not unlike how the Savior arrived on the earth 2,000 years ago and established his ministry and church—unknown to most of the rest of the world—only to be ultimately rejected by those whom they were intended to serve.

The restored Church, since that momentous day in 1830, has grown steadily, largely due to an ambitious missionary program that was instituted almost immediately after the Church was organized.[31] Through that program, the Church was given the responsibility of preaching the fullness of the gospel to the entire earth:

> The voice of warning shall be unto all people, by the mouths of my disciples, whom I have chosen in these last days. . . . And they shall go forth and none shall stay them, for I the Lord have commanded them. . . . And verily I say unto you, that they who go forth, bearing these tidings unto the inhabitants of the earth. . . . Wherefore the voice of the Lord is unto the ends of the earth, that all that will hear may hear. (D&C 1:4–5, 8, 11)

As the restoration of the gospel was to be made available to humanity everywhere, missionaries, leaving their livelihoods and families behind, went forth to all the surrounding communities—all of New England—and then on to Europe and other countries. As a result, and because the missionary program is now a fundamental part of Latter-day Saint life (there are currently over 56,000 missionaries worldwide), the Church has grown enormously, from only a handful of members surrounding the Prophet Joseph Smith to over 12 million today. More Latter-day Saints now live abroad than within the United States, and 116 temples of God are scattered through many countries.

Furthermore, the elimination of the Iron Curtain in 1989, with the liberation of millions in Eastern Europe and the old Soviet Union, has vastly expanded the missionary program to include, in fulfillment of the scripture, virtually "every nation, kindred, tongue, and people" (Mosiah 3:20). There are few countries today the missionaries don't reach, while the Church nevertheless influences even those few countries. Surely, they too will eventually have the opportunity to hear the gospel.

We are now in the "days of the Gentiles" (2 Nephi 27:1), as the bulk of Judaism has yet to hear the gospel. But that time too is yet to come:

> God will send his gospel, restored by an angel, to every nation, kindred, tongue, and people in the Gentile world before he will permit his servants to go to the scattered remnants of Israel; and they will labor with, preach to, and declare the work of God to the

Gentile nations, and seek to bring them to a knowledge of the ancient gospel, and to organize a Church among them, so far as they will hearken to and receive their testimony. Then, when the Gentile nations shall reject this gospel and count themselves unworthy of eternal life, as the Jews did before them, the Lord will say—"It is enough, come away from them, my servants, I will give you a new commission, you shall go to the scattered remnants of the House of Israel."[32]

The Gathering of Israel

And it shall come to pass in that day, that the Lord shall set his hand again the second time to recover the remnant of his people, which shall be left, from Assyria, and from Egypt, and from Pathros, and from Cush, and from Elam, and from Shinar, and from Hamath, and from the islands of the sea. And he shall set up an ensign for the nations, and shall assemble the outcasts of Israel, and gather together the dispersed of Judah from the four corners of the earth. (Isaiah 11:11–12)

Behold, I will take the children of Israel from among the heathen, whither they be gone, and will gather them on every side, and bring them into their own land: And I will make them one nation in the land upon the mountains of Israel. (Ezekiel 37:21–22; See also Jeremiah 23:3; 32:37)

Although numerous Old Testament and modern scriptures prophesy of the last days, one of the few prophecies that has been fulfilled beyond a doubt is that of the gathering of Israel, or at least the beginning of that momentous gathering. Students of the Bible will recall that around 700 B.C., ten of the original twelve tribes of Israel were captured and carried away from their homeland to Assyria and elsewhere, after which they were lost to history. To a large extent, they were probably assimilated into the cultures of their captive countries; modern researchers have found otherwise inexplicable traces of Israelite culture in various countries of eastern Europe, parts of Asia, and possibly even in Africa.

That is why the establishment of the State of Israel shortly after the end of World War II on the site of the original promised land was such a momentous event in Jewish and Christian history.[33] As such, it is one fulfilled sign of the last days that is difficult to dispute.

Nevertheless, this gathering has just begun, and hundreds of thousands of the descendants of the original ten lost tribes of Israel still remain scattered and are yet to be positively identified and to return to their homeland. This remarkable apparent fulfillment of prophecy is not, however, as simple or complete as it appears. First, one must keep in mind that the return of the Jews to their homeland is a far different matter than the conversion of the Jews to the restored Church. And second, the gathering of Israel and the return of the ten lost tribes can also be considered two separate events, as implied in the tenth article of faith: "We believe in the literal gathering of Israel and in the restoration of the Ten Tribes."

As noted above, the gathering of Israel has been underway for several decades, but when addressing the ten tribes we find confusion regarding when and how those lost remnants of Israel will return to Zion. This confusion or controversy revolves around the questions of where the ten tribes now are, when they will return, and how they will return. Numerous scriptures answer these questions in confusing or vague ways, the result being that even church authorities over the years have disagreed how to interpret this important sign of the times. It is doubtful that we can resolve much of this controversy, but at least we can examine it and perhaps gain a better understanding of what we look forward to.

Joseph Fielding McConkie provided some guidelines at the BYU Annual Religious Education Faculty Lecture in June 1987, where he warned against accepting, teaching, and thus perpetuating nonscriptural doctrines. As he pointed out, "It is not to be thought that every word spoken [or written] by the General Authorities is inspired, or that they are moved upon by the Holy Ghost in everything they speak and write."[34] The one exception, he pointed out, were the words spoken or written by the prophet, seer, and revelator pertaining to guidance of the Church. All other instruction and counsel given by those in authority throughout the Church must be weighed against the standard works. The scriptures, ancient and modern, are the defining test of truth.

If we do otherwise, as Brother McConkie points out, we may well fall prey to nonscriptural doctrines, which although they may often be harmless are still not supported by the scriptures. These we can readily label as Mormon myths.[35] To discuss the lost ten tribes of Israel, then, and their eventual return, we should rely thoroughly on the scriptures, though we will also focus somewhat on comments by Church authorities to help us understand what the scriptures say (although this may still not alleviate some of the controversy). In all probability, each of us should study the scriptures and then wait to see how these events will in actuality transpire.

Where Are the Ten Tribes?

First, when considering the present location of the ten tribes, related questions also arise as to whether or not they now are an identifiable group or groups and whether they are even aware of their identities as descendants of the ancient Israelites. The reality is that after 2,600 years away from their homeland, having been carried away as captives, they have almost certainly by now have been assimilated into the nations or countries in which they ended up and are probably no longer identifiable or aware of who they are. Don't forget, that period of time is roughly equivalent to over one hundred generations.

However, the Old Testament tells us that "they shall mingle themselves with the seed of men: but they shall not cleave one to another" (Daniel 2:43). The most important scriptural sources indicating that the ten tribes might be in an identifiable body are as follows:

- The Apocrypha, 2 Esdras (or 4 Ezra), which has been widely quoted in Mormon literature.[36]

- D&C 133, which speaks of a day when the tribes of Israel will return under the direction of the prophets.

- 2 Nephi 29:12–14, which states that we will someday have the records of the lost tribes.

- 3 Nephi 17:4, which mentions that Christ visited them.

Brother McConkie, in a BYU address, cautioned against attaching too much weight to finding the ten tribes in a group (or groups): "Indeed, we have no scriptural text that tells us that the ten tribes are located somewhere as a body." Despite the above scriptures, "it takes a two-thousand-year leap to suppose that they have remained so today."[37]

Thus, it is likely that by now the ten tribes are largely fragmented and scattered through many nations. This is substantiated by various scriptures and comments by the Prophet Joseph Smith that refer to the "dispersion" of the ten tribes and the "scattered" condition of Israel. Nevertheless, and in all fairness, it should also be kept in mind that various scriptures indicate (albeit unclearly) that the ten tribes remain somewhere as a group to this day.

Many theories, most of them speculative and of spurious origin (some plain hearsay although attributed to the Prophet Joseph Smith), have emerged over the years as to where the ten tribes now are. Most assume that they are still together as a distinct and identifiable group. Isaiah prophesied that the remnants of the Lord's people, or what was left of them, would be recovered "from Assyria, and from Egypt, and from Pathros, and from Cush, and from Elam, and from Shinar, and from Hamath, and from the islands of the sea" (Isaiah 11:11).

Other scriptures state that after their captivity they ended up in the "north" countries (Apocrypha, 2 Esdras 13:40–47).[38] More than that, we don't know. To dwell briefly on Old Testament geography, Assyria was located northeast of the Holy Land, Egypt to the southwest, Pathros was a portion of upper Egypt, Cush was either to the south of Egypt or a part of south Arabia, Elam and Shinar were to the east, and Hamath was immediately to the north. As far as "the islands of the sea" are concerned, there are over 20,000 islands scattered all over the globe. In other words, we have no clear scriptural hint where the lost ten tribes may now be, especially if they still remain together as an intact group.

Predictably, many theologians and scholars over the centuries have tried to pinpoint the whereabouts of the ten tribes, just as they have the remains of Noah's ark, the burial places of the prophets and of Jesus, the Garden of Eden, and so on. Even Mormons are not immune to this penchant. With varying degrees of authority—but most extremely dubious—various Latter-day Saints from the time of the Prophet Joseph Smith to the present have claimed the ten tribes to be located in the following places:

- On a star near the North Star.
- On a portion of the earth that has been taken away.
- In a hollow of the earth at the North Pole.
- In a mysteriously camouflaged area near the North Pole.
- On a knob of the earth near the North Pole (with the city of Enoch being on a similar knob at the South Pole).
- In a cave in Mexico.

From this representation, it should be obvious that no one really knows where the ten tribes are or if they are in fact in a body. It is doubtful that they are in any of the above places, as there remains extremely little of the earth's surface (including caves, knobs, and hollows) that hasn't been explored and mapped. This is especially true if they remained together as a large population of people, undoubtedly now numbering in the hundreds of thousands. If they are on another star (which is doubtful as stars are in reality suns much like ours) or on a piece of the earth that has been taken away, well, we'll just have to wait and see.

This being the case, let's examine when they are to return, presumably from the north. Once again, we find two schools of thought, and so once again it is best for us to rely on the scriptures as well as on a little common sense.

When Will the Ten Tribes Return?

A major controversy that exists is whether the ten tribes will return prior to Christ's Second Coming or later, during his millennial reign. We know that the state of Israel will play a pivotal role in the events leading up to the return of the Messiah, especially during the battle of Armageddon. It is obvious, however, that that small nation, since its establishment in 1948, has been a central point of contention for much of the world, enduring its enmity for decades. Not only is it surrounded by hostile and resentful Arab nations, but it also lies adjacent to Middle Eastern oil fields—a major source of ongoing contention among industrialized nations—and has land and shrines that are hallowed to Islam and Christianity, as well as Judaism.

Keeping that in mind, let's examine the scriptures and comments of Church leaders that hint that the return of the ten tribes will take place prior to the Second Coming of Jesus. The first thing to stress is that it was necessary for the Book of Mormon to come forth and for the Church to be restored in order to facilitate the gathering of Israel and the return of the ten tribes:

> Verily I say unto you, I give unto you a sign, that ye may know the time when these things shall be about to take place—that I shall gather in, from their long dispersion, my people, O house of Israel, and shall establish again among them my Zion. . . .
>
> And then shall they [the followers of Jesus] assist my people that they may be gathered in, who are scattered upon all the face of the land, in unto the New Jerusalem. And then shall the power of heaven come down among them; and I also will be in the midst. And then shall the work of the Father commence at that day, even when this gospel shall be preached among the remnant of this people. Verily I say unto you, at that day shall the work of the Father commence among all the dispersed of my people, yea, even the tribes which have been lost, which the Father hath led away out of Jerusalem. Yea, the work shall commence among all the dispersed of my people. (3 Nephi 21:1, 24–27)

The importance of the Book of Mormon and the missionary

efforts of the restored Church will be necessary in order to return the hearts of Israel and the lost tribes to Jesus, whom they earlier rejected. Only when this happens will the return of the ten tribes occur:

> Nevertheless, when that day cometh, saith the prophet, that they no more turn aside their hearts against the Holy One of Israel, then will he remember the covenants which he made to their fathers. Yea, then will he remember the isles of the sea; yea, and all the people who are of the house of Israel, will I gather in, saith the Lord, according to the words of the prophet Zenos, from the four quarters of the earth. (1 Nephi 19:15–16)

This, then, is a sign of the times that we are still awaiting. Only when Judaism accepts Jesus as the Messiah and Son of God will the complete gathering commence, regardless of whether it will occur before or during the millennium of Christ's reign. This gathering and return will occur entirely through the Church of Jesus Christ of Latter-day Saints, apparently as a part of its already established missionary program:

> The gathering of Israel as spoken of in the scriptures is destined to take place under the direction of the priesthood. Let it be stated again that they keys of the gathering of Israel rest with the president of the Church. . . . They do not rest with the United Nations or with any other politically appointed body. In D&C 13:26–34, we are told that the tribes of Israel will in a future day "come in remembrance before the Lord; and their prophets shall hear his voice." . . . This is simply to say that after missionaries have gathered them to the waters of baptism, bestowed the blessings of the restored gospel upon them, and established the Church in their midst, they will be organized according to the pattern of the Church. Inspired leaders will be called from among their number, as has been the case

> wherever the gospel has been taken. At the appropriate time, the president of the Church—he who holds the keys of the gathering of Israel and the leading of the ten tribes from the land of the north—will direct the leaders, or prophets, who serve under his direction among the various congregations of Israel to bring their people to the temples of the Lord that they might be crowned with glory and receive the fullness of the gospel blessings. (See D&C 42:11)[39]

If the ten tribes return at or near the war of Armageddon, things will hardly be peaceful, whereas if they return during the Millennium, peace and righteousness will reign.

James E. Talmage hinted that the ten tribes would return prior to the Millennium:

> I say unto you, there are those now living, aye, some here present, who shall live to read the records of the Lost Tribes of Israel, which shall be made one with the record of the Jews, or the Holy Bible, and the record of the Nephites, or the Book of Mormon.[40]

This would indicate that Elder Talmage expected the return of the ten tribes relatively soon after his 1916 pronouncement. But it must be noted that there is also some controversy over what the returning ten tribes would be bringing with them, besides the fact that nearly all of those who may have attended that conference session are by now deceased.

Further support for the prior-to-the-Millennium theory can be found in the prophecies of Zenos. The entire fifth chapter of Jacob is devoted to the allegory of the olive orchard. That lengthy chapter describes how all the three daughter branches—allegorically the Jews, Lamanites, and ten tribes—will be restored prior to verse 76, which describes the Millennium. This would indicate that all three branches of God's children will be grafted back into his fold prior to the Millennium.

Other scriptures and prophecies aren't entirely clear about whether the ten tribes will return prior to the Second Coming of

Jesus or afterwards, during the Millennium:

> Now I am prepared to say by the authority of Jesus Christ, that not many years shall pass away before the United States shall present such a scene of bloodshed as has not a parallel in the history of our nation; pestilence, hail, famine, and earthquake will sweep the wicked of this generation from the face of the land, to open and prepare the way for the return of the lost tribes of Israel from the north country.[41]

Likewise, various scriptures clearly state that the ten tribes will return after the destruction of the great and abominable church (see 3 Nephi 21:26). With that in mind, and considering the preceding statement of the Prophet Joseph Smith, it may very well be that the return of the ten tribes will take place after the great calamities and the battle of Armageddon are over, perhaps immediately prior to or shortly after the Second Coming of Christ. Probably one of the best indications of this timetable is given in latter-day scripture describing the return of Jesus:

> Behold, he shall stand upon the Mount of Olivet, and upon the mighty ocean, even the great deep, and upon the islands of the sea, and upon the land of Zion. And he shall utter his voice out of Zion, and he shall speak from Jerusalem, and his voice shall be heard among all people; And it shall be a voice as the voice of many waters, and as the voice of a great thunder, which shall break down the mountains, and the valleys shall not be found. He shall command the great deep, and it shall be driven back into the north countries, and the islands shall become one land; And the land of Jerusalem and the land of Zion shall be turned back into their own place, and the earth shall be like as it was in the days before it was divided. And the Lord, even the Savior, shall stand in the midst of his people, and shall reign over all flesh. And they who are in the north countries shall come in remembrance before the

> Lord; and their prophets shall hear his voice, and shall no longer stay themselves. (D&C 133:20–26)

In addition to these apparent hints of a return immediately following the coming of Jesus, there are further indications that the arrival of the Savior will signal the ten tribes' return. In the Book of Mormon, for example, it is stated that the returning tribes will come to the New Jerusalem, which is to be built on the North American continent, but they will do so apparently at the beginning of the Millennium:

> And they shall assist my people, the remnant of Jacob, and also as many of the house of Israel as shall come, that they may build a city, which shall be called the New Jerusalem: And then shall they assist my people that they may be gathered in, who are scattered upon all the face of the land, in unto the New Jerusalem. And then shall the power of heaven come down among them; and I also will be in the midst. And then shall the work of the Father commence at that day, even when this gospel shall be preached among the remnant of this people. Verily I say unto you, at that day shall the work of the Father commence among all the dispersed of my people, yea, even the tribes which have been lost, which the Father hath led away out of Jerusalem. (3 Nephi 21:24–26)

Joseph Fielding McConkie, on the other hand, emphatically states that the bulk of the gathering of Israel and the return of the ten tribes would be a millennial event (although this could also mean at the *beginning* of the Millennium):

> The gathering is primarily a millennial event. That is not to say that great numbers will not embrace the gospel of Abraham before that glorious day, but rather that the extent to which Israel will be gathered in the millennial era will so far surpass what will have taken place before that day that in comparison the

pre-millennial gathering will hardly be considered a beginning.[42]

We shouldn't spend a great deal of time contending over whether the ten tribes will return prior to the coming of Jesus or afterward. The gathering has already begun, and when instructed to do so, the prophet, seer, and revelator of the Church will direct missionary efforts toward finding, preaching the gospel to, and establishing the Church among those tribes, wherever they are. And then will begin one of the greatest movements of humanity ever known, reminiscent of the people of Moses following the pillar of fire. But in this case, hundreds of thousands will follow their prophets not only southward but into the Americas, to the New Jerusalem.

How Will the Ten Tribes Return?

The scriptures provide us with some details about how the ten tribes will return and what they will bring with them. We have already discussed the fact that the ten tribes will be gathered and organized for their return largely under direction of the prophet and the general authorities of the Church through its missionary program. Upon their return from the north, there seems to be some contention, however, among modern-day Church members over what they will bring with them. In the Book of Mormon, for example, we are told,

> Behold, I shall speak unto the Jews and they shall write it; and I shall also speak unto the Nephites and they shall write it; and I shall also speak unto the other tribes of the house of Israel, which I have led away, and they shall write it; and I shall also speak unto all nations of the earth and they shall write it. And it shall come to pass that the Jews shall have the words of the Nephites, and the Nephites shall have the words of the Jews; and the Nephites and the Jews shall have the words of the lost tribes of Israel; and the lost tribes of Israel shall have the words of the Nephites and the Jews. (2 Nephi 29:12–13)

This leads us to latter-day scripture that states that the returning tribes will "bring their rich treasures with them" (D&C 13:30). Many Latter-day Saints have interpreted this scripture to mean that the "rich treasures" the lost tribes will bring with them will be their own scriptures.

This opinion was emphatically stated in 1997 by Joseph Fielding McConkie and by James E. Talmage almost a century earlier, in 1916:

> When the Ten Tribes return, the scriptural records they bring with them will be the Bible, the Book of Mormon, the Doctrine and Covenants, and the Pearl of Great Price.[43]

> The tribes shall be brought forth from their hiding place bringing their scriptures with them, which scriptures shall become one with the scriptures of the Jews, the Holy Bible, and with the scriptures of the Nephites, the Book of Mormon, and with the scriptures of the Latter-day Saints as embodied in the volumes of modern revelation.[44]

On the other hand, Joseph Fielding McConkie stated some years later, in 1987,

> There is no reference to either the Ten Tribes or their scriptural records in the Doctrine and Covenants. The text in question appears to have reference to the return of all the tribes of Israel and says that they will bring their "rich treasures" with them. This has been interpreted to mean scriptural records. I would like to suggest that the text means what it says, that the Lord said "rich treasures" because he meant rich treasures.[45]

Brother McConkie then pointed out that this isn't unlike the Old Testament accounts of the children of Israel returning to the Holy Land from Egypt with their "jewels of silver and their jewels of gold" (Exodus 12:35), and to the later return of the Jews from their Babylonian captivity, when they returned to rebuild Jerusalem and the temple laden with silver and gold. He then used these precedents, contending,

> Thus, when Israel returns to claim the blessings of the temple in the last days, should they not return with their rich treasures as their fathers did before them?[46]

Regardless of what the returning ten tribes will bring with them, this vast reunion of previously scattered Israelites will be a momentous occasion. In fact, we have several scriptures and prophecies detailing how they will return:

> And they who are in the north countries shall come in remembrance before the Lord; and their prophets shall hear his voice, and shall no longer stay themselves; and they shall smite the rocks, and the ice shall flow down at their presence. And an highway shall be cast up in the midst of the great deep. And in the barren deserts there shall come forth pools of living water; and the parched ground shall no longer be a thirsty land. (D&C 133:26–27, 29)

To understand the reference to a highway being "cast up in the midst of the great deep," we need to return to the apocryphal account of how the Jews escaped from their Assyrian captors seven centuries before Christ:

> These are the ten tribes which were led away from their own land into captivity in the days of King Hoshea, whom Shalmanezer the king of the Assyrians led captive; he took them across the river, and they were taken into another land. But they formed this plan for themselves, that they would leave the multitude of the nations and go to a more distant region, where humanity had never lived, and there at least they might keep their statutes which they had not kept in their own land. And they went in by the

> narrow passages of the Euphrates River. For at that time the Most High performed signs for them, and stopped the channels of the river until they had passed over. (4 Ezra 13:40–49)

In a similar manner, then, the returning tribes will return home on dry land. Their journey was well described by Orson Pratt:

> Again, says the Prophet, "And the Lord shall utterly destroy the tongue of the Egyptian Sea." How? "With his mighty power shall he shake his hand over the river and shall smite it in the seven streams and make men go over dryshod. And there shall be an highway for the remnant of his people which shall be left from Assyria like as it was to Israel in the day that he came up out of the land of Egypt." The same thing, not a spiritual, but a literal transaction, as the Lord smote the tongue of the Egyptian Sea in ancient days, and caused his people to go through on a highway in the midst of those mighty waters which stood like walls on each side of the assembly of Israel. So in the latter days he will not only cut off the tongue of the Egyptian Sea, but the river in its seven streams will also be divided and men will go through dryshod.[47]

Orson Pratt later went on to say that upon completion of the future temple in Jackson County, Missouri, the ten tribes will be heard of, away in the north, a great company, as Jeremiah says, coming down from the northern regions.

> They will come, and the Lord will be before their camp, he will utter his voice before that great army, and he will lead them forth as he led Israel in ancient times. This long chain of Rocky Mountains, that extends from the cold regions of the north away into South America, will feel the power of God, and will tremble before the hosts of Israel as they come to sing on the heights of Zion. In that day the trees of the

> field will clap like hands, says the Prophet, and in that day the Lord will open waters in the wilderness, and streams in the desert, to give drink to his chosen, his people Israel.[48]

Conclusion

It is apparent that many prophecies, or signs of the times, have been fulfilled or that their fulfillment is under way. Among these are great and increasingly devastating wars, the last great apostasy led by the great and abominable church, the gathering of Israel, and the restoration and spread of the gospel (including the restoration of the priesthood and the coming forth of the Book of Mormon).

As yet, however, it is less clear whether the great natural calamities that have long been prophesied have yet begun. It is certain they will come, and when they do their crescendo will be unmistakable. There is also a strong possibility that many such calamities will occur near the very end, near the battle of Armageddon, when all humanity is in turmoil and the anti-Christ is in power. As a matter of fact, many scriptures make it clear that earthquakes, signs in the heavens, pestilences, and the like will precede Christ's return, when he will cause the anti-Christ and great and abominable church to fall.

As Brigham Young stated:

> All we have yet heard and have experienced is scarcely a preface to the sermon that is going to be preached. . . . All you know now can scarcely be called a preface to the sermon that will be preached with fire and sword, tempests, earthquakes, hail, rain, thunders and lightnings, and fearful destruction. . . . You will hear of magnificent cities, now idolized by the people, sinking in the earth, entombing the inhabitants. The sea will heave itself beyond its bounds, engulfing mighty cities. Famine will spread over the nations, and nation will rise up against nation, kingdom against kingdom, and states against states, in our own country and in foreign lands; and they will destroy each other,

> caring not for the blood and lives of their neighbors, of their families, or for their own lives.[49]

Simply because many prophecies haven't yet come to pass doesn't mean they won't. As President Ezra Taft Benson said,

> Too often we bask in our comfortable complacency and rationalize that the ravages of war, economic disaster, famine, and earthquake cannot happen here. Those who believe this are either not acquainted with the revelations of the Lord, or they do not believe them. Those who smugly think these calamities will not happen, that they will somehow be set aside because of the righteousness of the saints, are deceived and will rue the day they harbored such a delusion.[50]

How near is the Second Coming? The answer seems to lie not in a calendar but in events—the extent to which the gospel is preached throughout the earth. Joseph Fielding McConkie was somewhat optimistic in this respect, contending that that great event may not take place for generations:

> The first and perhaps most common misconception relative to the millennial day is simply how close we are to it. The time cannot be properly estimated in days, months, or years. It must be measured in events, the chief of which is the extent to which the gospel has been taught among the nations of the earth. Suffice it to say, so much still needs to be done before the promise is fulfilled that the gospel will be taken to those of every nation, kindred, tongue, and people that we can safely say that we are generations removed from the final winding-up scene.[51]

B. H. Roberts, on the other hand, was less optimistic a century ago:

> The most important events which are to take place

> before the glorious coming of the Son of God have been fulfilled. We know not the day nor the hour in which the Master will come, but we know that the preparatory work to that event has made considerable progress: The gospel has been restored to the earth, and is being preached to all nations for a witness that the end is near:—The messenger has come and restored the authority of God to man, that the way may be prepared for His coming and judgment:—Elijah has come and performed his mission:—And the saints are gathering together to the tops of the mountains, and are building up the House of God. And as the fig tree putteth forth its leaves proclaims the approach of summer, so things indicate the near approach of that time when the Son of God will be "revealed from heaven with His mighty angels in flaming fire, taking vengeance on them that know not God and who obey not the gospel of our Lord Jesus Christ." This is the word of God, and remember, O reader! That it is written that though heaven and earth pass away, not one jot nor tittle of the word of God shall fail, but all shall be fulfilled.[52]

Notes

1. President Joseph Fielding Smith, in Conference Report, April 1966, 12–13.

2. Joseph Fielding McConkie, *Straightforward Answers to Tough Gospel Questions* (Salt Lake City: Deseret Book, 1998), 12–13, 15.

3. Bruce R. McConkie, *Mormon Doctrine,* 2d ed. (Salt Lake City: Bookcraft, 1966), 826. To emphasize Brother McConkie's assertions about the inhumanity and ugliness of war, wartime atrocities are commonplace on both sides. One of the best examples was during the Pol Pot regime in Cambodia after the conclusion of the Vietnam War. Cambodia's Camp S-21 was renowned as little more than a torture stockade. Of fifteen thousand prisoners who entered its gates, only six survived.

4. Gordon B. Hinckley, "War and Peace," *Ensign,* May 2003, 80.

5. The concept of preemptive war is not necessarily bad. If, for example, a preemptive war had been waged against Nazi Germany in the mid-1930s as it was against Sadam Hussein's Iraq, World War II may not have happened.

6. Joseph Fielding Smith, in Conference Report, April 1937, 59.

7. George Albert Smith, in Conference Report, October 1941, 99.

8. For example, Hamas, a terrorist Palestinian group long hostile to Israel, is responsible for most of the 112 suicide bombings that have killed 465 people on the Israeli side during the past three and a half years of violence.

9. Orson Pratt, in *Journal of Discourses,* 18:63–64.

10. In Conference Report, April 1966, 14.

11. Mount Everest, for example, is now a couple of steps higher than it was when first climbed by Sir Edmund Hillary in the 1950s.

12. A key factor in continental drift (which means that the earth's crust is composed of large, continent-sized "plates" drifting around ever so slowly) is the mid-Atlantic Ridge. Discovered in 1954, it is a fissure in the ocean floor of the Atlantic Ocean. It is spreading apart at the rate of seven to twelve inches per year, thus pushing Europe and Africa away from the Americas. Multiply this apparent slow rate of separation by thousands of years and you begin to realize the vast changes that are taking place over the earth's surface. Incidentally, the mid-Atlantic Ridge is, in reality, more than fifty thousand miles long, running the north-south length of the Atlantic Ocean and zigzagging around much of the rest of the world as well.

13. The death of Christ was followed by three hours of tempests, earthquakes, fires, whirlwinds, and physical upheavals, not to mention the deaths of thousands, and then darkness throughout the New World.

14. M. Russell Ballard, "When Shall These Things Be Done?" *Ensign,* December 1996, 56.

15. Because earthquakes and volcanoes most often occur where the earth's crust is moving and changing, these often violent forces of nature occur regularly and almost predictably. Earthquakes shake the earth in any given area at semiregular intervals, which is also the case with volcanoes. As a result, scientists expect the San Andreas Fault to shift again as it has done at more or less regular intervals in the past—likewise volcanoes, which erupt in nearly regular cycles over thousands of years. This has been the case with Mount St. Helens and Mount Rainier in Washington, Mount Shasta and Mount Lassen in California, and dozens of other volcanoes worldwide.

16. An earthquake of 7.5 magnitude or greater is considered a major earthquake. About ten of this magnitude occur every year somewhere in the world.

17. Data from the U.S. Geological Survey, as well as much of the following commentary.

18. In Conference Report, April 1966, 14.

19. For those who are worried about man's pollution of the atmosphere, Mount Pinatubo spewed out more gases and particulate matter into the atmosphere than all motorized vehicles throughout history.

20. An active volcano is one that has erupted during historic times or is expected to erupt again because its magma reservoir remains intact beneath the earth's surface.

21. Mount St. Helens and other volcanoes up and down the west coasts

of North and South America, as well as many around the shores of the Pacific Ocean, in Japan, the Aleutian Islands, and the Philippines, erupt regularly every few hundred years. That is why there is growing concern about impending future eruptions of Mount Rainier in Washington, Mount Hood in Oregon, Mount Shasta in California, Popocateptl in Mexico, and others. This concern arises from the fact that population centers have sprung up near these mountains within the past several decades despite the likelihood of future eruptions.

22. Let's not forget the tornado that wreaked havoc in downtown Salt Lake City in 1999. A smaller, F2 tornado, it caused extensive damage, numerous injuries, and one fatality.

23. In Lituya Bay, Alaska, a landslide generated such a wave—1,740 feet tall—in 1958.

24. China is now engaged in the largest dam-building program in the history of humanity in order to avert such catastrophes in the future.

25. Melvin J. Ballard, in Conference Reports, June 1919, 88–89.

26. That plague, which was carried by lice on rats, killed one-fourth of Europe's entire population. Rats have accounted for more such deaths in human history than have all humanity's wars combined.

27. At least 25 percent of all food shipped from the United States overseas to needy countries is contaminated, spoiled, or eaten by rats due to inadequate shipping and storage facilities. A great deal also ends up on the black market, confiscated by corrupt government officials before reaching those it is intended to help.

28. The pope at that time was widely criticized for blessing Axis cannons that were to fire on other Christians, including Catholics.

29. Not the Jews alone but all Israel.

30. April 6 was the true date of Jesus' birth.

31. Samuel Smith, the Church's first missionary, began his mission on June 30, 1830. Proselyting not far from home, he was indirectly responsible for the conversion of Brigham Young, who received the Book of Mormon from his brother Phineas, who received it from Methodist minister John P. Green, who received it from Samuel.

32. Orson Pratt, in *Journal of Discourses,* 18:176–77; see also 1 Nephi 13:42).

33. In 1900, only 25,000 Jews lived in their original homeland. By 1948, however, when Israel was declared a sovereign nation by the United Nations, 650,000 Jews lived there. By 1952, that number had reached 1.4 million. Today, Israel's population has swelled to 4.9 million, although another 5.7 million still live in the United States.

34. Joseph Fielding McConkie, "A Search for the Ten Tribes and Other Things We Lost" (Provo, Utah: Brigham Young University Religious Education, 1987).

35. Two Mormon myths noted by Brother McConkie are the often-used concepts of eternal progression and the admonition that we should practice unconditional love, as God does. Eternal progression is only hinted at in the

scriptures but isn't clearly described as now commonly preached, and the idea that God's love is unconditional is likewise nonscriptural (see Helaman 15:4).

36. The Apocrypha were sacred books of the Jewish people not included in the Hebrew Bible and thus not in our modern Bibles. Though they provide a link connecting the Old and New Testaments and are often regarded as correct (D&C 91), they were subject to human tampering and must therefore be used with caution (see Bible Dictionary, s.v. "Apocrypha").

37. Joseph Fielding McConkie, "A Search for the Ten Tribes and Other Things We Lost."

38. Esdras records in considerable detail the ten tribes' arduous one-and-one-half year journey northward after escaping from the Assyrians (see also McConkie, *Mormon Doctrine,* 455–57).

39. McConkie, "Straightforward Answers to Tough Gospel Questions," 130–31.

40. In Conference Report, October 1916, 76.

41. Joseph Smith, *History of The Church of Jesus Christ of Latter-day Saints* (Salt Lake City: The Church of Jesus Christ of Latter-day Saints, 1932–51), 1:315.

42. McConkie, "A Search for the Ten Tribes and Other Things We Lost."

43. McConkie, *Straightforward Answers to Tough Gospel Questions,* 131.

44. James E. Talmage, in Conference Report, October 1916, 75–76.

45. McConkie, "A Search for the Ten Tribes and Other Things We Lost."

46. Ibid.

47. Orson Pratt, in *Journal of Discourses,* 14:66.

48. Ibid., 18:68.

49. Brigham Young, in *Journal of Discourses,* 8:123.

50. Ezra Taft Benson, "Prepare for the Days of Tribulation," *Ensign,* November 1980, 32.

51. McConkie, *Straightforward Answers to Tough Gospel Questions,* 133–34.

52. B. H. Roberts, *Handbook of the Restoration: A Selection of Gospel Themes Discussed by Various Authors* (Independence, Missouri: Zion's Printing & Publishing), 425.

5

Are Science and Religion Really Incompatible?

For centuries there have been continuing disputes between scientist-academics and traditional theologians. Note the following "scientific" statement:

> The only important news is news of science, medicine, and technology. All the rest—politics, culture, art, literature, and world affairs—rarely really changes and ultimately has little effect on how we lead our lives. Science shapes everything around us, defines who we really are, determines how long we'll live.[1]

Although especially vehement when such arguments revolve around the issue of evolutionary theory, they usually extend also to the nature or reality of God and his frequently perplexing role in the natural world around us. "There is no God," contend the atheist-scientists. "Man certainly did not evolve from a monkey," counter the stolid theologians. "Science and religion are incompatible and mutually exclusive," say some scientists, while a few others feel that the two competing philosophies can "live harmoniously together in the human soul."[2]

Unfortunately, it is doubtful that such differences can be quickly resolved, due to the polarity and usual lack of common-ground compromise between the two extreme positions. Those who are the ardent defenders of God and religion's status quo have long contended that God is the creator of all and that his hand is evident in everything around us. To them, anyone who questions these "facts" is against God, is anti-religious, satanic, lacks faith, or is, at best, spiritually ignorant. For them, and even more so for laymen of the various churches, a favorite proof of deity is the orderliness and precision of the universe and the natural world. Such a vast system of perfection, they say, proves that there is a God.

Anyone who has felt compelled to discuss such things with others has assuredly heard this same response from their religious acquaintances. When speaking thus, people usually think of our earth's orderly place in the solar system, or of flowers blooming regularly in the spring, and the like.

On the other hand, they seldom extend such thinking to include such natural events as the grisly process of a snake eating a frog, or why there's a need for leeches, or why rock layers in mountains are often not neatly parallel with each other, or why the earth's polarity reverses itself from time to time. Nevertheless, this is not to belittle those who fervently hold religious values such as these when, in fact, there *is* order and purpose everywhere in the entire system of life on this earth, even amidst apparent chaos everywhere.

And when speaking of religion, it should be understood that one must also include not only Christianity and Judaism, but also other major world religions. Most religious scholars, of whatever persuasion, will readily admit that nearly all world religions have many doctrines in common, many of which seek, either overtly or otherwise, to exclude competing scientific thought from their traditions. As has been the case with Christianity, religious zealots have historically sought ways to suppress scientific thought, frequently by means of force, when felt necessary. The often bloody suppression of scientific thought and research by early Catholicism, for example, is well know to historians,[3] and even in our day such suppression and intolerance is still found in certain conservative religions, such as Islam, which rejects some scientific thought.

Again, this is not meant to condemn religious thought, for such thought usually has two common and laudable underlying themes: that there is a Being (or beings) greater than us who created the world and all its complexity; and that we, as a part of his creations, should try to get along better with one another. It is doubtful that any scientists would find fault with the second of these universal traditions.

As a matter of fact, a great part of science is dedicated to making the earthly lot of humanity better, including improved medications, labor-saving devices, improved agricultural methods to eliminate hunger, and so forth. None of us, no matter what religion we adhere to, wants to turn our backs on our modern comforts—created by scientists—and go back to living without comfortable homes, ample food, doctors and hospitals, automobiles, and the like.

The problem scientists have with religion, especially those scientists who reject religion entirely, is that religion relies on faith as its foundation instead of on empirical facts and data. For example, there is an undeniable paucity of firm proof that God exists at all. He can't be measured, observed, or otherwise physically studied. Only his handiwork is available for us to study—the intricate system of life around us, the clouds in the sky, great mountain peaks, and rolling seas. Faithful churchgoers say, therefore, that he exists without our ever having seen him. And their faith is remarkably unshakable. After all, the Bible says that this should be the case.

This kind of thinking drives scientists to distraction, for without observations, measurements, or other empirical data relating to God himself, there is nothing about him for them to study. In other words, faith, to them, doesn't count for much. The same goes for many of God's works: the biblical account of the Creation is also a matter of faith to the Judeo-Christian world, while to many scientists it consists merely of fables and myths from dusty old scrolls. Again, there is no way to objectively study how Eve was created from the rib of Adam, or of how Adam was created in the first place. Certainly not from "the dust of the ground"!

Fortunately, some in each camp, scientists and religionists, fall somewhere between the extremist poles described above. Many scientists are trying to make their profession validate their religious views, with limited success, and simultaneously many religious lay people might well consider themselves agnostics but without really knowing or admitting it.

It might be well to point out here that the term *agnostic* isn't necessarily derogatory but subscribes more closely to the truth than many might believe or admit. It indicates only that a person doesn't know the answers to religious riddles or questions. It is doubtful that ignorance can be considered prejudicial in this case. When confronted with the question of how man arrived upon the earth, for example, it is certainly no disgrace to simply say, "I don't know." By so admitting, one buys neither into the "man from dust" doctrine of old-time religion nor into the "man and monkey from a common ancestor" theory of evolutionists.

Theologians and scientists should, in fact, work hand in hand to find the truth. Many are fed up with stilted, stale religion that demands that we unwaveringly believe what the church says while at the same time we ignore the signs of intelligent design in the world around us as science hard-liners would have us do.

Yet, scientists will be the first to admit that they don't know it all.[4] Every new discovery results in new questions for scientists to research. For example, new directions in genetic research have opened up vast new research opportunities that were entirely unthought of only a few decades ago. By the same token, religion doesn't have all the answers either. Even with prophets and apostles, there are hundreds of things we still fail to understand. For example, where is Kolob? How do heavenly beings move about and make their appearances to us mortals, especially without transport vehicles as we do?[5] Is time travel possible? Otherwise, how can prophets foresee the future? And on and on.

It seems increasingly clear, given the amazing strides in science over the past couple of centuries, that an eventual convergence of the two ideologies is unavoidable. Religion must simply be patient and wait for science to play catch-up, to validate much of what theologians have been saying for so long. This is not to say, however, that much of religion will be eventually proven infallible. The sheer number of divergent religious beliefs in the world today rules out this possibility. No, religion too will have to bend in places and soften its rigid stance in many respects. Furthermore, it will have to grudgingly admit that science also provides a means of learning about our Creator and his works.

Bruce R. McConkie best articulated this inevitable compatibility:

> Obviously there never will be a conflict between truths revealed in the realm of religion and those discovered by scientific research. Truth is ever in

> harmony with itself. But if false doctrines creep into revealed religion, these will run counter to the discovered truths of science; and if false scientific theories are postulated, these ultimately will be overthrown by the truths revealed from Him who knows all things.[6]

Instead of throwing rocks at each other, each side—religion and science—must inevitably try complementing each other. When this occurs, and science begins to substantiate the bigger picture of religion, the knowledge and truth that we will ultimately derive from such a joint effort will surely prove astounding. We study science to learn more about the world around us and ourselves, and we go to church to learn about God, ourselves, eternal and spiritual matters, and the world around us.

Religion and science are *not* mutually exclusive. They are simply different means of reaching the same goals. In fact, as science continues to study and confirm the order and laws of the universe, we should all gain a greater reverence and awe for our Creator.[7] This thinking has been reiterated by numerous LDS scientists and is insightfully articulated by Bart J. Kowallis, chair of the Department of Geology at Brigham Young University:

> I believe that all apparent contradictions between religion and science will disappear as our understanding approaches God's understanding (paraphrased from Dr. Henry Eyring). For us, each new discovery of science should be as a new revelation; each discovery gives us a more complete understanding of how God works. As science demonstrates the order and law of the universe, we should not feel threatened but should gain a greater reverence and awe for the marvelous work of the Creator.[8]

Perhaps we will eventually find that we indeed *do* have an understandable God whose works and plan have more importance to us than we could ever have realized!

Miracles and "Acts of God"

Throughout the scriptures, especially those comprising the Old Testament and the Book of Mormon, one reads of dozens of miracles performed either by the Lord himself or through his prophets. We are all familiar, for example, with the great Flood at the time of Noah, the destruction of Sodom and Gomorrah through fire and earthquake, the burning bush on Mount Sinai, the pillar of fire that led the Israelites through the wilderness, the plagues of Egypt, the earthquake and darkness at the time of Christ's death, the star of Bethlehem, the parting of the Red Sea at the command of Moses, and many more similar miraculous events.

We call such occurrences miracles, events that to us are supernatural and impossible to understand. Even in our day of instant worldwide communications, television, miracle medications, space travel, and the like, we can't conceive of how God could perform the miracles found in the scriptures. As a matter of fact, many nowadays in our sophisticated and enlightened age, are unable to account for such inexplicable occurrences and simply brush them off as fables or religious myth. Such scriptural miracles are still well beyond our comprehension despite the vast knowledge we now possess. But don't forget, many everyday conveniences we now take for granted would likewise have been regarded as miracles by our forefathers of only two hundred years ago.

We can speak to and see someone a thousand miles away via a wireless telephone. We can transplant organs into a dying person's body, allowing them further life. We can flick on a lightbulb or enjoy automated, programmed heating or cooling in our homes. We can travel a greater distance in our automobiles in an hour than the pioneers could travel in a week—and we do so in air-conditioned or heated comfort while listening to a CD. Or consider what a miracle a Bic cigarette lighter would have been to our pioneer forefathers, or a washing machine to their wives.

This is all to say that the scriptural miracles we attribute to God are simply manifestations of powers and knowledge that he has that far surpass our own. It is certain that God understands the natural laws of our planet far better than do we. This means that his miracles are simply applications of natural laws about which we have yet to learn.

To put this line of thought into perspective, we read in the scriptures about "signs and wonders" in the heavens. Nowadays, we see airplanes flying overhead and catch occasional glimpses of satellites, space shuttles, and space stations. Furthermore, we see airplanes so often that we take them for granted and pay little attention to them. On the other hand, our astronomers can tell us far in advance when to expect a meteor shower. Most of us understand generally what makes them occur as we gaze up at the fireworks in the night sky. On occasion we see comets, which we likewise pass off as interesting spectacles. Similarly, many of us have experienced a solar eclipse, knowing well in advance when and where it would occur and what to expect.

But think of the astonishment, mystery, and even fear such things would evoke among most of our ancestors. They would be amazed and probably terrified to see an airplane up close, let alone consider getting inside one to go for a ride.

Likewise, doomsday prophecies of volcanoes and earthquakes are now more understandable, as we know what causes earthquakes and volcanoes and where they are most likely to occur. We fear plagues and pestilences less as we have developed technologies and medicines that have controlled or eliminated many previously deadly diseases. Even famines are by now less a threat than they were in biblical times thanks to modern farming methods, improved crop varieties, and control of insects and plant diseases,[9] not to mention modern methods of preserving and transporting food.

Our early Latter-day Saints were promised that the wilderness where they were to settle would "blossom as the rose" (Isaiah 35:1). And it has, through the dedicated efforts of those early settlers, through deep-well pumping systems and ingenious irrigation systems that have made Utah—the second driest state in the nation—a region of productive farmland. The same is true of the state of Israel, concerning which the same prophetic promises were made. The Holy Land too is now productive farmland and a country with a burgeoning population. Even desalinization of seawater is being used to make it yet more productive and hospitable.

The bottom line of all this is that we have learned, through science and technology, to do things that would be miraculous by biblical standards. We are able to create lightning bolts on demand, something ancient man attributed only to the gods. Certainly, we still have much to learn, and God can easily perform miracles that we scarcely understand simply because he possesses and applies knowledge and understanding that are far beyond our mortal capabilities.

What this boils down to is the probability that the events leading up to Jesus' Second Coming will also occur through natural phenomena, despite the language and confusing symbolism of the scriptures. We may not understand some things with our present limited knowledge, but the predicted events will still come about through natural laws that we have yet to learn.

The prophets of old described the signs of the times as best they could, often through symbolism. But the accounts of pestilence, famine, earthquakes, floods, wonders in heaven, fire and brimstone, and so forth will also occur naturally. The Lord possesses the means to cause or manipulate them, but they won't occur out of nowhere. We may even be able to understand them, though not avoid them. Just like the weather, we understand it quite well but can do nothing about it.

As Melvin J. Ballard said in general conference,

> Our Father . . . though he be God, is yet limited to law, by obedience to which he became God, and he must honor the same, he cannot step beyond those limitations and set aside the law. The law must take its course.[10]

Notes

1. *Discover Science Almanac,* ed. Steven Petranek (New York: Hyperion Books, 2003), ix.

2. Edward O. Wilson, "Evolutionary Biology and Religion," lecture given at Catholic bishops' meeting, 1987; see also *Religion, Science and the Search for Wisdom,* David M. Byers, ed. (Washington, D.C.: U.S. Catholic Conference, 1987), 82–90; and Freeman J. Dyson, *Infinite in All Directions* (New York: Harper & Row, 1989), 11.

3. Early scientists were persecuted and executed for putting forth such heretical thoughts as the idea that the earth is round and not the center of the universe.

4. An example of the complexity of our world, which God understands

and we don't, is found in modern DNA research. Scientists admit that of the 3 billion "letters" of human DNA, "it would take decades or even centuries to completely understand the language of the code—how the tens of thousands of genes and their proteins interact to create the biological symphony of a human being" (James Shreeve, *The Genome War* [New York: Alfred A. Knopf, 2004]).

5. Think of it. Given the fact that heavenly beings can apparently travel about the universe at will, we can't possibly conceive of how this can be done. The universe, by latest estimates, is forty billion light-years in diameter and expanding. Because a light-year is defined as the distance light travels (186,000 miles per second) in a year, it should be obvious that this distance can't be reckoned using ordinary mathematics and our conventional units of measurement. Instead, astronomers rely on light-years and scientific notation to depict such enormous distances. To put this into perspective, the nearest star to our sun, Proxima Centauri, is 4.23 light-years away, a distance of 24.8 trillion miles. It would take us more than 94,000 years (at 30,000 miles per hour) to travel such a distance using our current rocket technology.

6. Bruce R. McConkie, *Mormon Doctrine,* 2d ed. (Salt Lake City: Bookcraft, 1966), 250.

7. See Richard H. Bube, *Putting It All Together: Seven Patterns for Relating Science and the Christian Faith* (Lanham, Md.: University Press of America, 1995), 66.

8. Kowallis, *Of Heaven and Earth: Reconciling Scientific Thought with LDS Theology,* ed. David L. Clark (Salt Lake City: Deseret Book, 1998), 38–39.

9. Many people nowadays are particularly wary of the "new" science of genetic engineering that has been responsible for many improved varieties of plants and animals. In reality, the ancient practices of crossbreeding and selective breeding of plants and animals are much the same thing (albeit low-tech) and have resulted in many of the high-producing and nutritious foods we enjoy today.

10. Melvin J. Ballard, in Conference Report, October 1923, 31.

6

Signs in the Heavens—Fire and Brimstone

Now let's turn to science to consider signs of the times that may well occur toward the end and that fit within the realms of both science and religion. This is not to say that these events are certain to occur, as they're presented here only as speculation, but they are certainly within the realm of possibility. They are undoubtedly controversial and argumentative, but they may offer some insights into how the Lord may manipulate events to conclude our mortality here on this earth. Keep in mind that they are surely not the only possibilities.

Mass Extinctions

One thing to understand at the outset is that the extinction of mortal man from the earth wouldn't be unprecedented. Such mass extinctions have occurred numerous times throughout the earth's history.[1] Anyone who has even briefly studied geology, the earth's history, paleontology, archaeology, or any other related science will be familiar with the fact that the earth's history is divided up into eras, periods, epochs, and the like, which are simply periods of time during which certain types of plants or animals or other geological conditions were predominant.

For example, during the Precambrian period (3,800 million to 540 million years ago), ancient, simple types of marine life predominated, as did both primitive plants and animals. The Jurassic period (206 million to 144 million years ago), as most moviegoers know, was a time ruled by dinosaurs. Our current period, the

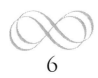

Anthropogene or Quaternary period, began 2.6 million years ago and has been characterized by ice ages and the rise of man. We are now living in the Holocene epoch, and the last ice age ended some 20,000 years ago.

The point to be made here is that each of these grand periods of the earth's history has a fairly distinct beginning and end, a period during which something changed on the earth that began a period of time different in several important ways from those before and those after.

For example, the Precambrian period was a time of marine life only—of no green plants or land-dwelling animals—characterized by simple and small primitive organisms. The later Jurassic period was a time of tropical forests, reptiles of all sizes, dinosaurs, and diminutive, insignificant mammals—still no people. Our current Anthropogene or Quaternary period has been characterized by dinosaurs becoming extinct, by climates closer to those with which we are familiar (despite repeated ice ages), and by a predominance of mammals and man, ranging from primitive to modern.

The question should logically arise that if each of these geological periods had a beginning and an end, what caused it to differ from the period before and the one after? For example, what caused the dinosaurs to become extinct at the end of the Cretaceous period to make way for mammals to rise to predominance after them? What conditions on the earth existed later that allowed man to rise to the top of the animal and plant kingdoms to become the apex of all creation?

The earth's thousands of ecosystems are in a continual state of flux. Whenever the smallest change occurs within an environment, such as a little less sunlight, a tiny decrease in temperature, less moisture, and so forth, the organisms living within the environment that had been their niche must either adapt to the new conditions or eventually die off. This is a continuing process that has occurred millions of times over the earth's entire surface from the beginning on.

For example, if you water your lawn, you affect the hundreds of organisms that live in your grass or in the soil underneath. Some organisms need the extra moisture, while others may not be moisture tolerant and will have to migrate elsewhere or die. Those that feed on the water-tolerant organisms will also thrive, whereas those that feed on the less water-tolerant organisms will likewise have to either migrate elsewhere or die.

If these environmental changes occur over wide enough portions of the earth's surface, it may well be that many species will become entirely extinct, unable to tolerate the new conditions. And they will be replaced by other species that have evolved to be more suited to the new conditions. For example, timber cutting throughout the Pacific Northwest over the years has caused a major disruption in the environments of many woodland species. That, along with hunting, has caused the near extinction of most bears, which once thrived there, as did wolves and other predators. On the other hand, deer, coyotes, and a few other species don't seem to mind and seem to do quite well.

In many waterways, we have found that slow-flowing, warmer streams, such as those upstream from dams, soon become populated with carp, bass, sunfish, and similar species, whereas the trout that once lived in those streams (when they were colder and fast-flowing) have either died off or migrated elsewhere.

The point to be made here is that major environmental changes are most often the root cause of changes in earth's history over the past billions of years. Vast environmental changes cause corresponding changes in the plants and animals that inhabit the earth and are thus a convenient demarcation line for scientists to differentiate one geological period from another. Of course, one may well ask, what caused the environmental changes in the first place?

Early in earth's history, global environmental changes resulted most often from changes in or around the earth itself, from volcanism, asteroid bombardments, atmospheric changes, and the like. (The early atmosphere of the earth was extremely toxic, lacking oxygen entirely.)[2] However, these events took place during earth's early, formative period.

Later on, in about the last ten periods of the earth's history—approximately the last 500 million years—the bulk of extreme global environmental changes (causing a major disruption in the earth's life and thus a transition from one period to another) were due to climate changes of one sort or another. In other words, global heating or cooling became extreme enough that a large percentage of the earth's plant and animal species died and were later replaced by other species that found the new conditions tolerable.

Numerous such mass extinctions have occurred over the past billion years of life on the earth. And mass extinction rates, whatever the cause, have ranged from 30–40 percent to as high as 90 percent of all then-existing species. This includes plants and animals, both marine-dwelling and terrestrial species.[3]

An excellent example of such a mass extinction event was the extermination of nearly all of the earth's dinosaur species, as well as of thousands of other species, at the end of the Cretaceous Period, 65 million years ago. The consensus among most paleontologists is that this global catastrophe seems to have resulted from a major asteroid collision with the earth that disrupted weather systems around the world, causing massive mortality of living things worldwide.

The numbers of species now inhabiting the earth is frankly unknown. Biologists and taxonomists—scientists who study anatomy—have catalogued some 2.5 million species of plants and animals, but it is estimated that the actual number ranges between 3 and 30 million distinct species. The real number is probably around 5 million, which includes all plants, animals, marine life, and microscopic life. It is worthy of note, however, that 75 percent of the total consists of insects. Insects have been around for 400 million years through all sorts of environmental extremes. This tells us a lot about the survival of the fittest.

When we speak of mass extinctions, then, we must keep in mind that between 1,000 and 100,000 species now become extinct annually—approximately .01 percent of the total—with or without the influence of man. In addition, large portions of such extinctions (at least 75 percent) occur on islands. This simply means that animals and plants on larger land masses or continents have much more room to migrate in search of more suitable environments than do island dwellers.[4]

Of course, many people contend that man is initiating another wave of mass extinctions by dumping his pollution everywhere, by harvesting and eating a substantial number of originally wild species, especially in the oceans, or by wide-scale destruction of environments through his building of cities, agricultural practices, and the like. This contention is debatable but is beyond the scope of our discussion.

What this boils down to is the real possibility that the scriptures that predict the destructions of the last days are simply prophesying a mass extinction of humanity, an extinction of the kind the earth has not seen before.[5]

For decades, especially during the Cold War period from 1950 to 1990, it was widely assumed that nuclear annihilation would be the ultimate fate of humanity. America and the Soviet Union certainly had enough nuclear warheads pointed at each other to destroy not only America and the Soviet Union but much other earth life as well. Fortunately, that threat diminished somewhat with the collapse of the Soviet bloc a decade and a half ago. Keep in mind, however, that most of those weapons still exist somewhere and that many of these same nations of the world don't like each other any more now than they did then.

Another possibility for mass extinction arises from other types of weapons of mass destruction that exist throughout the world, such as chemical and biological weapons, which in many cases are smaller and transportable, easier to manufacture, and every bit as deadly as nuclear weapons. There is little doubt that sooner or later a terrorist group or rogue nation will gain access to, and use, one or more of these weapons, with predictable consequences.

The irony of all this is that despite the numerous advances man has made over the past couple of centuries, and despite the vast stockpile of knowledge we now have, we may simultaneously now be on the brink of initiating the mass extinction of our very own species—and without God's intervention to save most of us!

As indicated previously, however, many of the scriptures that speak of the calamities to come also hint that those calamities will occur near Christ's Second Coming and be, to some extent, the means by which he defeats evil in the last great battle. Weapons of mass destruction may then come into play as well as a couple of other possibilities that fit the scriptures equally well.

Super Volcanoes

Besides the hundreds of active volcanic sites around the world, which we have already discussed, volcanologists and geologists have recently become aware of what they term super volcanoes. So far, about a half dozen of these have been located and studied, causing concern among volcano watchers and doomsday types, especially as more of these sites probably remain to be discovered.

The reason for their concern is certainly understandable. An eruption at a single one of these sites would be so huge—thousands of times larger than that of any recent volcano—that it could well cause global death and destruction, mostly from atmospheric and climatic changes. A single super-volcanic eruption would be at least 2,000 times more powerful than that of Mount St. Helens in 1981.

Because of their sheer size and corresponding explosive force, super-volcanic eruptions cause craters (caldera) instead of mountains, as most normal volcanoes do. That is because all surface material is blasted away during a single eruption. This results from sodium dioxide and carbon dioxide being mixed under enormous compacting pressure with subsurface magma (imagine a gigantic super-hot bubble waiting to burst), which, when it finds a way to the surface and the compacting pressure is released, expands explosively. What surface material is left after the eruption simply collapses back into the empty magma chamber.

The region of absolute devastation surrounding such an explosion would range as far outward as six hundred miles from the eruption site. Destruction of life would be caused by the blast itself, the release of poisonous gases, heat, and pyroclastic flows (superheated air and particulate matter that stream outward along the ground in giant waves) cooking everything in their paths. In addition, massive clouds of smoke and gases from such volcanic eruptions, or even from smaller ones such as that of Mount St. Helens, cause severe lightning storms.

One of these super-volcanic sites sits right in our own back yard, in Yellowstone Park. Recent detailed studies in the park have fairly well established that it erupts about every 600,000 years, the last of which occurred about 630,000 years ago. There have also been smaller such eruptions, one of which occurred in 7410 B.C.

This obviously means that another huge eruption may be a real possibility within the next several centuries.[6] Even now, intensive studies are being conducted within the park to monitor minor geological changes that might provide early warning of another eruption. The north end of Yellowstone Park is actually bulging upward slightly, though it tends to rise and fall from time to time, reflecting magma activity below. Incidentally, the molten magma chamber under the park, from which an eruption would originate, is half as big as the park itself. Hence its classification as a super-volcano. Much of the park is a twenty-eight–by–forty-seven-mile-wide caldera, underneath which the magma chamber sits five miles below the surface. That magma chamber is itself six miles thick.

Two of Yellowstone's last three major eruptions in the past 2 million years have been among the largest eruptions known to have occurred on the earth, each producing more than six hundred cubic miles of magma. The total volume of magma erupted from the Yellowstone Plateau volcanic field since 2.5 million years ago approaches 4,000 cubic miles.

Researchers have found that ash deposits, as much as six feet deep in Nebraska, once covered over half of North America. These have been traced back to a Yellowstone eruption 1.2 million years ago. Large-scale and widespread biological extinctions worldwide can be traced back to the same period.

Another identified super-volcanic site is the north end of the island of Sumatra, just south of Thailand in Southeast Asia, which gives us some evidence of what could happen if (or better yet, when) Yellowstone Park or one of the other super-volcanoes erupts again. The Sumatra volcano, Toba, apparently last erupted some 74,000 years ago, the largest volcanic eruption in the last two million years. From its caldera—eighteen miles wide by sixty miles long—an estimated 2,000 cubic miles of ash was ejected, 2,800 times more than that from the Mount St. Helens eruption.

In addition, its accompanying pyroclastic flows scorched 15,000 square miles, and its devastation was worldwide. Not only did it cause local and regional destruction near where the eruption took place—as well as tsunamis or tidal waves—but its effects on the world's climates was immediate. As a result of its massive release of sulfur dioxide into the atmosphere, temperatures around the globe dropped precipitously an average of seven degrees Fahrenheit for years. Summers in temperate climates cooled by as much as 15 degrees, causing enormous and widespread disruption to the earth's delicately balanced ecosystems.[7]

To translate this into a present-day scenario, that means that if another such super-volcanic eruption were to occur, nearly all agriculture around the world would cease, storms and other atmospheric changes would become more commonplace and extreme, earthquakes and tidal waves would range outward from around the eruption site for hundreds, if not thousands, of miles (earthquakes and volcanic activity are both often concentrated together geographically[8]), and tens of thousands of the earth's species would become extinct within a year.

The tidal waves from the 1883 Krakatoa eruption, which was a little larger than an average eruption but not anywhere near the size of a super-volcanic eruption, killed more than 36,000. In the last five centuries, over 200,000 have perished from normal volcanic eruptions, which, again, are on a far smaller scale than super-volcanic ones.

Relating to species' extinction from such an event, some researchers who study mitochondrial DNA, which provides a rough approximation of genetic change over an organism's history, contend that approximately 70,000 to 80,000 years ago, humanity's population was inexplicably reduced almost to extinction, perhaps leaving only a few thousand of us on the earth. Of course, the researchers can't determine the cause of this dramatic population reduction, but their timetable of 70,000 to 80,000 years ago corresponds fairly well with the Sumatra super-volcanic eruption of 74,000 years ago, does it not?

A third recently discovered super volcano, which is now apparently dormant, is the Fish Canyon Tuff in Colorado's San Juan Mountains. It last erupted 27.8 million years ago with about the same force and destruction as Sumatra's Toba.

> Surely in that day [when Gog shall come against the land of Israel] there shall be a great shaking in the land of Israel . . . and the mountains shall be thrown down, and the steep places shall fall, and every wall shall fall to the ground. . . . And I will plead against him with pestilence and with blood; and I will rain upon him, and upon his bands, and upon the many people that are with him, an overflowing rain, and great hailstones, fire, and brimstone. (Ezekiel 38:19–22; see also Malachi 4:1)

> The sun and the moon shall be darkened, and the stars shall withdraw their shining. (Joel 3:15; see also Isaiah 5:30; 2 Nephi 23:10)

> And I will shew wonders in the heavens and in the earth, blood, and fire, and pillars of smoke. The sun shall be turned into darkness, and the moon into blood, before the great and the terrible day of the Lord come. (Joel 2:30–31; see also Zephaniah 1:15; Malachi 4:1; Revelation 6:12)

A detailed study of the above verses will quickly reveal that there is little in these prophecies of the last days that can't easily apply to such enormous volcanic eruptions. A super-volcanic explosion will undoubtedly be accompanied and followed (and perhaps preceded) by frequent earthquakes ranging outward from the eruption site for hundreds of miles in all directions. If the eruption were to take place on an island or along a coastal area, it will almost certainly generate huge tsunamis that will fan outward at hundreds of miles per hour and travel thousands of miles. Wherever they strike land, they will cause great damage and loss of life.

A super-volcanic eruption would cause large amounts of debris to be thrown miles into the atmosphere, having two consequences. In the near term, much of that debris would consist of boulders, flaming lava, and smaller red-hot stones, all of which would come raining back down on the earth for a period of time after the initial eruption. Some of them might fall to the earth a considerable distance away, similar to a rain of "fire and brimstone."[9]

Such an eruption would, of course, cause terrifying storms, which, together with the force of the explosion and the great amount of ash ejected into the air, would be like a scene from hell. Day would be turned into night, as the residents of Yakima, Washington, found shortly after the 1981 explosion of Mount St. Helens. During that eruption, which consisted mostly of gases and ash and less of lava flows, huge clouds of ash and debris were blown into the sky and were carried downwind to the east of the mountain in billowing clouds for hundreds of miles.

Because of the dust, the residents of Yakima literally saw no sun, moon, or stars—or even each other—for a couple of days after the eruption. The ash was so thick that one had to don a face mask when venturing outside in order to avoid damage to the lungs and eyes. In addition, travel was brought to a halt as the blowing ash damaged car and truck engine parts, besides piling up in great drifts throughout the countryside.[10] A day or two later, as the ash clouds began to clear, sunrises were red, as was the moon at night! Consider what it would be like, then, to experience such a period of poisonous darkness and to be pelted with red-hot stones, debris, and ash falling from the sky! Would that not fulfill prophecy?

On the west side of Mount St. Helens, besides the forty-six people killed directly by the mountain's explosion, many homes, vehicles, and bridges were washed away by the flooding of the ash-laden Toutle River, swollen by snow melt from the eruption.

Near the eruption of a super volcano, every living thing for hundreds of miles in nearly every direction would be destroyed by the blast as well as by its superheated pyroclastic flows that would roll outward from the site at sixty miles per hour, charring everything in their path. The long-term effects of such a gigantic explosion would be like that of Mount St. Helens, but the ash cloud would be so immense that it would encircle the earth with sufficient gases and debris to pollute the entire atmosphere for months, if not years.

This would mean that storms and weather extremes would increase in frequency and ferocity, and the earth's atmosphere would cool, due to lack of sunshine, to the point that winters would be prolonged in temperate areas and tropical areas would be cooled. Food production would be brought to a halt as no crops would survive. Human, animal, and plant deaths would escalate exponentially worldwide due to disease, starvation, and the damaging effects of the gases and ash on living organisms.

Needless to say, these extreme conditions would shortly be accompanied by mass starvation, a breakdown in social order in nearly all communities and cities, and eventual chaos everywhere, as people and families were forced to survive in any way they could, even by predation on others. Add to this the fact that the world would probably already be in turmoil from war and the evil reign of the anti-Christ, and we can easily see the true impact the scriptures should convey to us.

Asteroid Impact

Astronomers and earth scientists contend that billions of years ago the earth and the other planets and bodies in the universe were formed by the slow accretion of space debris. As the debris coalesced together, gravitational pull increased, thus attracting still more debris until, over tens of millions of years, a planetary body was formed.

This accumulation process continued and comets, asteroids, and smaller bodies crashed into the new planets, causing them to eventually reach their current size. This process continues to this day, although at a much slower pace than billions of years ago as much of the space debris has, in the interim, been greatly reduced, having been pulled into other bodies within our solar system and throughout the universe. Nevertheless, the earth continues to be bombarded by meteors and space dust, most of which we are oblivious to, except for large ones. Much of this space debris rains down during daylight hours when it is less detectable, is burned up in the atmosphere before it reaches the earth, or lands in the oceans.

Traces of this accumulation process are difficult to find since most impact sites have occurred in oceans or have, over millennia, weathered and eroded away on our land masses. For those who need proof that this is the case, one needs only to look at the moon, which is pockmarked with over 100 million impact craters (which are not volcanic). The moon has no process of erosion or oceans, and the clear signs of asteroid impacts, which have occurred over billions of years, remain clearly visible to this day. Even Mars still retains an asteroid crater the size of Western Europe.

As far as the earth is concerned, quite a number of asteroid craters are still to be found. Fifty-two have been discovered in North America alone, plus numerous others around the world. Before we discuss these, we should note that many scientists now contend that earth's seas were the result of either volcanic eruptions, which spew out huge volumes of water vapor, or of comet impacts with the earth. Comets, astronomers have found, consist not only of rock and smaller debris, but also of ice as well. As a matter of fact, it is estimated that the Comet Hale-Bopp, which many of us saw in 1997, alone contained enough water—in the form of ice—to fill half of one of the Great Lakes. Although smaller space debris (meteors) burns up before reaching the earth, the small amount of ice they contain continues to add water vapor to our atmosphere.

The volume of asteroids, comets, and other space debris remains substantial, although it has by now been largely depleted from what it once was. For example, the well-known asteroid belt between Mars and Jupiter has been much studied. It contains at least 40,000 asteroids, ranging in size from that of a house to chunks hundreds of miles in diameter. In addition, the Oort cloud—a massive field of asteroids and comets outside our solar system—contains many times more that number. The thing to be concerned about is that whenever these great asteroid clusters are jostled (often by collisions among themselves), asteroids are often deflected away to travel elsewhere in the universe, including into our solar system. In addition, smaller asteroid fields orbit the sun both inside and outside of earth's orbit.

Astronomers continue to study the universe for traces of such wandering asteroids, and a number have been found traversing in and out of our solar system. Thus far, scientists have studied approximately 580 such near-earth objects (NEOs) and estimate that at least the same number exist that we should be keeping an eye on. Tom Morgan, chief scientist of the NASA small planet program, states that approximately 1,000 asteroids bigger than six-tenths of a mile pass near the earth in their orbit of the sun.[11] In fact, every eighteen months, an asteroid half a mile in diameter or larger passes closer to the earth than the distance to the moon.

How close do such heavenly bodies come to the earth, and how often? Recent near misses include the following:

- A three-mile-wide asteroid passed within one million miles of the earth in September 2004.

- Asteroid 1950DA, which orbits the sun near earth's orbit, has a one in three hundred chance of impacting the earth (in the year 2883).

- Asteroid 2002 NY40, half a mile in diameter, passed within 350,000 miles of the earth (slightly more than the distance to the moon) in August 2002.

- Asteroid 2001 CU11, half a mile in diameter, passed just outside the orbit of the moon in August 1925.

- A one-hundred-foot asteroid passed within 100,000 miles of the earth in March 2004.
- An asteroid six hundred yards in diameter passed inside the moon's orbit in 1996.
- Asteroid 2000 SG344 has a one-in-five hundred chance of colliding with the earth in 2030 (although scientists are not all in agreement on this projection).

Probably the most reliable and comprehensive summary of such potentially hazardous asteroids (PHAs) has been compiled by scientists at Harvard University. They list in detail nearly nine hundred asteroids that will pass relatively close to the earth (less than the distance between the earth and the sun) between now and 2178. All except five will pass closer to the earth than the orbit of the moon. Keep in mind, however, that we still have no complete summary of all asteroids circulating within or approaching our solar system.

As noted above, there have been millions of asteroid impacts on the earth during its creation, with a decreasing number since then. But how about impacts in out neighborhood more recently? Several are worthy of note. The first didn't strike the earth but the planet Jupiter. Comet Shoemaker-Levy 9 surprised astronomers testing the Hubble telescope in 1994 when they observed the comet colliding with the giant planet. Hitting at 200,000 miles per hour, it broke into twenty-one pieces, the largest a mile in diameter. The resulting explosions, each larger than the earth, lasted for weeks.

The two most well-known impact craters on the earth are those in Arizona and Australia. The Arizona impact site, Meteor Crater, was created 50,000 years ago by an asteroid half the size of a football field. It struck the earth at 30,000 to 40,000 miles per hour, leaving a crater seven hundred feet deep and 4,000 feet across.

Approximately 175 million tons of rock and earth exploded outward, forming a continuous blanket of debris surrounding the crater for a mile. Large boulders were thrown several miles away. How much destruction was caused beyond that distance is unknown, though it was undoubtedly considerable—from the heat, from the explosion itself, and from the resulting ash cloud that blew into the atmosphere. The asteroid, instead of being buried in the crater, fragmented or melted on impact, most of it being thrown outside the crater.[12] The Australia crater is similar to the Arizona crater in size, composition, and the manner in which it was created.

More recently, a smaller asteroid impact occurred in remote Siberia in 1908. Researchers there have recently examined evidence of a large, shallow crater, now overgrown with forest, and patterns of long-dead trees that, for miles round about (over one hundred square miles), were blasted outward as if from an enormous bomb. It is doubtful that this impact was of much consequence to the rest of the world, although local devastation was enormous. Siberia is sparsely populated, especially in the early 1900s, so that few people were even aware of what had occurred.

The asteroid's impact, however, was reported to have knocked people down forty miles away. Called the Tunguska Impact, the object was estimated to have been the size of two houses. Despite its relatively small size, its explosion was equivalent to a thousand atom bombs like the one dropped on Hiroshima. It exploded up to thirty thousand feet above the earth's surface.

Undoubtedly the most meaningful asteroid impact that should give us pause is the one that occurred 65 million years ago on the Yucatán Peninsula. For a century, scientists have debated over what ended the age of dinosaurs, as their extinction was relatively abrupt in geological time. It was speculated that they may have died of disease or climatic change, but no proof or even a hint of such an end was forthcoming. Some scientists even proposed that an asteroid impact might have been the cause, but no evidence was found.

Scientists received their first break in the puzzle when oil explorations near the northeastern coast of the Yucatán Peninsula revealed a circular pattern in the earth roughly 108 miles in diameter. Subsequent investigation of the site, called Chicxulub, confirmed that, indeed, a large asteroid had collided with the earth at that spot 65 million years ago. Further studies have fairly well established the damage done by the asteroid's impact, giving an idea of its size and leading to the opinion that it was most likely responsible for the extinction of the dinosaurs and also of tens of thousands of other species alive at that time.

Caused by an asteroid six miles across, that impact left traces and residue over much of the western hemisphere that are still being found and studied. Dust and debris deposits traced back to Chicxulub range outward from the impact site as far away as 2,700 miles. Locations three hundred miles away show deposits three feet deep. Impact ejecta, consisting of rocks, shocked quartz, and spherules (rounded once-molten rock), have been found not only all around the Gulf of Mexico, but as far away as the New England coast of the United States and as far north as the Canadian border near Montana.[13] The short-term and long-term damage this impact caused worldwide isn't difficult to imagine.

> Here is an assessment of what another such large-scale impact would do. The energy released by just one impactor (asteroid), kilometers across, is equivalent to the release of the world's entire nuclear arsenal—at the peak prior to current disarmament—many dozens of times over. Such an enormous release of energy on a habitable planet has the capacity to transform oceans and atmospheres and to destroy life on a planetary scale; 15 percent of all shallow water marine families would become extinct, including 80 percent of shallow-water invertebrate species. It would cause the contemporaneous disappearance of many animal species. Molten debris would heat the air and ground sufficient to ignite forests. Tidal wave action would be enormous.[14]
>
> Such an impactor would gouge a crater in excess of sixty miles in diameter and fling dust into the upper atmosphere. The molten flying debris and pressure wave would burn and knock down trees across thousands of kilometers of land. If the impact were into water, the resulting tidal wave would inundate adjacent land areas for hundreds of miles around. The material blown into the stratosphere would encircle the earth and enough dust would be available to shroud the earth in darkness for months. The energy released from such an impact would be over a million times more powerful than the

> Mount St. Helens eruption or the largest nuclear test explosion.
>
> In addition to the direct effects of the impact, such as widespread forest fires and tidal waves, the plume of debris and smoke rising into the earth's stratosphere would have a devastating effect on life by altering the climate. By physically blocking the rays of the sun, the dust would cause the lower atmosphere and the surface of the earth to cool suddenly and remain that way for weeks or months. Much of the continental area of the earth would average daytime temperatures of only 10 degrees C (50 degrees F).
>
> Reduced sunlight would slow or shut down photosynthesis for up to a year, killing off large numbers of species dependent on various marine and continental food chains. (Photosynthesis is the removal of carbon dioxide from the atmosphere by plants and replacing it with oxygen.) The atmosphere would then, after the cooling dust settled, tend to heat strongly due to the remaining high carbon dioxide content in the atmosphere. Thus, months of global winter might well be followed by years, decades, or more of global warming and acid rain.
>
> Reduced ozone abundance would cause exposure of organisms on the earth's surface to deadly ultraviolet radiation. Hydrogen sulfide, a flammable, poisonous gas, would be produced in large quantities by worldwide decaying vegetation.[15]

This would assuredly be a dismal prospect. So just how realistic is the threat that a sufficiently large asteroid will strike the earth before long? Scientists now estimate that

- A small asteroid impact, causing localized destruction (such as that in Siberia), occurs every fifty to 1,000 years.

- A larger asteroid impact, causing regional destruction (such as those in Arizona and Australia), occurs once every 1,000 to 100,000 years.

- A massive asteroid impact, causing global destruction (such as that in Yucatán), occurs once every 100,000 years or more.

To better understand and predict the potential hazards of asteroid or comet encounters with the earth, astronomers have developed what is known as the Torino Scale. This scale utilizes numbers ranging from 0 to 10, similar to the better-known Richter Scale for gauging the severity of earthquakes. A zero on the Torino Scale indicates any known asteroid-like object that will encounter the earth and dissipate within the atmosphere or bypass the earth entirely (a near miss). The numbers then range upward through those objects that will strike the earth's lower atmosphere and surface but will cause nominal or only local or regional destruction. At the top of the scale—numbers 8–10—are those objects that will definitely impact the earth's atmosphere or surface with sufficient force to cause widespread destruction, possibly on a global scale.

The question arises, do we have any real defense against any of these eventualities? The answer is no, not really. Despite Hollywood's various heroic portrayals of blasting them apart or altering their course toward earth with nuclear-tipped missiles, there exists, realistically, no defense against such a threat to the earth.

The closest real-life effort at a defense was Project Icarus, which was contemplated at the Massachusetts Institute of Technology as long ago as 1968 as a graduate research project. It was named after a then-known asteroid named Icarus that passed within four million miles of the earth in 1997, regularly orbiting near the earth every nineteen years. Project Icarus proposed, similar to recent Hollywood dramatizations, launches of at least six Saturn 5 rockets tipped with one-hundred-megaton nuclear bombs to destroy or deflect any threatening asteroid away from the earth.[16] The program was of doubtful efficacy even then and has been largely neglected since.

There is now no known feasible government program to ward off or even diminish a significant asteroid impact on the earth—unless that program is so top secret that no one has heard of it. As a matter of fact, astronomers' attention to asteroids has waned somewhat of late, but scientists are just recently beginning to belatedly realize that such a threat to the earth is, in fact, a real possibility and will occur sooner or later.

Despite a scientific and governmental consensus on this

likelihood, lip service has been the only result. NASA, to its credit, recently undertook an effort to catalog all such potentially threatening space objects, but otherwise they believe that because the general public thinks something should be done, something should be done.

Conclusion

I have discussed what the effects will be when either a super-volcanic eruption or a massive asteroid impact with the earth occurs. Few, however, have ever contemplated what would happen on a first-person basis. What, in fact, will it be like when the end comes?

The effects will be similar in either scenario. First, at the time of a super-volcanic eruption or asteroid strike, an enormous explosion will take place, resulting in widespread earthquakes, renewed volcanic activity for hundreds of miles around the site, and tidal waves that will range outward for thousands of miles, assuming the event takes place in or near an ocean, which is a likely possibility. This will mean that nearly all islands and coastal areas—which are usually the most heavily populated—will be inundated with tidal waves almost certainly hundreds of feet tall. Such waves will travel hundreds of miles per hour.

Within minutes of the explosion, enormous clouds of smoke, dust, water vapor, boulders, and other debris will be blasted into the upper atmosphere, some of it consisting of molten chunks as large as basketballs. At the same time, weather for hundreds of miles around the explosion site will be immediately altered, consisting of massive storms of wind, lightning, and probably hail. This turbulence in the weather will spread outward from the site, probably from west to east, or from east to west south of the equator. Within a few short days, it will have spread quickly around the globe. This means that the entire earth will be blanketed with massive storms, and the weather patterns and climates we have long been accustomed to will no longer exist.

Our spring and summer seasons will disappear due to the dense cloud, smoke, and debris cover, which will block incoming sunlight. At the same time, and even more terrifying, will be the rocks and other molten material, blown into the sky during the initial explosion, which will fall back to earth within the first few hours or days—in effect, like hailstorms of blazing rock. Doesn't this sound eerily like the Bible's warnings that the end will come amid fire and brimstone from the sky? The Bible mentions also, as noted earlier, that the sun, moon, and stars will disappear, and the mountains will be thrown down, and that massive earthquakes will tear the earth.

The book of Revelation prophesies,

> There followed hail and fire mingled with blood, and they were cast upon the earth, and the third part of trees was burnt up, and all green grass was burnt up. . . . And as it were a great mountain burning with fire was cast into the sea; and the third part of the sea became blood; and the third part of the creatures which were in the sea, and had life, died; and the third part of the ships were destroyed. . . . And there fell a great star from heaven, burning as it were a lamp, and it fell upon the third part of the rivers, and upon the fountains of waters . . . and the third part of the sun was smitten, and the third part of the moon, and the third part of the stars; so as the third part of them was darkened, and the day shone not for a third part of it, and the night likewise.
>
> And men were scorched with great heat. . . . And there were voices, and thunders, and lightnings; and there was a great earthquake, such as was not since men were upon the earth, so mighty an earthquake, and so great.
>
> And every island fled away, and the mountains were not found. And there fell upon men a great hail out of heaven, every stone about the weight of a talent [seventy pounds]. (Revelation 8:7–10, 12; 16:9, 18–20)

As if these events wouldn't be disastrous enough, keep in mind that after the initial storms and the fiery debris falling from the sky, the dense dust and smoke cover encircling the earth would probably last for months, if not years.

What does this mean to the man on the street? Undoubtedly,

tens of millions will perish during the first few hours after the event occurs simply because of tidal waves, earthquakes, volcanoes, and storms. These will also certainly result in massive inland flooding, particularly in lowland areas. But in the months to follow, all crops will die, and there will be massive losses of livestock and vegetation around the earth. As we learned in the recent Hurricane Katrina disaster in Louisiana, those who survive the first few days will then have to contend with rapidly diminishing food supplies and lack of sanitary water and sewage removal, as well as the cold and continuing storms. Very likely, temperatures around the earth will begin to resemble those of winter in the northern hemisphere, and they will probably remain that way for months or years.

In social terms, we can expect near total societal collapse. Stores will run out of food and other supplies within hours, money and international monetary systems will become valueless, power systems will probably collapse within days, and any semblance of an orderly society will begin to disappear. In other words, for those who are still alive, it will quickly become a matter of "survival of the fittest." And our governments, national and local, will be largely ineffective, even with the military, as they too rely on fuel and communications, both of which will be in increasingly short supply. So one may forget about hospitals, police, and firefighters, as transportation systems, including automobiles, and all the other things we have blithely taken for granted most of our lives, fail us.

Families, communities, and cities will almost certainly become hostile enclaves that cling together for survival, on guard against and at the expense of others. Looting and mayhem will spread as law and order break down. Home heating and comforts will become rare, and food and drinking water will become more valuable than gold. No more work will be available at the office. There will be no schools and no vacations. Simply put, life will become the drudgery of each family fending for itself, trying to stay fed and warm. Those unable to do so will die, first the elderly and ill, and then everyone else as they succumb to the elements, to sickness and to starvation.

Even isolated islands on the other side of the world and people taking refuge in caves or underground bunkers won't be spared. They may delay the inevitable for a time, but as this dismal scenario will play itself out for years, they too will eventually succumb. Numerous recent novels and movies describe such grim events and their aftermath. Some of the best of these include the recent films *Deep Impact* and *Asteroid,* as well as the novel, *Lucifer's Hammer,* by Larry Niven and Jerry Pournelle (Fawcett Crest Books, 1977). Unfortunately, they provide only a Hollywood glimpse or superficial glimmer of the probably awful reality that could spell our end.

This isn't a happy commentary on how man may end his days on the earth, but the scriptures aren't much more positive. Anyone who has dwelt on the comments of Jesus and the prophets, discussed previously, or on the dire prophecies in the book of Revelation, will acknowledge that many parallels exist between those scriptures and the events described above. The only thing lacking, perhaps, in the scriptures' last-days symbolism, are the horsemen of the apocalypse, the seven seals, the rise and reign of the anti-Christ, the final battle of Armageddon, and the return of Jesus Christ. We will return to these in the ensuing chapters.

> For not many days hence and the earth shall tremble and reel to and fro as a drunken man; and the sun shall hide his face, and shall refuse to give light; and the moon shall be bathed in blood; and the stars shall become exceedingly angry, and shall cast themselves down as a fig that falleth from off a fig tree.
>
> And after your testimony cometh wrath and indignation upon the people.
>
> For after your testimony cometh the testimony of earthquakes, that shall cause groanings in the midst of her, and men shall fall upon the ground and shall not be able to stand. And also cometh the testimony of the voice of thunderings, and the voice of lightnings, and the voice of tempests, and the voice of the waves of the sea heaving themselves beyond their bounds. And all things shall be in commotion; and surely, men's hearts shall fail them; for fear shall come upon all people. (D&C 88:87–91)

Notes

1. There will certainly be some who don't adhere to geologists' understanding of the earth's 4.7-billion-year history. For them, this may simply be food for thought, although it is difficult to overlook the multitude of evidence that indicates the earth's antiquity far beyond 6,000 years, the time since the biblical Garden of Eden.

2. Oxygen in our atmosphere, which we take for granted and which makes life possible for the entire animal kingdom, including man, didn't occur until green plants made their appearance on the earth 500 million years ago.

3. For a clear, readable, and thought-provoking discussion for the layman of the earth's mass extinctions, see Peter D. Ward's *Rivers in Time,* published in 2000 by Columbia University Press.

4. Yes, plants *do* migrate, although they don't do so as individuals. Their migration reflects their spread into peripheral areas through seed spreading or outward growth of root systems. Their migration, then, must be considered in generations rather than through actual movement. Migration of an aspen forest from one area to another, for example, may take thousands of years.

5. The scriptures do, however, promise that a small portion of humanity will survive and remain on the earth—those who, through the last difficult days, will remain true to Jesus Christ and his teachings.

6. "The consensus among those who have studied the area is that the Yellowstone magmatic system will likely erupt again" ("Historical Unrest at Large Calderas of the World," *U.S. Geological Survey Bulletin 1855).*

7. To understand this, remember that a volcanic eruption spews into the atmosphere huge amounts of gases, smoke, debris, water vapor, and dust. In the case of a super-volcanic eruption, the earth's atmosphere would become so saturated with materials that solar radiation (sunlight), on which our climates and crops depend, would be greatly reduced, just the same as if we had a heavy cloud cover that lasted for months and even years. The cooling effect this would have on weather, crops, and climates should be obvious.

8. Both Yellowstone Park and Sumatra are seismically active areas with frequent earthquakes.

9. Brimstone is simply the biblical term for sulfur, a foul-smelling chemical usually associated with hot springs and volcanic areas.

10. Several economic consequences resulted from the Mount St. Helens eruption as well. One was the need to dredge the ash-clogged Columbia River for miles so that inland barges and shipping could resume. Another was the fact that Weyerhauser, a large producer of timber products, had to abandon thousands of its own acres of timber downed by the volcano, again because of ash damage to engines of logging equipment. However, a positive consequence was the fact that some Yakima residents found that they could market tiny bottles of "genuine Mount St. Helens Ash" worldwide for as much as $5 each. This latter is an example of true American entrepreneurial spirit, especially when you have a foot or two of ash covering your home and yard!

11. The largest known asteroid is 750 miles across and is part of the Kuiper Belt, near Pluto's orbit.

12. Short-lived iron mining operations were at one time carried on in the crater, but because little of the asteroid remained, they soon went defunct. However, microscopic diamonds, formed by the intense heat of the impact, have been found. Few asteroids remain in their craters after impact; most consist of relatively brittle fragmented rock that disintegrates or vaporizes upon entering the earth's atmosphere at a speed of 20,000 to 40,000 miles per hour. An asteroid traveling at such speeds would pass through the earth's atmosphere in one second.

13. The central part of North America was at that time under water. Note also that the spherules blown so far away by the impact were molten when ejected, raining down thousands of miles away long after the initial explosion.

14. Signs of a gigantic tidal wave have been found around the Gulf of Mexico and in the Caribbean.

15. Jonathan I. Lunine, *Earth, Evolution of a Habitable World* (Boston: Cambridge University press, 1999), 235–37.

16. Icarus's rocket and large warheads were then as yet untested, and the calculation of computer trajectories was then equally questionable.

7

Approaching Armageddon

Although literally dozens of scriptures in our standard works describe the last days, many of which we have already cited, those with the greatest substance relating to the period just prior to and during the battle of Armageddon are to be found at the end of the Bible, in the book of Revelation. Certainly, many of the prophecies found in the Bible and the Book of Mormon relate to this period of time, but the words of John the Revelator are the most comprehensive and descriptive (and chilling) source we have regarding this final chapter in man's history.

For those who have had occasion to read John's account, however, they have undoubtedly found it difficult to understand, especially in placing it into a chronological context. John's writing relies heavily on symbolism with his discussion of fiery horsemen, the seven seals, plagues of locusts, and the like. Over the centuries, theologians have studied his words and written hundreds of books, trying to assess the true meaning of his imagery. Even Hollywood and novelists have gotten on the bandwagon with numerous recent films and books about the seventh seal, the anti-Christ (whom they have often dubbed Damien), the "rapture" prior to Christ's Second Coming, and so forth.

Unfortunately, many of these portrayals are based only loosely on the scriptures and have been marketed to a wide audience with their intrigue, violence, and a feeling that maybe this is how it will be. Few moviegoers or readers, however, have ever sat down to seriously relate such offerings to the book of Revelation.

Another difficulty one encounters when studying John's writings is the fact that he seems to ramble somewhat. For example, it is often difficult to establish chronological continuity in what he has to say. Unlike our modern history books, which go to great lengths to place events in proper order, John seldom organizes his prophecies from beginning to end. They are instead interspersed throughout the book in no discernible sequence. We often can't clearly tell which events will happen before (or after) others. This is further troubling as he also, on occasion, seems to be symbolically describing the same event in different chapters. These difficulties are undoubtedly a large part of the reason why few theologians and church laymen can reach a consensus on what we can realistically expect in the last days. Nevertheless, the Prophet Joseph Smith stated that "the book of Revelation is one of the plainest books God ever caused to be written."[1]

The Seven Seals

> According to our prophet's teachings, God gave to this planet, Mother Earth, seven thousand years as the period of "its temporal existence;" and four thousand years . . . had passed before Christ was crucified, while another two thousand years, . . . have gone by since. Consequently, we stand at the present moment in the Saturday Evening of Time, near the close of the [sixth thousand years], at the week's end of human history.[2]

An excellent example of John's symbolic writing can be found in his discussion of the seven seals (see Revelation 5–9). Many (including Latter-day Saints) throughout the centuries have tried to relate these seals, or periods of time and events, to the latter days with little success. Fortunately, however, we have the advantage of latter-day scripture to clarify these important happenings. The Prophet Joseph Smith, in a revelation in 1832, clearly explained how we should understand the seven seals:

> Q. What are we to understand by the seven seals with which it was sealed?
>
> A. We are to understand that the first seal contains the things of the first thousand years, and the second also of the second thousand years, and so on until the seventh. (D&C 77:7)

In light of this clarification, the following are 6,000 years of the earth's history from the time of Adam onward, divided into the seven seals:

Years	Reference	Comments	Historical Events
First Seal			
4000–3000 B.C.	Revelation 6:2	Adam's ministry; wickedness begins to spread.	John sees a white horse; he who sat on the horse had a bow and went forth conquering and to conquer. This perhaps refers to Enoch, who had many battles with the enemies of the people of God.
Second Seal			
3000–2000 B.C.	Revelation 6:3–4	Enoch's ministry; City of Enoch translated; Noah's ministry; the great flood; Jaredites come to America.	John sees a red horse, and peace was taken from the earth. The time just before the flood was wicked, violent, and corrupt.
Third Seal			
2000–1000 B.C.	Revelation 6:5–6	Abraham's ministry; Isaac, Jacob, and the 12 tribes of Israel; Joseph, and Israel's bondage in Egypt; Moses' ministry; conquest of Land of Canaan; Israelites begin to have kings.	John sees a black horse and describes famine conditions. There was no greater time of famine in the history of the earth than during the days of Abraham.

Years	Reference	Comments	Historical Events
Fourth Seal			
1000 B.C.–Time of Christ	Revelation 6:7–8	Israel divided into two kingdoms; Isaiah's ministry; 10 tribes conquered and lost; Judah taken captive. During this time, powerful earthly kingdoms such as Assyria, Babylon, and Rome had many wars.	John sees a pale horse, ridden by Death, and Hell followed with him. Power was given unto them over the fourth part of the earth to kill with the sword, hunger, and death.
Fifth Seal			
Christ's Ministry–1000 A.D.	Revelation 6:9–11	Christ's ministry; Church established; Christ's Crucifixion and Resurrection; Gospel taken to the Gentiles; Great Apostasy and the Dark Ages.	John sees his own day and describes those who were slain for the word of God and for the testimony that they held of the Savior.
Sixth Seal			
1000–2000 A.D.	Revelation 6:12–17	Renaissance and Reformation; Industrial Revolution; Joseph Smith's ministry; Church restored and becomes a church.	John sees a great earthquake, and the sun becomes of sackcloth and hair, and the moon becomes as blood. The stars fall unto the earth, the heaven departs as a scroll, and every mountain and island are moved out of their place.

Much of this compilation is from ldslastdays.com, "Prophetic References to the Signs of the Last Days," and *The Life and Teachings of Jesus and His Apostles,* The Church of Jesus Christ of Latter-day Saints, 1979, 220–21.

Due to changes in calendars over the millennia, it is doubtful that each of these thousand-year periods is exact.

The Seventh Seal

It is interesting to note that of the 292 verses dedicated to the seven seals in the book of Revelation, only eleven deal with the first five seals. The remaining 281 verses are dedicated to our day, from the year 1,000 A.D. to the end of man's time on the earth. This is indicative of why John the Revelator went to such lengths to describe what will occur during our mortality on the earth as it draws to a close.

Again, John's imagery, symbolism, and chronology are difficult to decipher as he describes the horrific events that will take place apparently early in the seventh thousand-year period (probably very near to, or during, the battle of Armageddon). During that time, wholesale death and destruction are to be meted out on those who continue to fight against Jesus, which will comprise the bulk of humanity. Two lengthy examples should suffice, the first of which we discussed in the preceding chapter:

> The first angel sounded [his trump], and there followed hail and fire mingled with blood, and they were cast upon the earth: and the third part of the trees was burnt up, and all green grass was burnt up. And the second angel sounded, and as it were a great mountain burning with fire was cast into the sea: and the third part of the sea became blood; and the third part of the creatures which were in the sea, and had life, died; and the third part of the ships were destroyed. And the third angel sounded, and there fell a great star from heaven, burning as it were a lamp, and it fell upon the third part of the rivers, and upon the fountains of waters; And the name of the star is called Wormwood: and the third part of the waters

> became wormwood; and many men died of the waters, because they were made bitter. And the fourth angel sounded, and the third part of the sun was smitten, and the third part of the moon, and the third part of the stars; so as the third part of them was darkened, and the day shone not for a third part of it, and the night likewise. (Revelation 8:7–12)

> And there came out of the smoke locusts upon the earth: and unto them was given power, as the scorpions of the earth have power. And it was commanded them that they should not hurt the grass of the earth, neither any green thing, neither any tree; but only those men which have not the seal of God in their foreheads. And to them it was given that they should not kill them, but that they should be tormented five months: and their torment was as the torment of a scorpion, when he striketh a man. And in those days shall men seek death, and shall not find it; and shall desire to die, and death shall flee from them. (Revelation 9:3–6)[3]

Resembling the devastating plagues of "locusts," an attack John describes by a massive cavalry (whose horses breathe fire and smoke)—apparently in conjunction with the two calamities cited above—will cause the deaths of "the third of men" (Revelation 9:15–19). These great calamities are eerily reminiscent of the plagues brought against Egypt during the time of Moses. Nevertheless, remembering the fact that humanity has changed little since then, John says that those remaining will still not repent, just like the Egyptians. Be that as it may, these calamities will probably not occur until the reign of the anti-Christ or during the battle of Armageddon.

The Anti-Christ

> And every spirit that confesseth not that Jesus Christ is come in the flesh is not of God: and this is that spirit of antichrist, whereof ye have heard that it

> should come; and even now already is it in the world.
> (1 John 4:3)

As it appears in the scriptures, the term *anti-Christ* can be used in a general sense, as above—meaning those who deny that Jesus, the son of God, is the Christ—but also in a specific sense, referring to a particular person. In the former case, anti-Christs have been with us from the days of Jesus' ministry until the present day: "Little children, it is the last time: and as ye have heard that antichrist shall come, even now are there many antichrists; whereby we know that it is the last time" (1 John 2:18).

In the book of Revelation, John provides remarkable detail about *the* anti-Christ, that great, powerful, and evil person who will play a pivotal role in the days leading up to Armageddon. He is referenced several times in Daniel 7 as the "little horn" and is also described as the beast by John. It seems that all the evil remaining to Satan in his last days will be consolidated in this one person and his minions to finally and decisively turn man away (as have Satan's thousands of followers throughout humanity's history) from the Savior and his teachings. It is almost as if Satan, in a last desperate effort, will focus all his energy and power—which is enormous—into this one person as a means of (he hopes) finally winning the war against the Father and the Son that began in the premortal existence.

This person—the anti-Christ—has been the central theme of numerous modern novels and films and is someone we should absolutely be watchful of. An emissary of Satan (or "the dragon"), the anti-Christ will have the power to perform miracles, one of the first of which will be his own marvelous recovery from a grievous or deadly wound. This will apparently happen early in his career and will focus worldwide attention on him for his miraculous recovery.

Undoubtedly citing the need for world order and unity, not to mention his own benevolence, he will consolidate his power by leading the majority of willing humanity away from God and succeed in establishing a mighty worldwide kingdom John calls Babylon (Revelation 17). This is exactly the type of one-world government many opponents of the modern United Nations fear.[4] This great kingdom will be created through an alliance of ten other kingdoms or nations under the anti-Christ's leadership and will be absolutely corrupt, ruthless, and evil.[5] Worse, yet, they will be united against the remaining believers and followers of God, who will be strenuously ostracized and relentlessly persecuted:

> And I saw one of his heads as it were wounded to death; and his deadly wound was healed: and all the world wondered after the beast. And they worshiped the dragon which gave power unto the beast: and they worshipped the beast, saying, Who is like unto the beast? Who is able to make war with him? And there was given unto him a mouth speaking great things and blasphemies; and power was given unto him to continue forty and two months.
>
> And he opened his mouth in blasphemy against God, to blaspheme his name, and his tabernacle, and them that dwell in heaven. And it was given unto him to make war with the saints, and to overcome them: and power was given him over all kindreds, and tongues, and nations. And all that dwell upon the earth shall worship him, whose names are not written in the book of life of the Lamb. . . .
>
> And I beheld another beast coming up out of the earth; and he had two horns like a lamb, and he spake as a dragon. And he exerciseth all the power of the first beast before him, and causeth the earth and them which dwell therein to worship the first beast, whose deadly wound was healed. And he doeth great wonders, so that he maketh fire come down from heaven on the earth in the sight of men, And deceiveth them that dwell on the earth by the means of those miracles which he had power to do in the sight of the beast; saying to them that dwell on the earth, that they should make an image to the beast, which had the wound by a sword, and did live.
>
> And he had power to give life unto the image of the beast, that the image of the beast should both speak, and cause that as many as would not worship the image of the beast should be killed. And he causeth

> all, both small and great, rich and poor, free and bond, to receive a mark in their right hand, or in their foreheads: And that no man might buy or sell, save he that had the mark, or the name of the beast, or the number of his name.
>
> Here is wisdom. Let him that hath understanding count the number of the beast: for it is the number of a man; and his number is six hundred three score and six. (Revelation 13:3–8, 11–18)

Note a number of significant items in the above account: the "beast," or anti-Christ, will remain in power for 42 months, assisted by another peaceful, but equally evil beast (see also Revelation 11:2), and all his followers will be identified by a mark to demonstrate their allegiance to him and his kingdom. This mark—probably a tattoo or other similar identifying mark[6]—is significant as it is to be placed on the right hand or forehead of all who follow the beast, in effect permitting them to carry on commerce within the beast's kingdom. In reality, those who receive the mark are those who are deceived and worship the beast (Revelation 19:20).

Obviously, those without the mark will be easily identifiable as persons who refuse to follow or worship the beast, making them easy targets for discrimination and persecution. This will undoubtedly be similar to the worst days of Stalinism and Nazism, during which pogroms, secret police, mass propaganda, and exterminations were commonplace. Nevertheless, those who choose instead to pursue God and righteousness are warned against following the beast, despite such persecution:

> If any man worship the beast and his image, and receive his mark in his forehead, or in his hand, the same shall drink of the wine of the wrath of God, . . . and he shall be tormented with fire and brimstone in the presence of the holy angels, and in the presence of the Lamb: And the smoke of their torment ascendeth up forever and ever: and they have no rest day nor night, who worship the beast and his image, and whoso receiveth the mark of his name. (Revelation 14:9–11)[7]

This will undoubtedly be a time of extreme testing for those followers of God still on the earth, and because of it many of them will undoubtedly capitulate and choose to follow the anti-Christ. We will devote further attention to this unfortunate situation below. On the other hand, some of those who don't receive the mark will be beheaded "for the witness of Jesus." Those who won't worship the beast and are beheaded will receive their reward and will reign with Christ (Revelation 20:4).

Notice also the miraculous powers that the anti-Christ will have. He will, for example, "make fire come down from heaven" and will have the "power to give life unto the image of the beast." In attempting to exalt himself above God, as we noted earlier, his followers—those of Satan—will be required to worship his image.

If the presumption is true that we are now entering the period of the seventh seal, it is a matter of speculation and interest that the anti-Christ may well be living somewhere among us right now, perhaps as a youth in another country attending school, or perhaps already rising through political circles somewhere but aspiring to much more. The scriptures tell us little else about him—whether he will be Caucasian or of another race; of what nationality he will be; if he will be large or small in stature; how old he will be when he assumes leadership of Babylon; and so forth.

In order to assemble all the kingdoms and peoples of the earth into one massive empire loyal to him, he will surely have to be a leader of such great intellect, oratorical powers, charisma, and ruthlessness that billions will willingly follow him. And as the scriptures point out, he will also have the godlike ability to use all of Satan's tools to gain and consolidate his power, including murder, deception, and coercion (Revelation 13:14–15). Nevertheless, he will hopefully be recognizable as he will openly declare himself an enemy of God. As the scriptures above state, he will "speak great things and blasphemies . . . against God . . . and his tabernacle . . . and them that dwell in heaven."

Secret Combinations

Those who have studied the Book of Mormon even briefly have undoubtedly encountered the term *secret combinations* many times. Throughout the entire text, such clandestine groups posed a continuing threat not only to those who loyally followed Jesus and the ancient prophets, but to both the Nephite and the Lamanite nations as well, even when their religion had waned. Often operating in secret, but later openly, as their power grew, these secret combinations eroded both nations and were a major cause of the eventual destruction of the Nephites.

Secret combinations have been a scourge to humanity since the days of Adam and are specifically mentioned as such in Moses 6:15. They also proliferated among the Jaredites after their arrival in the Americas (Ether 8:18) and have existed in many nations ever since.

It is a certainty that such evil groups will be involved with, or will facilitate, the rise of the anti-Christ as he gains power over the nations of the earth in the last days. Foreseeing such a danger, it is clear why Book of Mormon prophets went to such great lengths discussing and warning us of what we might expect:

> And it came to pass that they [dissidents in the Jaredite kingdom] formed a secret combination, even as they of old; which combination is most abominable and wicked above all, in the sight of God; For the Lord worketh not in secret combinations. . . .
>
> And now, I, Moroni, do not write the manner of their oaths and combinations, for it hath been made known unto me that they are had among all people, and they are had among the Lamanites. And they have caused the destruction of this people of whom I am now speaking, and also the destruction of the people of Nephi. And whatsoever nation shall uphold such secret combinations, to get power and gain, until they spread over the nation, behold, they shall be destroyed. . . .
>
> Wherefore, O ye Gentiles, it is wisdom in God that these things should be shown unto you, that thereby ye may repent of your sins, and suffer not that these murderous combinations shall get above you, which are built up to get power and gain—and the work, yea, even the work of destruction come upon you, yea, even the sword of the justice of the Eternal God shall fall

> upon you, to your overthrow and destruction if ye shall suffer these things to be.
>
> Wherefore, the Lord commandeth you, when ye shall see these things come among you that ye shall awake to a sense of your awful situation, because of this secret combination which shall be among you. . . . For it cometh to pass that whoso buildeth it up seeketh to overthrow the freedom of all lands, nations, and countries; and it bringeth to pass the destruction of all people, for it is built up by the devil, who is the father of all lies. (Ether 8:18–25)

Most prominent of such evil groups during Book of Mormon times were the Gadianton Robbers, well known to students of Nephite and Lamanite history. Helaman 2:4-5 provides a detailed account of the origin of the Gadianton robbers who, hundreds of years later, were instrumental in the complete apostasy of both nations.

To understand and fully appreciate the danger such clandestine groups pose, Nephi, the son of Helaman, just prior to Christ's ministry in the Americas, described in detail the evil and corrupting effects secret combinations can have on otherwise righteous and God-fearing people:

> And seeing the people in a state of such awful wickedness, and those Gadianton robbers filling the judgment-seats—having usurped the power and authority of the land; laying aside the commandments of God, and not in the least aright before him; doing no justice unto the children of men; condemning the righteous because of their righteousness; letting the guilty and wicked go unpunished because of their money; and moreover to be held in office at the head of government, to rule and do according to their wills, that they might get gain and glory of the world, and, moreover, that they might the more easily commit adultery, and steal, and kill, and do according to their own wills. (Helaman 7:4–5)

With the collapse of the Soviet Union in the 1990s, and the subsequent abandonment of communism by many nations, many in the free world have become complacent, assuming that such godless tyranny is no longer a threat. Such thinking, however, is naively premature; various nations, including China, remain devoutly communist and are a continuing threat to world peace and order no matter what their current proclamations of peaceful intent happen to be. This international threat is a continuing worry, not unlike the threat of the Gadianton robbers in Book of Mormon times.[8] There remain literally hundreds of communist organizations, in our own country and throughout the world, who strive someday to regain their power on the international stage. These again are precisely the organizations that may provide stepping stones for the anti-Christ's own future rise to world power.

They may operate quietly, spreading their propaganda and luring new recruits to their ranks. Such organizations can be found on nearly any university campus in this country, although they shroud themselves in innocuous or patriotic names such as peace or peoples' movements, environmentalist "save the world" organizations, and assorted socialist nomenclatures. Later, as their membership grows, and after amassing funding and political clout, they step out of the shadows and reveal themselves for what they are—old-fashioned communists. As David O. McKay said,

> In this retreat from freedom [our alliances and continuous involvement in cold and hot wars] the voices of protesting citizens have been drowned by raucous shouts of intolerance and abuse from those who led the retreat and their millions of gullible youth, who are marching merrily to their doom, carrying banners on which are emblazoned such intriguing and misapplied labels as social justice, equality, reform, patriotism, social welfare.[9]

A similar modern, and immediately more pressing, threat we now face is that of terrorism, particularly from fanatical, extremely fundamentalist Islamic groups. These scattered secret cells, with their hate directed primarily at Israel and the United States—the

Great Satan, Israel's ally—conform in remarkable detail to the blueprint for secret combinations laid out by the Book of Mormon.

They operate clandestinely with the sole purpose to destroy the usually innocent Christians and Jews wherever they may be. These groups are particularly dangerous because they apply their fanatical zeal and hatred in the name of Allah. They may disguise their goals in politics, claiming they are fighting for their homeland as, for example, against Israel's claim to part of the Holy Land, or to protect their Islamic way of life or discourage American involvement in the Middle East over oil. In reality, however, their random terrorist atrocities prove that they act only out of hatred and religious bigotry.

The unfortunate reality is that these or any secret combinations thrive in countries where freedom predominates. The fact that our Constitution guarantees freedom of speech and assembly gives any of these fringe groups the protected right to assemble and express their hatred as much as they want. They are also often well funded and retain staffs of attorneys, often as corrupt as they are, to protect their evil activities. Only when it can be clearly shown that their radical ideas harm someone or that they are a threat to the nation can they be stopped. This seldom happens, however, as they carefully disguise their activities and goals and act in secrecy.

For those skeptical about the existence of such groups in this country, or about the political impact they have, or can have, the following represent a few of the more notorious ones:

The Great and Abominable Church: Although not secret combinations per se, there exist dozens of radical religious splinter groups scattered throughout the world who fit well the Book of Mormon's descriptions of secret combinations. They practice a wide array of bizarre religious rituals such as personal mutilation, animal sacrifice, and the like. Among them are cults that practice Satanism, strange combinations of paganism and Christianity such as voodoo, spells, and so forth. Many also quietly espouse no loyalty whatsoever to any government, including that of the United States. They feel that God is their ruling authority and that all other governments are artificial, man-made constructs.

To again refer back to Nazism, it should be remembered that Adolf Hitler, born a Catholic, often invoked God, Catholicism, and religion in his political rallies, as did his Italian ally, Benito Mussolini. Nephi saw nearly twenty-six centuries ago that the great and abominable church would rally against the Saints of the last days: "And it came to pass that I beheld that the great mother of abominations did gather together multitudes upon the face of all the earth, among all the nations of the Gentiles, to fight against the Lamb of God" (1 Nephi 14:13).

LDS Dissidents: It is a fact of LDS history that numerous groups have split off from the Church over issues such as succession of the presidency (i.e., the Reorganized Church of Jesus Christ of Latter Day Saints, now the Community of Christ); polygamy (as in dozens of apostate groups who, often illegally, continue to practice polygamy both openly and in secret); and more recent groups who have left the Church over the issue of race (when the Church made the priesthood available to blacks).

Most of these groups may not necessarily be classified as secret combinations and may be entirely legitimate, but others secretly flout United States law and act contrary to the laws of God as well. It should also be pointed out that there are, and have always been, many otherwise devout members of the Church who either believe or espouse doctrines that are contrary to those found in the scriptures or in the teachings of the General Authorities of the Church. If they remain in the Church, they then become dissidents within the Church, and if they intentionally begin spreading their erroneous doctrine to other members, they themselves come close to forming their own secret combinations.

Organized Crime: Often with no religious affiliation, criminal organizations have operated within the United States since its earliest days. Our protected freedoms have often provided them the means to grow and prosper, and they have willingly taken advantage of that fact. Well known are Irish gangs during the beginning of industrialization in this country; crime syndicates and the Mafia, who amassed great wealth and political power during the 1900s; and, more recently, Asian gangs, which have sprung up since the Vietnam War.

Add to these the motorcycle gangs, such as the Hells Angels; black and Hispanic gangs, which terrorize many urban areas; Russian gangs; drug cartels; gambling syndicates; and so forth. Most of these groups are strictly illegal, flouting our laws by dealing in drugs, prostitution, muggings, and murder, and yet they still operate relatively freely with great wealth and even political power. Over the years, they have become increasingly sophisticated, often posing as legitimate corporations, yet with dozens of politicians, judges, and attorneys on their payrolls.

Skinheads: This term can be loosely applied to the dozens of ultraconservative movements around the country that espouse hatreds of various kinds as well as animosity toward civil government. Often couched in Old Testament religion—many vowing allegiance to "Yahweh"—or in anarchistic patriotic traditions dating to our country's founding fathers, skinhead groups are diverse, ranging from the Aryan Nations—cloaked in Nazism and preaching anti-Jewish and anti-black hatred, believing that the United States must return to an all-white, all-Christian nation (which historically never existed)—to the Posse Comitatus, a group who denies the authority of the federal government and feels that only local government is legitimate.

There also exists a wide assortment of tax-protest movements, "peace" movements, extremist environmental movements,[10] and the like. Some of these groups are stridently vocal and, as in the case of the Aryan Nations, militant, living in armed, hostile compounds, yet always seeking recruits. Many are well funded and have political ties.

The Trilateral Commission: This supersecret organization is allegedly composed of a worldwide group of political and economic leaders who, over the decades, have worked behind the scenes to manipulate international activities in their own best interests. They are reputedly involved in worldwide banking schemes, trade negotiations, and political decision making. They are said to be involved in imports and exports, international shipping and distribution, stock markets, international monetary exchanges, the petroleum industry, and so forth. Much more than this we don't know, as reports of their very existence and activities are rumors only, although their membership is said to consist of judges, political leaders, industrial and trade executives, and the like.[11]

The Ku Klux Klan: Similar to the skinhead organizations discussed above, the KKK, dating from the days of the Civil War, is a quasi-religious group virulent in their hatred of blacks, Jews, and other racial minorities. Their contention—an artifact from the Civil War—is that the United States was intended by God to be a white Christian nation only. They have therefore historically resorted to intimidation, violence, and murder, mostly directed at blacks.

The KKK remained a prominent and powerful organization, especially in the Southern states, where it became well entrenched in many local and state government offices, from the end of the Civil War until the 1960s, when the federal government enforced an end to segregation and other racial practices. The power and membership of the KKK declined drastically from that time onward but the group has tenaciously remained with us to this day. Membership in the organization, including quiet political clout, can still be found in virtually every state in the union, including Utah, and vestiges of their hate-filled influence can still be felt.

Islamic Terrorist Organizations: Hamas, Islamic Jihad, Hezbollah, al-Qaeda, and similar terrorist organizations must also be included among secret combinations as they too operate in similar fashion. Operating openly in Middle Eastern countries, most of these groups are also found throughout the world and exist clandestinely in our own country as well. As the United States has discovered, these groups function secretively outside of Islamic nations but are powerful political forces at home. Often sophisticated and well funded—many of their members being products of our American educational system—they are strictly militant hate-filled groups with access to the weaponry of modern armies and filled with hatred toward Christianity and Judaism wherever they exist.

In this country, they operate furtively, yet take full advantage of our freedoms and the constitutional protections provided by our Western system of government. Ironically, however, their goal is to destroy that government and our way of life and replace them with a repressive Islamic dictatorship—with an Islamic theocracy that can't tolerate the freedoms and democracy we value and of which they take full advantage. Despite their hate-filled bigotry and disregard for human life, these groups continue to secretly and boldly thrive throughout the free world in the face of the ongoing War on Terror. Most disturbing is the fact that they continue to secure copious financing and attract new recruits, often on university campuses in this country and elsewhere in the world.

Obviously, plenty of secret combinations exist in the United States and abroad. Most are small and relatively harmless, while others strongly influence our political and economic systems. Any one of these groups could easily prove a useful tool for the anti-Christ and his followers with which to vault themselves into worldwide power. Continuing to use Nazi Germany as our model, it seems appropriate to stress that Hitler's Brown Shirts—his henchmen during the early stages of his fledgling Nazi movement—were themselves an obscure political group that eventually tried, and nearly succeeded, to take over the world.

Life in Pre-Armageddon

As in the preceding chapter, it might be helpful to outline in some detail the reality of what life will be like for Latter-day Saints and for the world at large during this late stage in humanity's history. We need to know what we can expect as, apparently, few have seriously considered, or have been reluctant to consider, this bleak forthcoming time.

Although what follows is in large part speculation, it is fair to contend that our country will continue to plod along much as it has done in the past, with its political wranglings, economic ups and downs, and life as usual for most of us. We will go to work or school, take in football on television, or watch—with largely characteristic indifference—as world events unfold just as they've always done. But somewhere, one day, the news will appear on our television screens of a then-perhaps-insignificant personage who appears to have miraculously recovered from a serious or deadly injury. That worldwide attention, plus his own ambitions, organization, and the evil forces behind him will vault him onto the international stage.[12]

We will then be confronted by, or at least be made aware of, a suave, charismatic, and impressive person who appears to have all the answers to the world's problems. He will smoothly proclaim that under his leadership we will all prosper and be made secure, and that many of our troubles will disappear with him in charge. He will probably be charming, handsome, and present a great persona in person and on our television screens. He will present to us his staff of capable and devoted administrators, who will assuredly be able to straighten out the world. He will be a combination—all in one person—of the world's greatest orators, philosophers, thinkers, political leaders, and movie stars.

That being the case, his rise to power will be dramatic, probably winning or wresting control of high office in one country or another with little resistance. Or he may do so through one of our present international organizations such as the United Nations or NATO. To many throughout the world, he will appear as a great savior of humanity. And he will eventually espouse a one-world government as the means to achieve these ends. Why, he will ask, should we have a world of fragmented, competing, and often contentious nations, when under his leadership we can have a world of international peace, cooperation, and tranquility?

Of course, such a proposal will have immense international appeal, and this person, the anti-Christ, will become immediately popular for his farsighted thinking and solutions to the world's problems.

On the other hand, it is equally possible that he, like Adolf Hitler, may wrest control of one country or another by subterfuge and force, after which he will do the same to other countries as his power grows. Or he may blend the two strategies by proclaiming, along with his forcible rise to power, that he can make the world a better place for all of us if we will simply submit to his will.

Whatever tactics the anti-Christ may use, his true nature—probably after he has gained substantial power—will eventually be revealed when he, as the "savior of humanity," begins to cater to the base nature of his followers (which will surely prove popular to millions) by denouncing troublesome religion and reviling God as being divisive and an impediment to the unity of humanity and the world. At this point, the prophecies will be fulfilled when he speaks "blasphemy against God . . . and his tabernacle and them that dwell in heaven."[13]

This great person, the anti-Christ, will eventually gain control, probably through force, coercion, intimidation, and political maneuvering, of ten other nations as John the Revelator prophesied, although the leadership of those nations may also join him willingly, realizing that an alliance with him would secure their own power.

In many ways, such a scenario is also reminiscent of Adolf Hitler's rise to power. He was a master at political maneuvering, intimidation, and coercion when he began his career. Only later did he resort to military might in his efforts to dominate Europe. History also tells us that many of the nations he conquered merely acquiesced to his threats, finding it easier and less painful, they thought, to capitulate to him than to offer resistance.

Once joined by ten other nations, the scriptures tell us, the beast or anti-Christ will remain in power for forty-two months or three and a half years. During that time, the world we have known and the lives we have led will be changed entirely and forever. Again using history as our guide, we learn that the anti-Christ will immediately install an international system of government—a one-world government, including perhaps our own country—based on force and corruption. Martial law will be the norm, and he will require that all citizens conform to his decrees or else.

As has been the case in thousands of years past, whenever a tyrannical system of government has been newly imposed on a people, a certain amount of "cleansing" first occurs. All who are perceived as potential threats to the new government will either be silenced or eliminated. This includes political rivals, academics, religious leaders and their congregations, and the like. Anyone who might in any way question or undermine the absolute control of the new rulers must be removed. That was the case in Hitler's Germany, in Stalin's Russia, in Cambodia's Pol Pot regime of thirty years ago, in Sadam Hussein's Iraq, and it continues today in places such as Cuba and North Korea.

To establish control, the anti-Christ, as John prophesied, will require absolute allegiance to the beast, to the point of applying marks on the right hands or foreheads of those willing to follow him. This mark will ostensibly mean that his followers will be permitted to buy and sell—to conduct commerce—under his government, but it will also be an easy means to weed out those who refuse to be thus marked. The latter will automatically be identified as dissidents, dangerous to the regime, who will need to be eliminated. Those who refuse to take the mark will, out of sheer survival, be required to go into hiding. They may be tolerated for a period of time, but we can only expect that the persecution and murder of such persons or groups will be the end result.

To further consolidate his power, the anti-Christ will, in some manner, erect or project an image of himself that all who are loyal to him will be required to worship. This will simply be another means to identify those who refuse to worship the image as objectionable dissidents who must be eliminated and silenced. These actions will further intensify the anti-Christ's stance and harangues against God and against religion.

The reality of the world will be such, and even now is, that most people won't find this new way of life that objectionable. To most, even now, religion is something superficial, if it is practiced at all, something that could be willingly traded off if they could be assured of a comfortable, complacent way of life with as few restrictions and responsibilities as possible.

If such a world leader could provide that, and people could continue to live their lives in peace and prosperity—especially if they could do so with relative security and minimal personal effort, as in a socialist state—they would surely choose that option. The personal freedoms they would lose under the anti-Christ's dictatorship would be worth it if they could live in comfort, security, and complacency. Don't numerous nations in the world today live under similar socialist systems, albeit in democracies, and aren't they quite satisfied with them (although they aren't known for religious tenacity, entrepreneurial innovation, or high standards of morality and spiritual conduct)?

Such a dictatorship under the anti-Christ will, with the help of his ten acquiescent collaborators, be absolute. However, all won't be entirely peaceful. There will likely be dissenting nations who won't go along peacefully with his plan. And although most troublesome dissident persons and groups will be silenced or eliminated, peace won't reign everywhere. The scriptures tell us that, especially as Armageddon approaches, nation will rise against nation and neighbor against neighbor. In other words, in many places chaos will be the norm.

What about in our own country or wherever LDS wards, stakes, and branches exist? The Church will, for some time, continue to function as best it can and its missionary program will remain in place, at least until worldwide chaos or the anti-Christ's tyranny makes this impossible. This brings up an important prophecy that will signal that Armageddon is at the doorstep, that the Lord will withdraw his Spirit and that the call will go forth for the missionaries to return home: "For the Spirit of the Lord will not always strive with man. And when the Spirit ceaseth to strive with man then cometh speedy destruction" (2 Nephi 26:11). "When the testimony of the Elders ceases to be given, and the Lord says to them, 'Come home; I will now preach my own sermons to the nations of the earth.'"[14]

Until that happens, however, life for us—for those who refuse to follow the beast, worship his image, or receive his mark on their hands or foreheads—will become tenuous. Much of the peace and security we have always known and taken for granted will no longer exist. Our continued existence will depend more and more on simply living in secrecy and surviving as best we can, much as many Jews did during the Nazi regime.

Even within the anti-Christ's tyrannical reign, lawlessness and chaos will become more and more prevalent, particularly as Armageddon grows near. Within our own country it can well be expected that we will no longer have the protection of our civil authorities—no police protection, no courts, and no one to turn to to ward off the tyranny of the anti-Christ and his hordes of accomplices. In other words, we will have to rely on the Lord, on ourselves, and on the Church for protection and survival.

Persecution of all dissident groups, the Church in particular, can be expected. Our sole focus in life will be sheer survival for our families and ourselves. This means that most of us will be forced to adapt to a life of secrecy, not only in our religious beliefs but also for physical survival. And for those who have lived comfortably and securely most of their lives, they can forget about gainful employment, bank accounts, Social Security, retirement checks, investments, insurance, hospital care, and even drivers' licenses. The new authorities will assuredly carefully monitor such things. All these, and much more, will be unavailable to those who refuse to follow the beast.

Undoubtedly, many predatory groups will seek to prey on those who don't conform to the new world order, and such groups will probably be sanctioned, either openly or otherwise, by the new regime. Religious activities of any sort will be strictly prohibited, probably under penalty of death.

A good example of this sort of persecution can be found in the history of the Jews who lived during Europe's Nazi regime. Taken prisoner by the Nazi SS, the secret police, a rabbi and his family were undergoing interrogation in their home by the Nazi authorities. During the threats and questioning by their sneering captors, the rabbi was offered the choice of either denying the sacred scriptures upon which he had based his entire life or seeing his family killed one by one in front of his eyes. When he refused, his four children were shot before him.

Again his captors repeated their ultimatum, stating that he must either deny his scriptures and denounce his allegiance to God or his wife too would be shot. Again he refused and she too was killed, her body falling among those of her dead children. When the Nazis turned their guns toward the rabbi, they repeated their threats and stated that he must not only deny his holy scriptures but must urinate on them as well if he wanted to live. Crying uncontrollably, he did so, and the soldiers left him alive and alone with his dead family. Following the war, he killed himself in the same manner as the Nazis had done to his wife and children.

Abysmal as it will be, such will be the atmosphere in which Church members will be forced to live during this trying period of time. Homes will be ransacked, food and necessities of life will be scarce, and Latter-day Saints will be relentlessly persecuted and killed. There will be no recourse for them but to rely on themselves and on other members of the Church just to survive.

Such has been the case throughout the history of the Lord's Church, from Old Testament times to those of our own early pioneers. The ancient prophets were persecuted and almost invariably paid with their lives for their allegiance to God. Jesus himself was crucified simply for preaching peace and brotherly love. And our early members of the restored Church likewise suffered much. Many, including the Prophet Joseph Smith, were persecuted, driven from their homes, and murdered. Of the 70,000 who left Nauvoo to make the 1,200-mile trek to the safety of the Salt Lake Valley, 6,000 died along the Mormon Trail.

In other words, the many months' rule of the anti-Christ will be a time of extreme testing for The Church of Jesus Christ of Latter-day Saints. As President Ezra Taft Benson said,

> I testify that as the forces of evil increase under Lucifer's leadership and as the forces of good increase under the leadership of Jesus Christ, there will be growing battles between the two until the final confrontation. As the issues become clearer and more obvious, all humanity will eventually be required to align themselves either for the kingdom of God or for the kingdom of the devil. As these conflicts rage, either secretly or openly, the righteous will be tested.[15]

The scriptures are replete with references to the continual testing the followers of God must undergo: "The Son of Man hath descended below them all. Art thou greater than he?" (D&C 122:8, revealed to the Prophet Joseph Smith while in jail at Liberty, Missouri); "My people must be tried in all things, that they may be prepared to receive the glory that I have for them, even the glory of Zion; and he that will not bear chastisement is not worthy of my kingdom" (D&C 136:31, revealed to Brigham Young while at Winter Quarters).

Many Latter-day Saints will be required to forfeit their lives for the Church under the anti-Christ's regime (Revelation 20:4). These, however, are promised a place in the First Resurrection.

Among the many books written about our forefathers who founded the restored Church and carried it westward and abroad, mention is seldom made of the fact that the Church underwent a great winnowing during those trying times. This was also the case in biblical and Book of Mormon times. Undoubtedly, many of the ancient Israelites chose to remain under Egyptian rule rather than follow Moses into the uncertain wilderness. Likewise, many of Jesus' disciples abandoned Christianity under Roman pressure. And many Latter-day Saints certainly capitulated and left the Church during the persecutions and trials of Nauvoo, although their stories remain largely unknown to history. The choices of all such people are understandable, even among the most righteous of us, because they were human. They feared for their well-being and that of their families.

The fact remains, however, that our very earthly experience is a time of testing to prove our faith and devotion to God and to the teachings of Jesus. The ultimate test, then, and that which will demonstrate most clearly our devotion to the Savior, will be our willingness to forfeit our lives and those of our families, if necessary, for him. After all, it is vital to understand that the choices we make now in our mortal existence will remain with us through eternity.

This may be difficult to accept, especially when we see the forces of evil in our fellow men all around us, threatening us with derision, physical harm, and death. But this is the refiner's fire of which we have so often heard. To be prepared for such an eventuality, we must keep in mind that "all they who suffer persecution for my name, and endure in faith, though they are called to lay down their lives for my sake yet shall they partake of all this glory" (D&C 101:35).

What we will see, then, as the anti-Christ's empire strengthens, and as members of the Church are faced with ever more intense persecution and death, is that the Church will undergo a massive exodus from its membership. It wouldn't be unrealistic to see half of all Latter-day Saints abandon their membership entirely, choosing to accede to the anti-Christ and to ultimately receive his mark on their hands or foreheads.

Is this assessment too harsh? Probably not, as we, in this life, place our lives and families above all else, often even above our membership in the Church. (This, many Latter-day Saints will have to admit after some soul-searching introspection.) That contention is borne out by the fact that a substantial part of the Church's rolls are now either entirely inactive or only marginally active.[16] These are they who will most likely fail the test, especially as their present earthly commitment to the Church is questionable at best. How many of us can honestly say that we would pass the test that the rabbi failed to pass?

The Fate of the United States

Within our own government, which we all have come to regard as stable and democratic, the anti-Christ's dictatorial influence will be overwhelming, even if he doesn't control the United States entirely.

Our nation, as we have been taught in our Sunday School

lessons, was divinely established, and our founding fathers were inspired to found a republic in which freedom and religion could prosper. That was God's promise to us. However, the promise was conditional—our freedoms and prosperity were based on the righteousness of the American people. The same promise was made to the Israelites led under Moses to the promised land. The people of Lehi were given the same promise when they arrived in the New World. Both ancient nations, as well as we ourselves, were promised freedom and prosperity so long as the recipients of the promise would remain obedient to the laws of God.

As we know, however, the Israelites first prospered but eventually turned their backs on God, after which they were destroyed and carried away captive by their enemies. Today, their promised land is the center of unending strife and international enmity. The fate of Lehi's descendants, the Nephites and Lamanites, was much the same. They, or at least the Nephites, prospered repeatedly and then fell away from God, succumbing ultimately to apostasy and their subsequent destruction at the hands of the Lamanites in terrible wars.

In our day we face a similar fate. For two hundred years, our nation was the showplace of the world, a place where freedom and opportunity thrived. We could practice whatever religion we liked, or none at all, and for the most part we were a Christian nation, structuring our legal codes on the commandments of God as written in the Bible. God saw fit to establish his restored Church in this land, and it has become a beacon of religious hope throughout the world. However, as with the Israelites and our predecessors in the Americas, that religious heritage has been greatly eroded.

Now we find that our opportunities, prosperity, and freedoms have resulted in apathy, religious squabbling and intolerance, and neglect of God's laws. Our religions have become distorted and full of perversions, immorality, and such liberal interpretations of Jesus' teachings that much is no longer recognizable as Christianity. Even worse, our own government and legal institutions, which once drew so heavily on Christian ideals, are now subverting those very principles. Abortion is now a federally funded right; homosexuality is an inherent privilege; immorality is ignored if not outright condoned; tissue from slain unborn babies is used in research; the law is often for sale to the highest bidder; and corruption at all levels of government is commonplace.

Furthermore, efforts are underway to remove even the mention of God and religion from public places, schools, and literature, while at the same time pornography and vile language can be found everywhere, protected as some of our most precious "freedoms." These trends can in no way be found to conform to our country's original God-given heritage. This is simply to say that we are no longer a "nation under God." Like the Nephites, Lamanites, and Israelites, the time is ripe for God to cancel his contract with us and withdraw his spirit from the United States of America.

In contrast to a dictatorship or similar form of tyranny—which is strong because of the iron hold of its ruler—our country, a republic, is simultaneously fragile and strong. We are strong so long as the majority of our citizens are unified in support of our leaders and institutions. And our constitutional form of government, which limits the government's power over us, allows us the freedoms we enjoy and protects our institutions. At the same time, we have representatives of the people—the Senate and the House of Representatives—who, together with the president, share power and limit each other. These bodies of government are further restricted by our system of laws and courts to protect against abuse by any of them.

One must realize, however, that all of this great system of checks and balances rests on the will of the people. And in this respect our system of government is fragile. As long as the people are relatively unified, the system works well because that is the way the people want it. However, two problems exist in this arrangement. The first is that we are also a complacent nation. We take our system of government and our freedoms for granted. This means that relatively few of us get involved in what government is doing, except perhaps at election time.

The result is that when enough Americans are complacent, it leaves a large power vacuum in which a small yet powerful minority can wield more than its share of power. With sufficient financial backing, a strong will, unity, and adroit political maneuvering, it is entirely conceivable that a small, well-organized group can rise through the political ranks in this country and gain great power quite rapidly.

The second symptom of fragility is the fact that money has come to play such an important role, not only in our personal lives but in the way the country functions as well. For example, very few of our political leaders, particularly at the federal level, are poor. Attaining high political office takes a great deal of money, either from the aspiring politicians themselves or from someone else.

This leaves latitude for political influence to be bought, often by special interest money or other types of campaign contributions that proliferate despite campaign finance restrictions; by bribery, which occurs quite regularly, publicized or not; or by one of the 313 billionaires in this country who wish to buy their way into office. A wealthy person—one who happens to have charm, charisma, and eloquence in front of a television camera, and who seems to have a few good ideas—can easily buy his way into high political office with a few billion dollars.

Regardless of how it happens, whether the anti-Christ gains power over this country from within or from outside, this land is promised a bleak future. While our nation will already be weak from a moral and legal standpoint—a symptom of the Great Apostasy and undermining influence of the great and abominable church—it will continue to decline, so much, in fact, that the words of Lehi will again apply as they did in the day of his sons:

> Wherefore, this land is consecrated unto him whom he shall bring. And if it so be that they shall serve him according to the commandments which he hath given, it shall be a land of liberty unto them; wherefore, they shall never be brought down into captivity; if so, it shall be because of iniquity; for if iniquity shall abound cursed shall be the land for their sakes. (2 Nephi 1:7)

As Paul taught, "Where the spirit of the Lord is, there is liberty" (2 Corinthians 3:17). But as discussed earlier, we are promised that the time will come when the Lord will abandon much of his efforts throughout the world, the missionaries will be called home, and the Spirit of the Lord will be withdrawn. That includes such activities within the United States as well. We may assume, therefore, that this will occur as the grip of the anti-Christ's rule tightens, making the practice of religion virtually impossible in this country and elsewhere.

How Will the Church Fare?

Previously, we discussed the persecution that the Church and its membership will endure under the tyranny of the anti-Christ—assuming that the United States too will be a part of his kingdom. How the Church will continue to function during those dark days is uncertain. As mentioned, most of the membership of the Church will have to go into hiding, including General Authorities. How they will communicate with the wards and stakes throughout the world remains to be seen, however. Very likely, those wards and stakes will often be required to function autonomously and surreptitiously in dealing with their memberships. That will, without a doubt, be difficult. It will place a heavy burden on stake presidencies and bishoprics, for they too will almost certainly be under scrutiny by the authorities of the anti-Christ and subject to the predations and persecution of his followers.[17] During that time of hatred and violence, the unity of each ward and stake will be tested. In the turmoil of the last days, Latter-day Saints will have to rely on themselves and their fellow Church members for guidance and survival.

The scriptures and prophets offer insights into what will be required of us as Armageddon approaches:

> That the gathering together upon the land of Zion, and upon her stakes, may be for a defense, and for a refuge from the storm, and from wrath when it shall be poured out without mixture upon the whole earth. (D&C 115:6)

> It shall come to pass among the wicked, that every man that will not take his sword against his neighbor must needs flee unto Zion for safety. And there shall be gathered unto it out of every nation under heaven; and it shall be the only people that shall not be at war one with another. (D&C 45:68–69)[18]

> I have sworn in my wrath, and decreed wars upon

> the face of the earth, and the wicked shall slay the wicked, and fear shall come upon every man; . . . And the saints also shall hardly escape; nevertheless, I, the Lord, am with them, and will come down in heaven from the presence of my Father and consume the wicked with unquenchable fire. . . . Wherefore, seeing that I, the Lord, have decreed all these things upon the face of the earth, I will that my saints should be assembled upon the land of Zion. (D&C 63:33–34, 36)

It will thus be our flight to Zion or our unity as Latter-day Saints that will preserve the Church during this time, through the protection of the Lord. Church authorities have cautioned us more recently, however, that this gathering to Zion shouldn't be interpreted as literally meaning that all Church members should come to Salt Lake City or even to Jackson County, Missouri—at least not yet. It appears that for a period of time, as noted above, we will need to rely on our local wards and stakes throughout the world in order to survive.

However, statements by early Church authorities indicate that at some time, perhaps just prior to the war of Armageddon, an actual gathering of the Saints will be required here in America or Zion. This will serve as a final refuge from the great destructions that have been promised to smite humanity during the battle of Armageddon, especially upon the return of the Savior:

> How some of us may be gathered to Jackson; I see two or three hundred thousand people wending their way across the plain enduring nameless hardships of the journey.[19]

> He will multiply us in the land; He will make us a great people, and strengthen our borders, and send forth the missionaries of this people to the four quarters of the earth to publish peace and glad tidings of great joy, and proclaim that there is still a place left in the heart of the American continent where there are peace

> and safety and refuge from the storms, desolations, and tribulations coming upon the wicked.[20]

> There is no other way for the Saints to be saved in these last days [than by the gathering], as the concurrent testimony of all the holy prophets clearly proves, for it is written, "They shall come from the east, and be gathered from the west; the north shall give up, and the south shall not keep back." "The sons of God shall be gathered from afar, and his daughters from the ends of the earth." It is also the concurrent testimony of all the prophets, that this gathering together of all the Saints must take place before the Lord comes to "take vengeance upon the ungodly."[21]

How and precisely when this gathering will take place, then, is unclear. It could very well be that the Saints are to remain in their present wards and stakes, wherever they may be, until world conditions become unbearable and the General Authorities feel that they should be called together as a final stand and protection against the destruction to occur during the battle of Armageddon and the return of Jesus.

Nevertheless, and despite the evil and turmoil of the last days, the Church will, in two respects, play a key role during this time. The first is that those who persecute the Saints will pay a severe penalty for their actions:

> Every nation which shall war against thee, O house of Israel, shall be turned one against another, and they shall fall into the pit which they digged to ensnare the people of the Lord. And all that fight against Zion shall be destroyed, and that great whore, who hath perverted the right ways of the Lord, yea, that great and abominable church, shall tumble to the dust and great shall be the fall of it. (1 Nephi 22:14)

In other words, the lawlessness and turmoil of the last days will be compounded by "nation fighting against nation." Those who would otherwise have preyed on The Church of Jesus Christ of Latter-day Saints will instead end up fighting among themselves. During that time, when the world is at war with itself and the sanity of civilization has been lost under the anti-Christ's rule, the Saints or the Church will survive only through the Lord's protection: "The spirit of God will entirely withdraw from those nations and they will war among themselves instead of persecuting the Saints."[22]

The second factor, or the critical role the Church will play in saving at least a portion of the United States, is the fact that Church leaders will somehow or other still be able to influence the leadership of this country in those last days despite all the persecution. We are not told how this will come about, however.

For 150 years after the founding of the LDS Church, "the Mormons" were considered little more than a cult or sect, which because of Joseph Smith's "hallucinations" and "golden Bible," lived in isolation from the rest of society and practiced polygamy. This stereotype remained for the most part intact until the last few decades, when the Mormons, who had grown rapidly in numbers, gained attention from the rest of the country and the world for their integrity, high standards, and wholesome way of life.

The missionary program that now reaches into almost every country on earth was undoubtedly responsible for a big part of this change in the Church's image, as well as the fact that Mormons by and large became good examples of how Christians should live. At the same time—a fact that also changed the world's view of us—was that as the Church grew and set exemplary standards, Christianity in the rest of the world was, and still is, in a state of decline. Other churches and much of the world at large have had to grudgingly admit that the Mormons are not such a bad lot after all. They maintain moral standards most of the rest of Christianity does not.

Although this recognition remains the same today, the hold of Satan and his great and abominable church is now so strong that many of those who have come to praise the LDS Church are reluctant to join an institution that is spiritually demanding, that still stridently follows the teachings of Christ.

Of course, family traditions and different cultures around the world play a large part in this reluctance as well, which in many cases provides a convenient scapegoat for not making the change to join the Church. It also provides an easy excuse for not taking on higher Christian standards and a more responsible and demanding personal lifestyle.

Despite this lethargy, The Church of Jesus Christ of Latter-day Saints has come to be a much more significant player in the workings of the United States than earlier when it was regarded merely as a quirky polygamous sect. Over the past decades, the Church has appeared favorably in many national publications and television commentaries. The stigma of polygamy is no longer with us, although thousands who are no longer Church members continue to practice it clandestinely in communes throughout the western states.

The quality of our people, especially our young people—Brigham Young University being a prime example—has reflected well on us. Our leaders, the First Presidency and Quorum of the Twelve in particular, travel throughout the world meeting with heads of state and are treated with respect wherever they go. The sheer size of the Church—now over 12 million and still growing rapidly—has vaulted us beyond a cult or sect and indicates that we are becoming a major religion in this country as well as abroad.

Moreover, the Church has many outreach programs that draw national and international attention, such as aid to disaster areas worldwide. And its stress on high standards, morality, a healthy lifestyle, and personal responsibility are noticed everywhere. And although the Church itself makes a point of staying out of politics, the fact that its members live according to high standards means that Mormon influence is strongly felt on election days.

Most recently, the 2002 Winter Olympics in Salt Lake City drew attention as never before. Suddenly, the world realized that the Mormons were not a troublesome sect but instead an influential member of the world community. We could uphold high moral standards and host a spectacular sporting event at the same time. That single event threw the spotlight on The Church of Jesus Christ of Latter-day Saints as never before. Now the world notices that Mormons are everywhere—in movies, politics, the military, educational institutions, sports, and so forth. And wherever they show up, they are almost universally respected.

Perhaps for all of these reasons, when this nation and the nations of the world are in turmoil, fighting among themselves, and at the same time persecuting the Saints, the time will come when the collapse of our country will be imminent. At that moment, the leadership of the Church will be called upon to salvage our great nation:

> Will the constitution be destroyed? No: it will be held inviolate by this people; and, as Joseph Smith said, "The time will come when the destiny of the nation will hang upon a single thread. At that critical juncture, this people will step forth and save it from the threatened destruction.[23]

> It is my conviction that the elders of Israel, widely spread over the nation, will at that crucial time successfully rally the righteous of our country and provide the necessary balance of strength to save the institutions of constitutional government.[24]

That will undoubtedly be a remarkable event or set of events, the details of which are lacking. We know that through the most trying times of the last days the Church will survive and that Zion will be established upon this continent. For these reasons, the Lord will use the Church itself to ensure that these things will happen. But this doesn't minimize the fact that its members will suffer much, though the Church will endure.

Be Prepared

When we speak of the suffering of the Saints in the last days, we can't overlook the fact that we have been told by our church leaders, as well as by the prophets of old, that we need to be prepared for that which is to come. As a matter of fact, preparation is an oft-repeated theme throughout the scriptures—preparation for the first coming of the Messiah; preparation for Judgment Day; preparation for the Second Coming of the Messiah; preparation to meet the Lord; preparation for eternity; and so forth. The last of these has been the focus of all the prophets and of the scriptures since the days of Adam. We must prepare ourselves for eternal life and the world to come.

The prophets and General Authorities of the Church have likewise repeated this theme of preparation from the time of Joseph Smith onward. But that idea has taken on a new sense of importance and urgency during the last few decades. Obviously, if Joseph Smith or the apostles of Christ's time spoke of their living in the last days, then we are now evidently much closer to that time than humanity was before. Consequently, our Church leadership repeatedly stresses the theme that we must prepare ourselves and our families for whatever eventualities may come, not just for the last days. It makes good sense that every family should be prepared, at least minimally, for even short-term emergencies, spiritually and physically.

Originally, members of the Church under the leadership of Brigham Young were counseled to set aside a seven-year supply of food and other needed items. This was then not necessarily directed toward preparations for the last days but as simple precautions to meet any unforeseen shortages:

> If you are without bread, how much wisdom can you boast, and of what real utility are your talents, if you cannot procure for yourselves and save against a day of scarcity those substances designed to sustain your natural lives? . . . If you cannot provide for your natural lives, how can you expect to have wisdom to obtain eternal lives?[25]

As is the case today, many Latter-day Saints then failed to follow the counsel of the prophet and encountered extreme food shortages when they were invaded by grasshoppers. Closer to our own day, similar advice was repeated by the General Authorities of the Church, notably by J. Reuben Clark in 1937, Spencer W. Kimball in 1976, Ezra Taft Benson in 1980, and others:

> More than ever before, we need to learn and apply the principles of economic self-reliance. We don't know when a crisis involving sickness or unemployment may affect our own circumstances. We do know that the Lord has decreed global calamities for the future and has warned and forewarned us to be prepared. For this reason, the Brethren have repeatedly stressed

> a "back-to-basics" program for our temporal and spiritual welfare. Today, I emphasize a most basic principle—home production and storage. Have you ever paused to realize what would happen to your community or nation if transportation were paralyzed or if we had a war or depression? How would you and your neighbors obtain food? How long would the corner grocery store—or supermarket—sustain the needs of the community? . . . We encourage you to be more self-reliant so that, as the Lord has declared, "notwithstanding the tribulation which shall descend upon you, . . . the Church may stand independent above all other creatures beneath the Celestial world" (D&C 78:14). The Lord wants us to be independent and self-reliant because these will be days of tribulation.[26]

Of course, such preparation as the General Authorities have counseled should include physical supplies for a twelve-month period. More recently, they have also stressed the advisability of each family having a 72-hour kit on hand for minor emergencies. Both of these suggestions are good advice, as can be confirmed by many families who, for one reason or another, have had to rely on either short-term or long-term preparations because of financial setbacks within the family, natural disasters such as hurricanes, floods, tornadoes, and other destruction of their home or livelihood.

Any number of items exists that a family should consider when setting up a preparedness plan, whether long-term or short-term. Although many families have followed the Church's advice of setting aside a permanent one-year supply, it is certain that many others have ignored this advice entirely. And yet, accumulating an adequate supply need not be an insurmountable problem. Yes, a full year's supply for a family of four or five can cost several thousand dollars, but then again it depends on how supplies are purchased or otherwise acquired.

For example, numerous companies, most LDS-owned, cater to the one-year-supply program. Many are worth looking into, especially as the quality of products is usually high (although prices aren't necessarily low) and storability is good. With the help of such companies, a family can put together a year's supply quickly through any number of purchase plans. They can thus avail themselves of a wide variety of beneficial products that can be stored almost indefinitely. In contrast to arduously assembling items individually, the convenience and ease of making preparations in this way usually involves paying a somewhat higher price. On the other hand, many Latter-day Saints prefer to go it alone and put their preparedness items together over a longer period of time, hand selecting what they think they may need.

The latter method is by far the least expensive. But it also requires that the purchaser keep in mind buying a wide variety of essentials, at the same time assuring that those items will store properly. In the latter instance, accumulating a year's supply is as simple as buying just an extra can or two of what the family normally eats each time major shopping is done. Through this method—assuming the family goes food shopping twice a month—it can put together anywhere from two to three dozen cans a year. That may not seem like much, but when one thinks in terms of five years of such shopping, that amounts to 150 to 200 cans.

Of course, a family will need much more than its favorite canned foods. It must also conscientiously gather dried milk, rice, beans, and flour (or, alternatively, vacuum-sealed wheat and a grinder). Things to keep in mind in this respect are taking advantage of case lot sales at local grocery stores as well as produce sales. These can result in a quicker accumulation of food with notable savings. Of course, bulk purchases of fresh fruits and vegetables often mean that a food dryer may be a worthwhile investment.

Such an apparatus can be purchased for $50 to $100, or can even be built at home for half that much. Dehydrators aren't complicated. They are cheap and simple to operate and ideal for drying nearly all vegetables, most fruits (except for the juiciest ones such as melons and citrus fruits), and even meats. When dried properly, such foods can be stored for years, although many may look less than appetizing because they tend to darken in the dryer. Nevertheless, they remain edible and will certainly be better than starvation when the time comes. The alternative is to buy vegetables and fruits already in cans conveniently ready for storage, but the price will be at least twice as high.

Other food supply possibilities are largely overlooked by many Church members but may be vividly recalled among some who still remember World War II. Nearly all Church members have access to at least a small plot of ground somewhere around where they live. Everywhere one goes throughout this country, we see beautiful spacious yards with grass, trees, and immaculate landscaping. In many less affluent areas, and in city apartments, one also sees window boxes of flowers, small plots of greenery, and the like. Yet it is surprising how few gardens exist among all this greenery.

Latter-day Saints, even those dedicated to putting aside a year's supply, have relatively few gardens, even when they may be sitting on acres of arable land. A modest garden can easily provide each year—through some work, maintenance, and seed—enough corn, beans, potatoes, and other vegetables to amount to several months' food supply all by themselves. After harvesting, one needs only to dry or bottle this essentially free food and add it to the family food supply. Of course, it can also be eaten through the winter, which is a form of rotation (which should be done anyway), and then replaced the next summer.

Add to this cheap supply of food the fact that few families even bother with fruit trees anymore, while at the same time—especially in newer homes—planting trees other than fruit trees. However, fruit trees are relatively inexpensive. They begin producing in five or six years and can be an attractive part of the landscape. Once they begin to bear, they continue doing so for years, even decades, requiring little upkeep beyond the first few years. Such trees, together with a food drier or basic bottling supplies, can provide another substantial and free component of a family's year supply to be eaten in winter and replaced the following summer.

Of course, other items may be added that aren't necessary for survival but that are good to keep in mind. These include personal toiletries, such as soap, toothpaste, feminine napkins, and the like. Similarly, one should consider pet food (if the family has pets it will absolutely not part with), paper plates and cups, plastic tableware, paper towels (which can be used for hand wipes, fire starters, toilet paper, and other uses), spices (to avoid bland foods), honey (which has a long shelf life), matches, candles, and other items a family may find useful yet are easy to overlook.

Nonfood items that may turn out absolutely essential include camp stoves and fuel (several gallons, especially if there is a possibility the stove may be an important or sole source of heat), lanterns and fuel, flashlights and batteries, extra clothing (especially for winter), gasoline (for vehicles and home equipment—several five-gallon cans, minimum), camping supplies (especially sleeping bags and tents), first aid supplies, medications, tools, sewing supplies, hunting supplies, and so forth. To prepare a proper list, one must simply note the multitude of items that would be absolutely necessary should the family have to live at least twelve months on its own resources with no contact whatsoever with civilization and stores. After some introspection, such a list could turn out to be quite long.

Not to be forgotten, of course—besides food and the items noted above—will be the necessity of having a long-term source of drinking water. Showers, flushed toilets, and the like may go by the wayside in the last days but drinking and cooking water will remain vital. For that reason, consideration should also be given to where an old-fashioned outhouse can be erected, should the need arise. Water is cheap and easy to store in empty soda pop containers (when properly cleaned by mixing a few drops of bleach with a cup of water, then rinsing thoroughly), gallon jugs, or five-gallon cans. And don't forget that many home water heaters hold forty to fifty gallons of water.

Those who live in rural areas will have an advantage as many already rely on wells and septic systems for their needs. However, even farm dwellers will find that wells and many heating systems don't work particularly well without electricity. For that reason, a basic piece of equipment every family should have, whether they live in the country or not, is a generator. And then, of course, once a family has a generator, it is another matter to make it run properly and to wire it into the house or to the well pump where it is needed.

If the generator will be needed only for urban family use, a smaller gasoline one will probably be adequate—around 1,500 watts is sufficient, with an array of extension cords to supply a number of lights, a radio, and to keep the refrigerator and freezer cold. Of course, any appliance that generates heat uses a much larger amount of electricity, so forget about irons, electric dryers, electric ranges, furnaces, air conditioners, and even hair dryers on smaller generators. In a rural area, in which a well pump is available, one should consider at least a 4,000-watt generator, either gasoline or diesel, with both 110 and 220 volts.

Gasoline generators are more expensive to run and also don't have the long life of diesel ones, which run more slowly. Larger generators can run most anything in the house, including the well pump, at 220 volts, although wiring the generator to the well pump will require a little expertise. Still, it wouldn't be advisable to run large heating appliances on them such as electric ranges, water heaters, clothes dryers, and the like. A 4,000-watt gasoline generator will use somewhat less than one gallon of fuel per hour, but running it for only two or three hours per day should be sufficient.

Fuel is another item that will become critically important in the last days. Under restrictions from the anti-Christ's regime, it is almost guaranteed that gasoline, diesel, and the like won't be available to those without the mark on their hands or foreheads. Therefore, a supply of fuel is a serious consideration along with a year's supply of food and other necessities. For vehicles and generators, the former of which may or may not be available to Church members during the tumultuous last days, several five-gallon cans of gasoline or diesel should be stored, but away from the home and other buildings for obvious fire-safety reasons.

Home heating is a further factor, as it may well be that winters and cold weather will have to be contended with. Homes with electric, natural gas, or fuel oil furnaces will be the most vulnerable. The same will be the case with vehicle fuel. Homes with wood heating, which are rare nowadays, will obviously have a big advantage, but getting along on less than four cords of wood a year is difficult. On the other hand, having a reliable chain saw will be a must, including an oil-fuel mix and chain oil. Forget fireplaces. They are both fuel- and heat-inefficient. Propane heating systems are the best alternative, although few homes have tanks of a capacity larger than 1,000 gallons , which provides a one-year supply at most. As with other types of fuels, propane will also be difficult to come by as times get worse.

Perhaps the best solution to the home heating problem will be for families to resign themselves to living in only one portion of their homes—one or two rooms maximum—blocking off other rooms to retain heat in their smaller living quarters. And then, the best heat supply may well be a small kerosene heater. Such heaters and their fuel are relatively inexpensive and can be kept with the rest of the year's supply for later, just in case. Several five-gallon cans of fuel can then be put aside with the gasoline discussed above.

Obviously, those living in rural areas will have a distinct advantage over urban dwellers when all these things are considered. Most rural homes have a well. Many have propane or wood heat, are surrounded by arable land for gardening, and may be some distance from neighbors. The latter may eventually be critical, as when the turmoil of the last days becomes most intense, it is almost certain that the isolation of a farm may be the best protection against the social upheavals of the cities.

Those living in apartments will be the most vulnerable in terms of security and maintaining a year's supply of essentials. Nor will those living on residential streets and in subdivisions be much better off. Lawlessness, gangs, and persecution will be most concentrated in the cities, especially if a family is found to be LDS. As a result, it can be expected that hordes of city residents will flee to the countryside to escape the breakdown in law and order in urban areas.

Properly maintaining a family's food supply is critical. Not only rotating it—using older items and replacing them with new ones—but properly packaging everything can be a challenge. Most canned and bottled items are of no concern, but those in boxes and plastic wrap are another matter. It is recommended that all such items be placed in plastic, sealable buckets. Even wheat in such buckets isn't foolproof, as weevils can do well in such containers and it can almost be guaranteed that weevil eggs exist in nearly all grains. Drop in a chunk of dry ice or shoot some carbon dioxide gas into the container prior to sealing, and don't open it again until it is to be used.

The food supply should be kept in a cool, dry place if possible. Humid climates are a problem, and mold or mildew grows quickly on anything not sealed airtight. Apples and potatoes can be kept for months in a cool basement if placed on a pallet of some sort in which air can circulate under and among them (although red russet potatoes do not store well). And finally, the food supply should be inspected regularly. Bulging or leaking cans should be disposed of, although rusty ones aren't necessarily bad. Be sure shelving is secure and strong as a couple of hundred cans can weigh as much as two hundred pounds. And watch for mice. They can destroy not only vulnerable portions of the food supply, but also clothing, paper products, blankets, and sleeping bags.

A further note or two regarding refrigerators and freezers: If one has even a small generator, a portion of the food supply can be maintained in the freezing compartment of the refrigerator or in the freezer itself. Many food items that a family routinely purchases, such as meats, frozen vegetables, and the like, can be a vital supplement to the food supply when local conditions get bad, but only for a short period of time. Eat what is in the refrigerator or freezer first before digging into the supply in the basement. Most families can probably exist on what is in these two appliances alone for perhaps as much as a month or two, thus saving the rest of the year's supply.

As noted above, a small generator can keep food in a refrigerator or freezer frozen quite well while running only two or three hours per day. On a small generator, this entails only a gallon or so of gasoline daily. Put large trays or pans of water in both, which, when frozen to ice, will maintain freezing temperatures throughout the appliance for hours. If one has put aside twenty to thirty gallons of gasoline for generator usage, this means that the freezer and refrigerator will do quite well and can stretch out your food supply for as much as a month or more.

When talking about a year's food supply, it should be mentioned that Americans are large people. Our more than adequate daily diets keep us well fed, and then some. Obesity is becoming epidemic in this country, despite the dozens of diet and weight loss programs one sees or hears of every day. This is all to say that a family's food supply will last much longer when one gets used to eating less each day—perhaps only two meals, with no snacks in between.

Living solely off the family's food supply when the time comes may seem daunting, but it may well be healthier as it is assumed that the family won't have a large supply of potato chips, cookies, French fries, candy, and other junk foods. At two average meals per day, a family of five will be able to make their food supply stretch out months longer than they would if they ate three meals per day as they do now.

Another controversial and problematic topic that many families will have to face is that of safeguarding one's family and food supply. This is a sticky issue and one Church authorities haven't addressed directly. It should be clear that as things go downhill and social turmoil increases, Church members will be likely targets of persecution and looting. If it becomes known, as it already is to some extent, that Latter-day Saints keep extra food on hand, many Church members will find themselves the targets of gangs and mobs seeking food.

During times of war and social conflict, and the deprivation that accompanies them, food will become a valuable commodity, often worth more than money. As a matter of fact, many German families and others throughout Europe during World War II resorted to bartering with local farmers for food. Family heirlooms, jewelry, handicrafts, and anything else of value were traded for just a few loaves of bread, or eggs, or milk, or a chicken (a true luxury).

This means that those who have a reserve supply of food must, of necessity, consider how they are going to safeguard it when faced with mobs and persecution. With their own lives and those of their family at stake, some hard decisions will need to be made. Hiding the food supply is an option, but it must also be accessible, which means that it must be in the home somewhere, which is the first place looters will look.

The family must then decide if they will turn to force, when the time comes, in order to protect themselves and their food supply. Will an armed guard be necessary? If so, will that person or persons be willing to kill someone intent on taking their food supply away? If the answer is yes, then firearms and ammunition must be included preparatory items as well, accompanied by the knowledge of how to use them. Don't forget, however, that confiscation of firearms will be one of the first measures the anti-Christ's regime will undertake in order to gain and retain control over its kingdoms.

The above is simply an example of the tough decisions that will need to be made about what a family should do when threatened by an angry and irrational mob, especially when violence and death of family members may result. Latter-day Saints, for the most part, are capable of taking care of themselves as many, at least those living in the western United States, have been raised with guns in the home. But when to use them against other human beings is another question. The best guidance we have are the admonitions given by Jesus to love our enemies and turn the other cheek, which have been more pointedly reiterated in these latter days:

> I speak unto you concerning your families—if men will smite you, or your families, once, and ye bear it patiently and revile not against them, neither seek revenge, ye shall be rewarded; But if ye bear it not patiently, it shall be accounted unto you as being meted out as a just measure unto you. And again, if your enemy shall smite you the second time, and you revile not against your enemy, and bear it patiently, your reward shall be an hundred fold. And again, if he shall smite you the third time, and ye bear it patiently, your reward shall be doubled unto you four-fold. (D&C 98:23–26)

A more penetrating account of this pacifist, humble attitude can be found in the Book of Mormon's depiction of the Lamanites who chose to follow Christ and willingly died at the hands of their enemies rather than take up arms against them (see Alma 24).

It has always been a fundamental program of The Church of Jesus Christ of Latter-day Saints to spur its members toward preparedness and self-sufficiency. And the Church itself has practiced this same counsel by maintaining a large welfare program, bishops' storehouses, and Church farms. Some of the items thus maintained are periodically used for Church humanitarian programs worldwide, wherever human suffering occurs as a result of natural disasters and war.

Despite these wise reserves, the question still remains about how the Church's stored supplies will be distributed to needy members when the crises of the last days come about. Communications and transportation will certainly be big issues that may seriously affect, or even curtail, distribution.

For years, in keeping with the Church's repeated counsel about being adequately prepared, many stakes and wards—not all—have been making similar preparations. Many stake presidencies and bishoprics have plans in place not only to communicate with their memberships but to coordinate, when the time comes, emergency assistance and supplies. For example, which members presently have adequate food supplies? Which have generators, fuel, vehicles, food, and expertise[27] that can be shared with other members? Are there members with special needs, such as those requiring special medications? Are there elderly, those with disabilities, and single parent families? Which members have housing space available that could be shared? Such will eventually become critical concerns.

Ever since the days of Joseph Smith, the Church has taught the law of consecration, which has both spiritual and temporal connotations. It is philosophically a concept far above what we are used to here on this earth that we must someday be willing, without question, to unselfishly give of what we have to those who have less. Jesus introduced that idea when he counseled the rich man that he should "sell whatsoever thou hast, and give to the poor" (Mark 10:17–22). This will require much more than the mere 10 percent tithing and fast offerings Church members have traditionally been urged to pay.

However, the law of consecration wasn't original to the restored Church. It was also practiced in the Old Testament, among the Nephites—for two centuries after Christ's ministry among them—and during the ministries of Jesus' apostles in the Holy Land: "And all that believed were together, and had all things in common. And sold their possessions and goods, and parted them to all men, as every man had need" (Acts 2:44–45; see also 4:2; 2 Corinthians 8:12–14; Moses 18:27–28; 4 Nephi 1:3).

As detailed by the Prophet Joseph Smith in Kirtland, Ohio, in 1831, the law of consecration was to be administered by a binding covenant between Church members and their bishoprics, each member's property to be turned over to the Church except for that portion, which, in the determination of the bishop, was "as much as is sufficient for himself and his family" (D&C 42:32). The remainder was to be retained in the bishops' storehouse for redistribution to those in need or for other Church purposes (see D&C 42:30–38; 51:4–5).

Certainly, this is a tough concept to sell in today's world, in which material possessions are so important. But in the last days, that idea of consecration may take on a new meaning—it may well spell the difference between life and death for many Latter-day Saints. The tight-knit unity of the Church will be a major factor in keeping it alive and functioning during the days of the anti-Christ, and it will require the commitment and unselfish dedication of Church members one toward another.

For example, a family will be expected, and should be willing, to provide room and board for others who may not be as fortunate. Those with warm clothing will be expected to provide it for those who have none. A family with a generator can easily run an extension cord to a neighbor's home to provide them too with lights and electricity. Only in this spirit will the Lord be able to help and protect the Church against want and against the depredations of the followers of the anti-Christ.

Aside from being adequately prepared with a year's supply of food and other necessities, the General Authorities have for decades counseled Latter-day Saints about avoiding debt. We have long lived far beyond our means—another symptom of our obsession with worldly possessions. American debt has skyrocketed in the last half century, and that includes debt among many Latter-day Saint families as well.

For example, how many of us live in 4,000-square-foot homes that, although comfortable and in an exclusive area, may cost our families $2,000 per month for the next forty years? Many such houses are far too big and luxurious for us to say that they are true necessities of life. Is it necessity or is it prestige or pride that is our real motivation for owning such a home? Likewise with families who insist they must have three or four new automobiles in their garage, especially SUVs or sports cars. And how about expensive recreational vehicles, such as boats, snowmobiles, four-wheelers, wave-runners, motor homes, travel trailers, not to mention costly jewelry and other such extravagant things?

When a family goes into debt for these, especially when they are purchased by multiple credit cards or through other loans, they are placing themselves and their families in bondage until they pay them off (which seldom seems to happen, as Americans' debt loads trend consistently upward and not downward). These worldly things may seem important to us now, but are they prudent or responsible? Utah, a predominantly Mormon state, also has one of the highest rates of bankruptcies in the country.

For these reasons, we have been continually advised through the Church to avoid debt in every way possible, for it is gambling with the future of our families. This is a particularly important and indispensable factor in being prepared for the last days. A large burden of debt will obviously make a family even more vulnerable to unjust authorities and persecution when our country teeters on the edge of disaster. When economic turmoil strikes, or when a family loses its income—either or both of which will happen in the last days—the worldly goods we have accumulated by going into debt will be lost or make us hostage to the anti-Christ's regime or to local corrupt officials.

In conjunction with preparations for the last days—as the prophets and scriptures have repeatedly emphasized—Latter-day Saints will have to be spiritually prepared. We have previously noted the evil that abounds in the world, and that this evil, together with our preoccupation with the things of this world, is increasing. Only when we are capable of abandoning our selfishness and practicing Christ's love for our fellow man will we be able to practice the law of consecration or be truly ready to meet the trials of the last days.

These events, then, will mean a great turn-around in many of our lives, but they will be part of the test we must meet before Christ returns to the world. In fact, these are things we should already be practicing to a degree as worthy members of The Church of Jesus Christ of Latter-day Saints. However, in the last days they will constitute the difference between whether or not we and the Church will survive to see Jesus' Second Coming.

Rebuilding Jerusalem and the Temple

Prior to the anti-Christ's rule and the battle of Armageddon, two separate yet related events will take place—the rebuilding of Jerusalem and its ancient temple and the healing of the Dead Sea. These may be regarded as more signs of the times and should be clearly recognizable when they occur. They will provide clear evidence that the end isn't far away. Prophecies of both events can be found in the Old Testament—in Zechariah and Ezekiel—and in latter-day pronouncements by Church authorities.

We have already discussed the gathering of the Jews and the return of the ten lost tribes, both of which will play significant roles in the rebuilding of Jerusalem and its temple. The gathering of all the tribes of ancient Israel will occur in two separate stages. The Jews have already returned in part and established their homeland in the Middle East, and the new state of Israel has, since 1948, proved remarkably successful and prosperous. This is fulfillment of prophecy in and of itself, despite subsequent decades of attacks and hostility from Islamic neighbors.

The return of the remainder of ancient Israel, the lost ten tribes, is another matter, however. The prophecies of their return have yet to be fulfilled as other prophecies indicate that the rebuilding of Jerusalem and the temple will not occur without their help: "The whole of the twelve tribes of Israel are to return back to Palestine in Asia and rebuild their city of Jerusalem and a temple within that city before, and preparatory to, the coming of the Lord."[28]

Joseph Fielding Smith, on the other hand, felt that the temple wouldn't be built until after the Jews accepted Christ as the true Messiah, which will apparently not happen until after his Second Coming: "After the Jews have repented and received the gospel, having acknowledged Jesus Christ as their Redeemer, the temple in Jerusalem will be built according to the prophecy in Ezekiel."[29]

Orson Pratt further indicated that the missionary work of the Church would eventually be redirected from the Gentiles, where it now is, to finding and gathering the lost tribes to the Holy Land for the purpose of rebuilding Jerusalem and the temple:

> When the gentile nations shall reject this gospel and count themselves unworthy of eternal life, as the Jews did before them, the Lord will say—"It is enough, come away from them, my servants, I will give you a new commission, you shall go to the scattered remnants of the House of Israel. I will gather them in from the four quarters of the earth, and bring them again into their own lands. They shall build Jerusalem on its own heap; they shall build a temple on the appointed place in Palestine, and they shall be grafted in again."[30]

This same contention was also reiterated by Wilford Woodruff.[31] Rebuilding the holy city and its temple, however, won't be without its hindrances. For example, many of the tribes of Israel, although they will return to the Holy Land, may not be believers in Christ. This is much the same as the Jews of today, who continue to reject Christianity. Nevertheless, the city of Jerusalem and the temple will be rebuilt because both are vitally important to ancient Israel's traditions. Orson Pratt also commented on this reality:

> Some of them will believe in the true Messiah, and thousands of the more righteous, whose fathers did not consent to the shedding of the blood of the Son of God, will receive the gospel before they gather from among the nations. Many of them, however, will not receive the gospel, but seeing that others are going to Jerusalem, they will go also; and when they get back to Palestine, to the place where their ancient Jerusalem stood, and see a certain portion of the believing Jews endeavoring to fulfill and carry out the prophecies, they will also take hold and assist in the same work. At the same time, they will have their synagogues, in which they will preach against Jesus of Nazareth, "that imposter," as they call him, who was crucified by their fathers.[32]

Another hindrance to the rebuilding of Jerusalem and the temple will be Islamic resistance. Currently, the only substantial remnant of the original Jerusalem temple is the Wailing Wall, an important artifact to Judaism. Standing on part of the old temple site are the Dome of the Rock and Al-Aksa Mosque, important artifacts to Islam. How this standoff between two major world religions will be resolved when the time for rebuilding of the temple comes remains to be seen:

> The work is moving on for the gathering of the Jews to their own land that they may build it up as it was in former times; that the temple may be rebuilt and the mosque of the Moslem which now stands in

> its place may be moved out of the way; that Jerusalem may be rebuilt upon its original site; that the way may be prepared for the coming of the Messiah.[33]

With the modern hostility of much of Islam toward the West and toward Israel, and toward Christianity in particular, it is entirely possible that rebuilding the Jerusalem temple at the expense of the Dome of the Rock and Al-Aksa Mosque may be the flash point that will eventually and ultimately spark the battle of Armageddon. Many within the Church contend that the rebuilding of Jerusalem and the temple will be done entirely under direction of the state of Israel, but just how these things will come about remains to be seen.

In conjunction with rebuilding the Jerusalem temple, another sign of the times, one that will be historically momentous and astounding, will ensue—the healing of the Dead Sea. The Dead Sea, with its high saline content, has been barren of life for as long as man has been on the earth, much the same as the Great Salt Lake. No fish and few plants can exist in its toxic water; in it live only a few insects and microorganisms such as brine shrimp. This is in stark contrast to the Sea of Galilee and other freshwater lakes and seas throughout the world, in which fish and aquatic life thrive, supporting important fishing industries.

> Afterward he brought me again unto the door of the house [the temple]; and, behold, waters issued out from under the threshold of the house eastward. . . .
>
> Then said he unto me, These waters issue out toward the east country, and go down into the desert, and go into the sea: which being brought forth into the sea, the waters shall be healed. And it shall come to pass, that every thing that liveth, which moveth, whithersoever the rivers shall come, shall live: and there shall be a very great multitude of fish, because these waters shall come thither: for they shall be healed; and every thing shall live whither the river cometh. And it shall come to pass, that the fishers shall stand upon it from En-gedi even unto En-eglaim; they shall be a place to

> spread forth nets; their fish shall be according to their kinds, as the fish of the great sea, exceeding many. (Ezekiel 47:1, 8–10)

In confirming Ezekiel's prophecy, the Prophet Joseph Smith said, "Judah must return, Jerusalem must be rebuilt, and the waters of the Dead Sea be healed. It will take some time to rebuild the walls of the city and the temple, etc.; and all this must be done before the Son of Man will make his appearance."[34]

It will be a remarkable occurrence when the temple is rebuilt, an event apparently unforeseen by the world at large. Jerusalem is in a relatively arid portion of the Holy Land, and wells, springs, and waterways don't exist in abundance. Somehow, perhaps during the reconstruction of the temple, water will flow from beneath the temple itself and in a river eastward to the Dead Sea. Upon reaching that body of water, life will emerge and the Dead Sea will produce fish in abundance. Of course, the scriptures don't tell us how or how rapidly this will happen, but the fact that it would happen at all, even over an extended period of time, could only be regarded as miraculous.

The New Jerusalem

> "We believe . . . that Zion (the New Jerusalem) will be built upon the American continent." (Articles of Faith 1:10)

In 1994, Richard O. Cowan published a significant and detailed summary of Latter-day Saint belief this long awaited, yet future, event—the building of a New Jerusalem and the establishment of Zion upon this continent. The significance of these events in the history of The Church of Jesus Christ of Latter-day Saints, which are to occur prior to the battle of Armageddon, can't be overestimated. The New Jerusalem will then become the new headquarters of the Church and play a pivotal role in humanity's last great conflict (excluding, of course, the great battle at the end of Jesus' millennial reign) and become a focal point at Jesus' Second Coming, as well as during the Millennium and beyond.

Jackson County, Missouri, where the New Jerusalem is to be built, is the center place of Adam-ondi-Ahman, the original Garden of Eden. Elder Cowan wrote,

> Since the early days of the Restoration, Latter-day Saints have been fired with the vision of this holy city, or Zion, on earth. The Book of Mormon, published in March 1830, declared that the New Jerusalem would be built upon "this land" (see Ether 13:2–3), meaning the American continent. In December of that same year, when the writings of Enoch were made known, Latter-day Saints were not only thrilled with descriptions of the power and glory of the ancient city of Zion, but also learned that in a future era of righteousness the elect would be gathered into a similar "Holy City" to be known as Zion or the New Jerusalem (see Moses 7:13–19; 7:62). Two months later, the Lord specifically mentioned that there would be a temple in the New Jerusalem. As he revealed the law of consecration, he indicated that, among other things, the consecrated funds would be used for the "building up of the New Jerusalem" to which the Lord's people would gather at the time he would come to his temple (D&C 42:35–36; 36:8; 133:1–2). Another revelation given the following month furthered intensified the Saints' anticipation of establishing this latter day Zion: "And it shall be . . . a land of peace, a city of refuge, a place of safety for the saints of the Most High God; And the glory of the Lord shall be there" (D&C 45:66–67).
>
> A revelation [to Joseph Smith] dated 20 July 1831 specified that Independence [Missouri] was to be the "center place" and that the temple should be built not far west of the courthouse (see D&C 57:3).
>
> On Wednesday, August 3, 1831, Joseph Smith and a small group of elders went to a knoll about a half-mile west of the Independence courthouse, turned south from the old road (now Lexington Avenue), and made their way about 200 feet through the thick

> forest. The prophet then indicated the specific spot where the temple was to stand, and placed a stone to mark the northeast corner of the future structure. Relevant scriptures were read, and a dedicatory prayer was offered, in accordance with previously revealed instructions (D&C 58:57). "The scene was solemn and impressive." In December of that same year, Bishop Edward Partridge purchased in behalf of the Church some 63.27 acres, which included the spot dedicated for the temple.
>
> For the next two years, Independence, Jackson County, was a focal point of the Saints' activity. Interest grew when, in June of 1833, Joseph Smith released his plan for the city of Zion. At the center of the mile-square city, he envisioned two large blocks containing 24 sacred "temples." These were to be assigned to the various priesthood quorums and were to serve a variety of functions. The prophet anticipated that the city would have a population of from 15,000 to 20,000 so that these 24 buildings would be needed as "houses of worship, schools, etc." Because all inhabitants of the city should be living on a celestial level (see D&C 105:5) all these structures could properly be regarded as "temples"—places of communication between heaven and earth—even though their functions were not restricted to ordinance work.
>
> But the temple in Zion was not to be built at that time. Anti-Mormon violence flared in Jackson County. By late fall, the Saints had to flee their homes in the chosen land.[35]

Since their expulsion from Missouri, Latter-day Saint interest in, and anticipation of, finally establishing their holy city in Jackson County, Missouri, hasn't waned. The prophets have repeatedly assured us that the New Jerusalem will be built there despite early hostility toward the Mormons:

> Hearken, O ye elders of my church, saith the Lord

> your God, who have assembled yourselves together, according to my commandments, in this land, which is the land of Missouri, which is the land which I have appointed and consecrated for the gathering of the saints. Wherefore, this is the land of promise, and the place for the city of Zion. (D&C 57:1–2)

In the century and a half since the Prophet Joseph Smith laid the stone marking the spot for what will eventually be the temple in the New Jerusalem, land ownership in Jackson County has been confused by competing interests, all surrounding the religious significance of that site. Many competitors have been other groups and churches, often apostate from The Church of Jesus Christ of Latter-day Saints:

> In 1867, a small group of former Mormons, who were now followers of Granville Hedrick, returned to Independence and began the process of quietly purchasing two and one-half acres including the spot where Joseph Smith had placed the temple cornerstone over three decades earlier. This group would form the "Church of Christ, (Temple Lot)."
>
> During the 1870s and 1880s, the Reorganized Church of Jesus Christ of Latter-day Saints, followers of Joseph Smith III, also began to return and eventually established their headquarters at Independence.
>
> In 1904, the Church of Jesus Christ of Latter-day Saints began to purchase 20 of the 63 acres originally acquired by Bishop Edward Partridge for the temple and other uses in Independence.
>
> In April 1929, the Church of Christ, the Hedrickites, broke sod for a temple. However, a split within the church in 1930 halted further work, and in 1946 the Hedrickites had their excavation filled in, the ground leveled, and the lot seeded in grass.
>
> In 1971, the Church of Jesus Christ of Latter-day Saints dedicated a visitors center in Independence, and in 1978 purchased over 4,000 acres of land across the

> river in Clay County. Church leaders stressed that the purchase was for investment purposes only.[36]

As of now, The Church of Jesus Christ of Latter-day Saints owns twenty of the original sixty-three acres purchased by Bishop Partridge. The Church of Christ, the Hedrickites, own nearly three acres, including the site designated by the Prophet Joseph Smith for the temple. And the Reorganized Church of Jesus Christ of Latter Day Saints (now the Community of Christ) owns forty acres.

When the time comes for construction to begin on the New Jerusalem, the Church will obviously play a central role in this undertaking:

> The time is fast approaching when a large portion of the people I am now addressing will go back to Jackson County. A great many people that are now dwelling in the State of Utah will have this privilege. Whether I, President Cannon, President Smith, or all the brethren of the Twelve will go back I know not. But a large portion of the Latter-day Saints that now dwell in these valleys will go back to Jackson County to build a holy city to the Lord, as was decreed by Jehovah and revealed through Joseph Smith.[37]

However, the membership of the Church as it now exists won't be the only ones involved. The prophets of the Book of Mormon and Latter-day Church authorities have made it clear that two other groups will also assist, namely, the remnants of the Lamanites, who fought so fiercely against the Nephites; and heavenly beings: "And they [the Lamanites] shall assist my people, the remnant of Jacob, and also as many of the house of Israel as shall come, that they may build a city, which shall be called the New Jerusalem" (3 Nephi 21:23).

Orson Pratt confirmed the prophecy in 3 Nephi, adding further details and emphasizing that the Lamanites will play a key role in building the New Jerusalem:

> These Lamanites, or American Indians, that are

> now so sunk beneath humanity, are to be lifted up by the power of the Almighty when the day shall come for Israel to be restored, for God will not forget them. They are descendants of the tribe of Joseph, and consequently they are numbered with the people of the covenant. God will remember the covenant which he made with our ancient fathers. These Lamanites, these American Indians, will come to the knowledge of the covenant, and they will arise and will build upon the face of this land a magnificent city called Jerusalem, after the pattern and in the same manner that the Jews will build old Jerusalem. That is what the Lamanites will do, and we will go and help them too, for it is predicted in the Book of Mormon that when this work should come forth, when the time fully arrives for the redemption of this small remnant of the house of Joseph, "As many of the Gentiles as will believe, they shall assist my people, who are a remnant of the house of Israel, that may build up on the face of this land a city that shall be called the New Jerusalem."[38]

In conjunction with the New Jerusalem becoming the headquarters of The Church of Jesus Christ of Latter-day Saints and focal point of Jesus' reign on the earth, Wilfred Woodruff, in a dream, foresaw that heavenly beings and angels would also aid in the work:

> I saw a short distance from the Missouri River, where I stood, twelve [men] . . . whose hands were uplifted while they were consecrating the ground; and later they laid the cornerstones of the house of God. I saw myriads of angels hovering over them, and above their heads there was a pillar-like cloud. I saw people coming from the river and from distant places to help build the Temple. It seemed as though there were hosts of angels helping to bring material for the construction of that building.[39]

The New Jerusalem will be a heavenly city, eventually to be administered by Jesus Christ at his Second Coming and thereafter. As such, it will be, as noted in Brother Cowan's comments above, in a celestial state. Its inhabitants should be living on a celestial level. The law of consecration will then be lived in its purest form, and it will be a city of magnificence and complete harmony, befitting Jesus when he returns. Of course, this will exclude many Latter-day Saints who, for various reasons, can't live up to that standard.

Although early leaders of the restored Church indicated that Church members should flock to Zion—which many did, to Salt Lake City—more recent Church pronouncements have cautioned that Zion is wherever in the world stakes and wards exist. The leadership and organization of those entities provide the guidance and security Church members need, both now and as the last days draw nearer.

The reality of man's nature, however, makes it likely that, especially in precarious times, Church members will tend to congregate near the headquarters of the Church, where the prophet and the Quorum of the Twelve are. This was the case in Nauvoo, and again in Salt Lake City. As a matter of fact, in the early missionary days of the Church, so many converts from all over the world emigrated to Salt Lake City that those remaining in their homelands suffered from a dearth of priesthood holders to administer the affairs of the Church. This was especially the case in Europe, where a lack of priesthood holders seriously hindered the establishment of stakes and wards until just the last forty years or so.

In the four decades since then, largely due to the Church's greatly expanded missionary program (with a consequent rapid growth in the Church) and the insistence of the General Authorities that Latter-day Saints stay where they are,[40] well-established wards, stakes, and temples can now be found throughout the world. As a matter of fact, only 14 percent of Latter-day Saints now reside in Utah.

Nevertheless, it is entirely predictable that great masses of Latter-day Saints will seek to migrate to the New Jerusalem as the influence of the anti-Christ intensifies throughout the world, together with the persecution, enmity, and warfare that will accompany his regime as the battle of Armageddon approaches. The Saints will do so for the spiritual atmosphere of the city but also simply for the protection it offers them and their families: "We expect that these mountains will not be the residences of all the Latter-day Saints, we expect that the great majority of the people will emigrate [to the New Jerusalem]."[41]

Furthermore, the Lord promised the New Jerusalem his protection during the difficult times ahead:

> It shall be called the New Jerusalem, a land of peace, a city of refuge, a place of safety for the saints of the Most High God; And the glory of the Lord shall be there, and the terror of the Lord also shall be there, insomuch that the wicked will not come unto it, and it shall be called Zion.[42]
>
> And it shall come to pass among the wicked, that every man that will not take his sword against his neighbor must needs flee unto Zion for safety. And there shall be gathered unto it out of every nation under heaven; and it shall be the only people that shall not be at war one with another.
>
> And it shall be said among the wicked: Let us not go up to battle against Zion, for the inhabitants of Zion are terrible; wherefore we cannot stand. (D&C 45:66–70)

Although the Prophet Joseph Smith planned for a city of 15,000 to 20,000, it is probable that the population of the New Jerusalem could easily swell to many times that number, especially as the Second Coming of the Savior approaches. Many Latter-day Saints will predictably and assuredly want to be on hand for that great event,[43] but again it should be remembered that only the elect who can live the law of consecration on a celestial level will be allowed to live there. In addition, certain prophecies, which we have already discussed, indicate that tens of thousands of the ten lost tribes will also seek to come to the New Jerusalem:

> After Zion is built in Jackson County, and after the temple is built upon that spot of ground where

> the corner stone was laid in 1831; after the glory of God in the form of a cloud by day shall rest upon that temple, and by night the shining of a flaming fire that will fill the whole heavens round about; . . . about that period of time, the ten tribes will be heard of, away in the north, a great company, as Jeremiah says, coming down from the northern regions, coming to sing in the height of the latter-day Zion. Their souls will be as a watered garden, and they will not sorrow any more at all, as they have been doing during the twenty-five hundred long years they have dwelled in the Arctic regions. They will come, and the Lord will be before their camp, he will utter his voice before that great army, and he will lead them forth as he led Israel in ancient times. This long chain of Rocky Mountains, that extends from the cold regions of the north away into South America, will feel the power of God, and will tremble before the hosts of Israel as they come to sing on the heights of Zion. In that day the trees of the field will clap like hands, says the Prophet, and in that day the Lord will open waters in the wilderness, and streams in the desert, to give drink to his chosen, his people Israel. And when they come to the height of Zion they shall be crowned with glory under the hands of the servants of God living in those days.[44]

As noted above, the New Jerusalem will have a special place during Jesus' millennial reign and throughout eternity. For example, the inhabitants of the purest city on earth, the city of Enoch, which the scriptures tell us was taken into heaven for its righteousness, will meet with the inhabitants of the New Jerusalem:

> Righteousness and truth will I cause to sweep the earth as with a flood, to gather out mine elect from the four quarters of the earth, unto a place which I shall prepare, an Holy City, that my people may gird up their loins, and be looking forth for the time of my coming; for there shall be my tabernacle, and it

> shall be called Zion, a New Jerusalem. And the Lord said unto Enoch: Then shalt thou and all thy city meet them there, and we will receive them unto our bosom. (Moses 7:62–63)

Orson Pratt indicated furthermore that the New Jerusalem, like the city of Enoch, will also eventually be taken up into heaven, to be "a choice and holy place":

> When we build that great central city, the New Jerusalem, there will be no such thing as the word decay associated with it . . . The Lord has promised that he will preserve the city of the New Jerusalem, the dwelling houses, the tabernacles, the temples, etc., from the effects of storms and time. It is intended that it will be taken up to heaven, when the earth passes away. It is intended to be one of those choice and holy places, where the Lord will dwell, when he shall visit from time to time, in the midst of the great latter-day Zion, after it shall be connected with the city of Enoch.[45]

Notes

1. Joseph Smith, *Discourses of the Prophet Joseph Smith,* comp. Alma P. Burton (Salt Lake City: Deseret Book, 1977), 248.

2. Orson F. Whitney, in Conference Report, April 1920, 123.

3. The verses following, 7–10, illustrate well John's symbolism. These were not ordinary locusts. They were shaped like horses with golden heads and faces of men. They had long hair and lion's teeth. They wore iron breastplates and had wings and stinging tails like scorpions.

4. This is the reason that many are wary of recent talk about a new world order or of our government becoming too involved in far-reaching alliances with other nations. Take, for example, the United Nations and, to a lesser extent, the North Atlantic Treaty Organization, NATO. Either organization can now claim international authority to interfere in other countries' internal affairs, including waging war against their governments and people under the pretext of maintaining regional or world stability or to correct human rights abuses. These are laudable goals but are under the wrong leadership. These same organizations could theoretically do the same in our country, could they not?

It is then but a small step for such an organization to assume absolute control over our or any other nation—especially if that organization had wide popular support—and thus destroy our democratic heritage. Even Thomas Jefferson long ago warned against becoming involved in "entangling alliances."

Few realize that such entanglements can potentially threaten our national sovereignty, as in recent negotiations and agreements between the United States and other countries over the establishment of global protected areas within our country and others in the name of environmentalism. These treaties or agreements, although they appear innocuous and well intentioned, give other countries a certain amount of control over our country. This may well be the case also with negotiations in Japan between the United States and several other countries—as in the Kyoto Accords—in order to establish international pollution controls, ostensibly to halt global warming. Again, these talks may be environmentally well intentioned, but they could well have implications for our own economy, including sanctions against this country if we fail to live up to the agreements. Despite the need for global clean air and the perceived need to control global warming—which scientists are still not entirely in agreement on—do we really want other countries to be able to dictate to our government what we can and can't do within our own borders? Are these not decisions to be made by our own people under our Constitution?

Similarly, many opponents of one-world government also fear what they consider international conspiracies, such as the infamous and shadowy Trilateral Commission, a secret (as nobody yet has been able to prove that it really exists) worldwide organization of politicians and economic leaders who allegedly operate clandestinely behind the scenes to control what is going on in our country and the rest of the world. Have they perhaps distorted some of our political process and usurped to some extent the will of the people?

5. For those who have studied history, this will almost certainly be reminiscent of Adolf Hitler's rise to power over Nazi Germany's Third Reich during the 1930s. Hitler achieved his power through ruthlessness, ambition, political maneuvering, intimidation, and, ultimately, assassination. In doing so, he surrounded himself with a staff as equally corrupt and evil as he was.

6. Precisely what this mark will be is unclear, though many scholars and laymen (and novels and films) have construed that mark to be 666. The significance of 666 is not specified in the scripture above, nor in other scriptures, nor how it will be used during the anti-Christ's reign. It will not necessarily be conveniently found on the beast himself, as Hollywood has depicted in some of films.

7. These verses make it sound as if there is a special, more extreme punishment for those who turn from God and follow the beast, as opposed to those who simply deny God or the Savior in other circumstances.

8. Elder Ezra Taft Benson provided a lengthy, insightful, and thought-provoking discourse on this topic, ranging from the divinely inspired birth of this nation to the global threat of communism. In his discourse, Elder Benson likened the threat of such groups to the Gadiantons of the Book of Mormon:

"It [the Gadiantons] was a secret political party which operated as a murder cult. Its object was to infiltrate legitimate government, plant its officers in high places, and then seize power and live off the spoils appropriated from the people. It would start out as a small group of dissenters, and by using secret oaths with the threat of death for defectors, it would gradually gain a choke hold on the political and economic life of whole civilizations." He later went on to stress that "the Lord has declared that before the Second Coming of Christ it will be necessary to '. . . destroy the secret works of darkness, . . .' in order to preserve the land of Zion—the Americas" (Ezra Taft Benson, in Conference Report, October 1961, 72).

9. David O. McKay, *Gospel Ideals* (Salt Lake City: Deseret Book, 1976), 273.

10. An excellent example of such a secret environmentalist movement is the ELF, the Earth Liberation Front. This group has recently been involved in the destruction of business and private property as a means of halting urban expansion in several western states. Its targets are construction equipment, lumberyards, and homes undergoing construction.

11. A similar organization is the Skull and Bones Society—a secret university fraternity—from whose membership have reportedly come many currently prominent political, government, and economic leaders.

12. It is also conceivable that this person and his wound may not initially be widely publicized. It could well be that his wound will be the result of an accident, a military injury, or the like, yet from which he unexpectedly recovers. John the Revelator simply states that the wound will be "deadly" and that it will be a "wound of a sword" (Revelation 13:3, 12, 14). Just how literally we can take these descriptions is difficult to say.

13. It is also possible that the anti-Christ will utter his blasphemies in private, at least initially, astutely realizing that by not doing so he may well alienate many who still take religion seriously. Only later, when his dictatorial regime is well established, might he publicly declare his enmity toward God.

14. Brigham Young, in *Journal of Discourses,* 8:123.

15. Ezra Taft Benson, "I Testify," *Ensign,* November 1988, 87.

16. Recently it was estimated that as much as 40 percent of the Church's membership fails to attend even one Church meeting per month. This means that only 60 percent of all Latter-day Saints are, in fact, active, or even marginally active, which is a poor number when we consider ourselves God's chosen people. Even so, active membership in the LDS Church is much higher than that in most other churches.

17. As noted in a preceding chapter, the most personal aspects of our private lives can be found in a database somewhere: our birth records, residence, financial records, family members, driver licenses, credit information, educational records, investments, and probably our political and religious affiliations. This information may then be available to the anti-Christ or his officials.

18. These verses suggest that Latter-day Saints will be joined by

non-Church members who also seek refuge.

19. Joseph F. Smith, in *Journal of Discourses,* 24:157.

20. Orson Pratt, in *Journal of Discourses,* 12:345.

21. Joseph Smith, *Discourses of the Prophet Joseph Smith,* 193–94.

22. Orson Pratt, in *Journal of Discourses,* 7:188.

23. Brigham Young, in *Journal of Discourses,* 7:15.

24. Ezra Taft Benson, in Conference Report, October 1961, 71.

25. Brigham Young, in *Journal of Discourses,* 8:68.

26. Ezra Taft Benson, "Prepare for the Days of Tribulation," *Ensign,* November 1980, 32–33.

27. Professions such as building, sewing, and the like will be extremely beneficial in the last days, as will be the services of doctors.

28. Orson Pratt, in *Journal of Discourses,* 14:350.

29. Joseph Fielding Smith, *The Signs of the Times* (Salt Lake City: Deseret Book, 1963), 238.

30. Orson Pratt, in *Journal of Discourses,* 18:177.

31. Wilford Woodruff, in *Journal of Discourses,* 2:200.

32. Orson Pratt, in *Journal of Discourses,* 18:65.

33. Charles W. Penrose, in *Journal of Discourses,* 24:215–16.

34. Joseph Smith, *Discourses of the Prophet Joseph Smith,* 236–37.

35. Richard O. Cowan, "The Great Temple of the New Jerusalem," *Regional Studies in Latter-day Saint History: Missouri*, ed. Arnold K. Garr and Clark F. Johnson (Provo, Utah: Department of Church History and Doctrine, 1994), 144–51.

36. Ibid.

37. Lorenzo Snow, in Conference Report, October 1900, 61.

38. Orson Pratt, in *Journal of Discourses,* 14:334.

39. *Wilford Woodruff: History of His Life and Labors as Recorded in His Daily Journals,* comp. Matthias F. Cowley (Salt Lake City: Deseret News, 1909), 505.

40. Harold B. Lee, quoting Bruce R. McConkie, said, "The place of gathering for the Mexican Saints is in Mexico; the place of gathering for the Guatemalan Saints is in Guatemala; the place of gathering for the Brazilian Saints is in Brazil; and so it goes throughout the length and breadth of the whole earth. Japan is for the Japanese; Korea is for the Koreans; Australia is for the Australians; every nation is the gathering place for its own people" (Harold B. Lee, *Ye Are the Light of the World: Selected Sermons and Writings of Harold B. Lee* (Salt Lake City: Deseret Book, 1974), 141.

41. Orson Pratt, in *Journal of Discourses,* 24:23.

42. *Zion* is defined in latter-day revelation as "the pure in heart." It also refers to geographical locations such as Jackson County, Missouri, which is called Zion in many of the revelations in the Doctrine and Covenants. It also refers to the city of New Jerusalem, to be built in Jackson County, Missouri, and in a wider sense, it sometimes refers to all of North and South America.

43. Could this be the undisclosed reason for the investment the Church

has made in four thousand acres in neighboring Clay County, Missouri?

44. Orson Pratt, in *Journal of Discourses,* 18:68.

45. Ibid., 21:153–54.

8

THE BATTLE OF ARMAGEDDON

Brigham Young made this prophecy:

> Do you think there is calamity abroad now among the people? Not much. All we have yet heard and experienced is scarcely a preface to the sermon that is going to be preached. When the testimony of the elders ceases to be given, and the Lord says to them, "Come home; I will now preach my own sermons to the nations of the earth," all you now know can scarcely be called a preface to the sermon that will be preached with fire and sword, tempests, earthquakes, hail, thunders and lightnings, and fearful destruction. What matters the destruction of a few railway cars? You will hear of magnificent cities, now idolized by the people, sinking in the earth, entombing the inhabitants. The sea will heave itself beyond its bounds, engulfing mighty cities. Famine will spread over the nations, and nation will rise up against nation, kingdom against kingdom, and states against states, in our own country and in foreign lands.[1]

Likewise, Wilford Woodruff prophesied,

> I wish to warn all nations of the judgments of God which are at their doors. Thrones will be cast down, nations will be turned over, anarchy will reign, all legal barriers will be broken down, and the laws will be trampled in the dust. You are about to be visited

> with war, the sword, famine, pestilence, plague, earthquakes, whirlwinds, tempests, and the flame of devouring fire. . . . The question may be asked why these judgments are coming upon the world in these last days? I answer, because of the wickedness of the inhabitants thereof.[2]

Man has fought increasingly bloody and destructive wars, from the days of stone tools to those of spears and swords to today's weapons of mass destruction. This propensity of man to kill other men is undoubtedly a part of Satan's plan for us and is his means to thwart God's plan of salvation. We have noted the reasons for wars in the past—for land, food, honor, riches, and even for God. But the great battle of Armageddon will be unprecedented as it will turn all nations against each other for no apparent reason. As we are told, "nation will rise up against nation," but no discernible rationale will exist behind these great conflicts except each other's destruction.

Certainly, food and power will be motivators for great battles but, as is the case in many wars, men will kill each other for the sheer sake of killing. And death and destruction won't be limited to nations only, but will include neighbor fighting against neighbor. In other words, this senseless killing will be everywhere and no one will be exempt. We are promised that the Church will be the only refuge during this period of time, but the battles and turmoil throughout the world will affect us as well.

Numerous scriptures speak of this impending great battle which will be the final climax of increasing warfare throughout the world. We have had recent previews of what is to come through two great world wars, not to mention the Korean War, Vietnam War, repeated wars in the Middle East and the Balkans, and the current War on Terrorism. These, however, are only preludes to the battle of Armageddon.

The great battle of Armageddon will escalate rapidly, although the scriptures and the prophets give us only hints as to what will happen and when. Certain events will, however, occur beforehand, giving us clues of what is to come. Precipitating this conflict, as reviewed in the previous chapter, will be the rebuilding of Jerusalem and its temple in the Holy Land and, at about the same time, the construction of the New Jerusalem here in America.

In near proximity to the same time, we should also see the rise of the anti-Christ to power. Apparently, only after he consolidates his power and control over his ten subservient kingdoms will the true countdown to Armageddon begin. Keep in mind also that he will likely achieve his power through one of the many secret combinations we have discussed. As was the case in the Book of Mormon, the Gadianton robbers, although starting off innocuously, eventually became so powerful that they caused the complete collapse of the Nephite and Lamanite kingdoms. The rise to power of the anti-Christ will likely take much the same course.

As the future begins to darken and warfare increases, the Church will probably be required to exist in secrecy, especially after the anti-Christ's grip becomes so strong that all his followers will be identifiable by his mark and by worshiping his image. Despite the fact that he will be an absolute ruler—at least over the ten kingdoms that will comprise the bulk of his power—warfare will continue to increase among his own unruly followers, or perhaps stem from the other nations of the world who refuse to join him. As time goes on, chaos and anarchy will ensue. As the scriptures make clear, warfare throughout the world may prove uncontrollable as social order dissolves and savagery rules.

Exactly how these events will affect the United States is unclear. It is apparent from the scriptures and comments from prophets that our country may well be one of the nations controlled by the anti-Christ; or, if not, it will also fall prey to the global warfare that will surround it. In any case, we know that things will become so precarious in this country that our own constitutional form of government will be in jeopardy, as discussed in the preceding chapter. Although the scriptures and prophets have given us little further detail as to how all this will be accomplished, we know that only the elders of the Church will be capable of preventing the complete collapse of our government.

Survival of the Saints and the Church itself will be extremely difficult, putting them both to the utmost test: "And it came to pass that I beheld that the great mother of abominations did gather together multitudes upon the face of all the earth, among all the nations of the Gentiles, to fight against the Lamb of God" (1 Nephi 14:13).

Many Latter-day Saints will be required to sacrifice their lives, and perhaps those of their families as well, in defending their faith. Nevertheless, the unity and cohesion of the Church, and its members' righteousness, love, and dedication to one another, will provide the framework by which the Lord will protect some of his chosen people, sparing them from the turmoil of the last days and the anti-Christ's rule. This will be particularly true for those residing in the New Jerusalem, which will be under the direct protection of the Lord and the headquarters of the Church.

Immediately after the days of Jesus' earthly ministry, the Lord directed that his Church should be taken to the Gentiles instead of to the Jews who rejected it. From that time on, the Church was almost predominantly a gentile church, with the Gentiles being "grafted in" to the house of Israel. This condition persisted throughout the Great Apostasy of the last 1,750 years, which ended with the restoration of the Church.

By now, the Spirit of the Lord has touched nearly every nation on the earth through the Church's missionary program, and The Church of Jesus Christ of Latter-day Saints has become an international church. Yes, many millions of Gentiles have accepted the gospel, but time is running out. The Lord's Spirit will ultimately be withdrawn from the nations of the world when the Lord determines that all "nations, kindreds, tongues, and peoples" have had the opportunity to hear the gospel and either accepted or rejected it:

> When God has called out the righteous, when the warning voice has been sufficiently proclaimed among the Gentile nations, and the Lord says, "It is enough," he will also say to his servants—"O, ye, my servants, come home, come out from the midst of these Gentile nations, where you have labored and borne testimony for so long a period; come out from among them, for they are not worthy; they do not receive the message that I have sent forth, they do not repent of their sins, come out from their midst, their times are fulfilled. Seal up the testimony among them and bind up the law."[3]

This withdrawal of the Spirit of the Lord will be a key turning point in humanity's history, a period when the Lord will leave humanity to his own devices, which, based on past history, will initiate a period of warfare and hostility among men as the world has never before seen: "After the nations have been fully warned, the spirit of God will entirely withdraw from those nations and they will war among themselves instead of persecuting the saints."[4]

In the past, when the Lord strove with humanity through his prophets and the Church to provide some kind of civilizing influence among us, man was capable of experiencing relatively brief periods of civility and spiritual progress. However, such periods were few and far between, and most of man's history has been characterized by little spiritual advancement.

Certainly, man has progressed in other respects. Our standard of living is higher than ever before, our technological prowess is growing exponentially, our lives are longer and healthier than ever before, and so forth. But despite such advances, the spirit of man is much the same now as it always has been—obsessed with self, greedy, and neglectful of, and even hostile toward, others. We are no closer now to Jesus' admonitions to "love thy neighbor as thyself" and "love thy enemies" than were the Jews of his time. As a matter of fact, our high standard of living has resulted in an era of self-aggrandizement, complacency, pride, and obsession with worldly things more than ever before in humanity's history.

Whenever the Lord's Spirit has been removed from man's affairs here on the earth, man has never failed to slide backward and become the worse for it. War, evil, and societal decay have rapidly set in, and no matter how wonderful we think we are, the collapse of our world—as has always been the case in human history—will result.

Examples of this repeated process, as discussed earlier, were the rise and fall of Macedonia, Greece, Babylon, Rome, Egypt, and many other once-great nations. Even the ancient Jaredites, predecessors of the Nephites and Lamanites in the Americas, destroyed themselves when the Spirit of the Lord was withdrawn: "Behold, the Spirit of the Lord had ceased striving with them, and Satan had full power over the hearts of the people; for they were given up unto the hardness of their hearts, and the blindness of their minds that they might be destroyed; wherefore they went again to battle" (Ether 15:19).

During the last of the Jaredite wars, even women and children were sent into battle. Warriors on both sides slept at night only to have the strength to fight the next day. In only six days, an entire civilization numbering in the millions annihilated itself.

As the scriptures have warned, however, our time will signal a collapse of global proportions, "the abomination of desolation," as prophesied by Daniel in the Old Testament (see Daniel 11:31; 12:11). Jesus reiterated Daniel's warning, making it clear that the abomination of desolation would take place at the conclusion of man's time on the earth: "And again, this Gospel of the Kingdom shall be preached in all the world, for a witness unto all nations, and then shall the end come, when ye therefore shall see the abomination of desolation, spoken of by Daniel the Prophet" (Matthew 24:14–15).

There is perhaps no event in history that has received more prophetic attention than the battle of Armageddon. Thanks to dozens of prophecies that exist throughout the scriptures relating to this epic battle—from Ezekiel, Jeremiah, Zechariah, Joel, Daniel, and the book of Revelation to the Book of Mormon and latter-day scriptures and pronouncements—enormous detail is available about what we can expect when it ultimately comes to pass.

Unfortunately and frustratingly, as is so frequently the case with scriptural prophecies, it is difficult to decipher the symbolisms and vagaries inherent in such writings. For example, it is all too often unclear in which chronological context these events will take place, whether prior to, during, or at the conclusion of the battle of Armageddon. Nevertheless, enough information is available to outline this final chapter in humanity's history.

We have already discussed the fact that societal decay and hostility will reign during the anti-Christ's regime. Corruption, anarchy, and warfare will spread throughout the world, including our own nation. Persecution and hatred will be the norm and global turmoil will be rampant. Food, water, clothing, warmth, and the comforts of life will be things of the past, as will be recreational activities, computer games, freedom to travel, and all the luxuries we now take for granted. With strife and conflict everywhere, it may well be assumed that the battle of Armageddon itself will be an extension of this worldwide turmoil. Satan's ultimate focus will be the destruction of that most important religious site on earth, the homeland of Jesus and the promised land of God's chosen people.

The events that will ignite this great war haven't been revealed to us. We do know, however, that the rebuilding of Jerusalem and its historic temple must take place beforehand, and this alone could well be the spark that will set it off.

We have already commented on the ages-old hostility among the nations of the Middle East. Stemming from as far back as the entry of Moses' followers into the Holy Land, there has been continual turmoil among peoples, as currently manifested in the conflict between Islamic nations and the Christians and Jews who have made repeated claims to that land. The Crusades were a prime example of this hostility, followed nearly 1,000 years later by the establishment of the state of Israel in 1948. That event, however, seems to have been a catalyst among Israel's Islamic neighbors, intensifying their resolve to eliminate Jews from the Holy Land finally and forever.

Exacerbating this enmity is the fact that since 1948, worldwide economic attention has been increasingly focused on Middle East oil reserves. As a result, the already tenuous situation there has been worsened by the world's industrial nations, who see the great oil fields as vital to their economies and well-being—so much so that they are willing to go to war among themselves for access to that oil. Even Hitler's Nazi regime during World War II considered the Middle East important for its oil, and the major world powers have since repeatedly threatened war against each other when they felt that their access to Middle East oil was jeopardized.

The combination of these two flash points—religious antagonisms and Middle East oil—seem, as the years go by, to be converging into the fuse that may well ignite the greatest international battle the world has ever known. More recently, the United States War on Terrorism has brought it into even sharper focus. Our traditional alliance with Israel, our seemingly insatiable need for Middle East oil, and the hatred of hard-line Islamic nations toward us and Israel has drawn the United States into the equation.

Islamic religious enmity struck this country on September 11, 2001, and will undoubtedly do so again. Despite the partial neutralization of Afghanistan and Iraq as hostile Islamic nations, most of Israel's other Middle Eastern Islamic neighbors remain antagonistic toward us, with the friendships of Egypt, Libya, and Saudi Arabia being precarious at best. All the ingredients are therefore on hand for the battle of Armageddon, and the signs of this great impending conflict will grow clearer:

> When you see the nations of the earth, especially the heathen nations, and also those north of Jerusalem—the great nation of Russia and other nations on the continent of Asia, together with many in Europe, gather up against Jerusalem after the Jews have returned and rebuilt their city and temple, and when their armies become exceeding great multitudes in the valley of decision, then you may look for the Lord to come down with his mighty ones, and for the constellations of heaven to be darkened.[5]

The Valley of Megiddo

In studying the Holy Land, as it was and as it now is, one notes that it is divided into two climatic regions. The southern portion of the country, including the region of Jerusalem and the Dead Sea—the Old Testament Kingdom of Judah—is relatively arid, with desolate stony mountains and valleys not unlike many regions of Utah. The northern half, on the other hand, is greener and has always been the more agriculturally productive of the two.

The prophets foresaw that in the latter days, however, the arid southern portion of the Holy Land wouldn't remain dry and forbidding. On the contrary, like the originally arid Salt Lake Valley, what is now southern Israel has come to "blossom as the rose" (Isaiah 35:1):

> O mountains of Israel, ye shall shoot forth your branches, and yield your fruit to my people of Israel; for they are at hand to come. . . . I will also save you from all your uncleannesses: and I will call for the corn, and will increase it, and lay no famine upon

> you. And I will multiply the fruit of the tree, and the increase of the field, that ye shall receive no more reproach of famine among the heathen. . . . And the desolate land shall be tilled, whereas it lay desolate in the sight of all that passed by. And they shall say, This land that was desolate is become like the garden of Eden; and the waste and desolate and ruined cities are become fenced, and are inhabited. (Ezekiel 36:8, 29–30, 34–35)

Since 1948, the rapidly expanding new nation of Israel, a democracy, has indeed proven the fulfillment of this prophecy through innovative modern irrigation and agricultural techniques as well as through its free-enterprise system. The result is a small desert country that now boasts a substantial agricultural base and thriving cities, the envy of its more backward neighbors who continue to struggle under dictatorial Islamic regimes. As a matter of fact, thousands of Muslims living along Israel's borders, and near Jerusalem in particular, have found employment in the Jewish state.

The name "battle of Armageddon" is of obscure origin and is perhaps best presented by Mark Dalby in his website at www.ldslastdays.com:

> Megiddo, which is approximately 60 miles north of Jerusalem, will apparently be where the battle of Armageddon will begin. The term *Armageddon* is used only once in the Bible, in Revelation 16:16. The name *Armageddon* is a Greek transliteration of the Hebrew *har Megiddo,* meaning mountain of Megiddo. Scripture also refers to this area as the Valley of Jezreel or the Plain of Esdraelon and is known by several names, including Megiddo Valley, Megiddo Plain, Esdraelon Valley, and Jezreel Esdraelon. Generally this is referring to the entire flat and fertile plain stretching southeast from the coast north of Mount Carmel to the Jordan River at Beth-shan. It is this area that Napoleon called an ideal battleground, saying, "All the armies of the world could maneuver their forces on this vast plain."[6]

Preparations for War

"I will gather all nations against Jerusalem to battle" (Zechariah 14:2). "I will bring thee forth, and all thine army, horses and horsemen, all of them clothed with all sorts of armour, even a great company with bucklers and shields, all of them handling swords" (Ezekiel 38:4). "And he gathered them together into a place called in the Hebrew tongue Armageddon" (Revelation 16:16).

Although the ancient prophets above suggested that "all nations" will be gathered against Jerusalem to battle, some qualifications may be necessary to these statements. Certain scriptures indicate that distinct nations will be part of the massive force to be aligned against the Jews, although their present identity and location remain nebulous. Scholars over the years, however, have proposed the following nations as likely participants:[7]

Biblical Nations/Regions	Modern Nations/Regions
Magog	Russia/Mongols
Rosh	Russia
Meschech	Moscow
Tubal/Tobolsk	Area in Russia
Persia	Iran, Iraq, Afghanistan
Gomer	Germany, Eastern Europe
Togarmah	Turkey, Southeastern Europe

Whether or not these nations will be included under the anti-Christ's regime is unclear, but they will assuredly be under his influence as the great war draws near.[8] The simple fact that wars between nations will increase globally, and that worldwide turmoil will exist, will apparently be sufficient to provide justification for Israel's ancient enemies to attack her. Moreover, Satan will be instrumental in this evil and disastrous undertaking:

> I saw three unclean spirits like frogs come out of the mouth of the dragon, and out of the mouth of the beast, and out of the mouth of the false prophet.
>
> For they are the spirits of devils, working miracles, which go forth unto the kings of the earth and of the whole world, to gather them to the battle of that great day of God Almighty. (Revelation 16:13–14)

Of course, it is doubtful that all nations of the world will be direct participants in the war, but it is inevitable that many of them will take one side or the other. This has always been the case in war, including during the current United States War on Terrorism. There remains, therefore, a distinct possibility, or even probability, that the United States and other nations will be drawn into the conflict, either against or on behalf of Israel. We have no way of knowing who will end up on which side, but it can plausibly be predicted that the United States will ultimately align with Israel because of our historic alliance with that country. On the other hand, possibly all Islamic nations worldwide will align themselves against Israel.

Likewise, there is no way to determine which nations will be combatants or whether those who aren't will lend material, financial, and political support to whichever side they end up on. Although the countries mentioned above may provide the nucleus in making preparations for the battle, it is entirely conceivable that many others of the world's nations will supply troops or finances and armaments. It will be simple to determine, however, whose side each nation is on from God's point of view:

> Those nations defending Israel in the coming Armageddon will find the God of battles allied with them, and the assemblage marching under the banner of Gog and Magog [scriptural references to the leaders of the foes of Israel] will be the rebels against righteousness.[9]

Nevertheless, a few nations will apparently object to the war, choosing not to be involved. These are somewhat nebulously referred to in Ezekiel 38:13 as the nations of Sheba, Dedan, and the merchants of Tarshish. The modern-day equivalents of these nations would undoubtedly be friends or allies of Israel. Despite a lack of consensus among Bible scholars, the great army of attackers against Israel will be massive, one never before seen in humanity's history. John the Revelator describes them as "two-hundred-thousand thousand" (Revelation 9:16), which translates into 200 million men.

Scholars in some cases, however, don't accept this figure literally and feel that it should be more correctly translated as two myriads of myriads. Whichever the case, as they approach the Valley of Megiddo, their sheer size will be more than all the hordes of the Mongols, Alexander's armies, Roman legions, Confederate and Union forces, Napoleon's armies, and both sides of World Wars I and II combined. This will undoubtedly be a horrifying prospect to a small nation like Israel, which has a total population of only 6.7 million:

> A day of darkness and of gloominess, a day of clouds and of thick darkness, as the morning spread upon the mountains: a great people and a strong; there hath not been ever the like, neither shall be any more after it, even to the years of many generations. (Joel 2:2)

> Thou shalt ascend and come like a storm, thou shalt be like a cloud to cover the land, thou, and all thy bands, and many people with thee. (Ezekiel 38:9)

Despite the massiveness of this imposing army, some comment seems necessary regarding their armaments. The ancient prophets Ezekiel and Joel mention that the army will be equipped with horses, armor, bucklers (shields), and swords (see Ezekiel 38:4; Joel 2:8). In our day of modern weapons—machine guns, smart bombs, aircraft, armored vehicles, missiles, and especially weapons of mass destruction—it is difficult to think that the last great war of humanity will be fought with shields and swords. Even the last of the United States Cavalry was disbanded over five decades ago, in 1951.

To account for this apparent inconsistency on the part of the prophets, there may be two plausible explanations. First is that the prophets of the Old Testament described only those weapons and armaments that existed during their day. In other words, they had no way to conceive of the weapons that have been developed during the millennia since then. Or perhaps they symbolically suggested that the massive armies heading for Armageddon would simply be well armed. This thinking is similar to that of Bruce R. McConkie:

> In prophetic imagery John here seeks to describe a war fought with weapons and under circumstances entirely foreign to any experience of his own or of the people of that day. Joel, subject to the same limitations of descriptive ability, attempted to portray the same scenes (see Joel 2:1–11). It is not improbable that these ancient prophets were seeing such things as men wearing or protected by strong armor; as troops of cavalry and companies of tanks and flame throwers; as airplanes and airborne missiles which explode, fire shells, and drop bombs; and even other weapons yet to be devised in an age when warfare is the desire and love of wicked men.[10]

Second, it may well be that the armies preparing for that battle will, in fact, be armed with horses, swords, and shields. That may seem unlikely, but the nations attacking Israel may be so decimated by wars raging throughout the world that many modern weapons won't be available. However, this is not a likely scenario and how they are armed shouldn't be a major point of contention. The fact remains that their numbers will be massive, that their evil leadership will be intent on the destruction of Israel, and that they will be heavily armed, disciplined, and resistant to wounds (see Joel 2:3–8).

War Commences—The Two Prophets

Although the battle of Armageddon may begin in the Valley of Megiddo, it will spread quickly southward toward Jerusalem. The Israeli army, although well equipped through United States assistance from decades of defending itself against its neighbors, will be no match for the overwhelming numbers of the attackers. As a matter of fact, complete and rapid collapse of the nation of Israel will seem inevitable.

That grim reality has been clearly described by the prophets of old: two thirds of the people of Israel will die. The one third that survives will be literal prisoners in their own land—probably only in Jerusalem—surrounded by hundreds of thousands of their enemies. Whether or not these numbers will include the tens of thousands of the lost ten tribes who will return to help rebuild Jerusalem and the temple we aren't told. "And it shall come to pass, that in all the land, saith the Lord, two parts therein shall be cut off and die; but the third shall be left therein" (Zechariah 13:8).

It can be assumed that those who die in the battle, as well as those who perish in the calamities yet to come, will be those who continue to reject Jesus Christ. As noted earlier, many current inhabitants of the state of Israel and of the ten lost tribes, although they will participate in the rebuilding of the holy city and its temple, won't do so because they recognize Jesus as the Messiah. The remaining one third will surely be those who accept him at his Second Coming.

What follows can be described only as a siege of Jerusalem. Having killed two thirds of the residents of Israel, apparently with little resistance, the attackers will succeed in conquering half of the holy city (see Zechariah 14:2). But that seems to be as far as they will get. In their frustration at what they thought would be an easy victory, the armies of evil will, predictably, turn to fighting among themselves:

> It shall come to pass in that day, that a great tumult from the Lord shall be among them; and they shall lay hold every one on the hand of his neighbour, and his hand shall rise up against the hand of his neighbour. (Zechariah 14:13)

The siege of Jerusalem will continue for forty-two months (see Revelation 11:2), yet their further conquest will be stymied by the direct intervention of the Lord in the form of two "witnesses":

> I will give power unto my two witnesses, and they shall prophesy a thousand two hundred and three score days [nearly three and a half years], clothed in sackcloth. (Revelation 11:3)

Note that the siege of Jerusalem will last for forty-two months, precisely the same time period as the two prophets will preach in Jerusalem.[11] This is surely more than coincidence, as it means that during the entire siege of Jerusalem, when the attackers are doing their best to destroy the last remaining Jews, they will be unable to do so, so long as the two prophets are alive and performing their work. Latter-day revelation gives us a little more information regarding these two witnesses:

> Q. What is to be understood by the two witnesses, in the eleventh chapter of Revelation? A. They are two prophets that are to be raised up to the Jewish nation in the last days, at the time of the restoration, and to prophesy to the Jews after they are gathered and have built the city of Jerusalem in the land of their fathers. (D&C 77:15)

The scriptures give us little information about the identities of these two prophets or where they will come from. For example, we don't know if they will rise out of the Jewish people themselves or if they will be representatives of The Church of Jesus Christ of Latter-day Saints. Nevertheless, they have received great attention from Bible scholars as they will play a central role in the events yet to come. John the Revelator, however, provides a great deal of information about how they will affect the outcome of the battle of Armageddon and the Second Coming of the Messiah.

As direct representatives from God, the two prophets will have enormous powers, even command over the elements:

> I will give power unto my two witnesses. . . . These have power to shut heaven, that it rain not in the days of their prophecy: and have power over waters to turn them to blood, and to smite the earth with all plagues, as often as they will. (Revelation 11:3, 6)

The power of these two prophets will then be directed at the anti-Christ and presumably against the massive army surrounding Jerusalem, for they will call down six of seven plagues. The plagues will make those who bear the mark of the beast receive a grievous sore. In addition, one third of the seas will become as blood, and one third of all sea life will die. A third part of the rivers will become as blood, and many will die due to the bitterness of the waters. One third of the sun, the moon, and the stars will be darkened. Men will be scorched with great heat and fire.[12] These calamities will apparently be part of the seventh seal prophesied by John and be called down by the Lord just prior to his Second Coming:[13]

> And the angel took the censer, and filled it with fire of the altar, and cast it into the earth: and there were voices, and thunderings, and lightnings, and an earthquake. And the seven angels which had the seven trumpets prepared themselves to sound.
>
> The first angel sounded, and there followed hail and fire mingled with blood, and they were cast upon the earth: and the third part of trees was burnt up, and all green grass was burnt up.
>
> And the second angel sounded, and as it were a great mountain burning with fire was cast into the sea: and the third part of the sea became blood; And the third part of the creatures which were in the sea, and had life, died; and the third part of the ships were destroyed.
>
> And the third angel sounded, and there fell a great star from heaven, burning as it were a lamp, and it fell upon the third part of the rivers, and upon the fountains of waters; And the name of the star is called Wormwood: and the third part of the waters became wormwood; and many men died of the waters, because they were made bitter.
>
> And the fourth angel sounded, and the third part of the sun was smitten, and the third part of the moon, and the third part of the stars; so as the third part of them was darkened, and the day shone not for a third part of it, and the night likewise. (Revelation 8:5–12; see also Revelation 16, which may be reiterations of the same events)

As might be expected, despite these calamities people won't repent but will continue to resist God and blaspheme him because of their misfortunes. It is likely that the bulk of humanity will not recognize the desolations that befall them as retribution from God:

> Men were scorched with great heat, and blasphemed the name of God, which hath power over these plagues: and they repented not to give him glory.
>
> And the fifth angel poured out his vial upon the seat of the beast; and his kingdom was full of darkness; and they gnawed their tongues for pain, And blasphemed the God of heaven because of their pains and their sores, and repented not of their deeds. (Revelation 16:9–11)

It is apparent that the two prophets will be instrumental in opposing the forces arrayed against what is left of Israel, for, as long as they preach, the forces of evil, despite their overwhelming size, will be held at bay. Eventually, however, the two will be killed, after which the evil forces will rejoice over their apparent victory, the troublesome prophets having at last been removed out of the way and the siege of Jerusalem being soon expected to end with Israel's defeat. As perhaps a gruesome symbol of impending victory, the bodies of the dead prophets will be left in the streets of Jerusalem for all to see:

> And when they shall have finished their testimony, the beast that ascendeth out of the bottomless pit shall make war against them, and shall overcome them, and kill them. And their dead bodies shall lie in the street of the great city, which spiritually is called Sodom and Egypt, where also our Lord was crucified. And they of the people and kindreds and tongues and nations shall see their dead bodies three days and an half, and shall not suffer their dead bodies to be put in graves. And they that dwell upon the earth shall rejoice over them, and make merry, and shall send gifts one to another;

> because these two prophets tormented them that dwelt on the earth. (Revelation 11:7–10)

At this pivotal time in the war, with the annihilation of the Jews virtually assured now that the two prophets' bodies lie in the streets of Jerusalem, the remainder of the now-greatly diminished Jewish nation will be huddled in the half of the city known as the Kidron Valley, also known as the Valley of Jehoshaphat, below the Mount of Olives. Preparing for their final victorious assault, the overwhelming army of the beast will, however, be amazed when the two prophets return to life—resurrected to join Jesus as he prepares to return to the earth:

> And after three days and an half the Spirit of life from God entered into them, and they stood upon their feet; and great fear fell upon them which saw them. And they heard a great voice from heaven saying unto them, Come up hither. And they ascended up to heaven in a cloud; and their enemies beheld them. (Revelation 11:11–12)

This miraculous occurrence will initiate a series of further events that will prepare the world for the Second Coming of Christ. The first will be a massive earthquake that will cause a tenth part of Jerusalem to fall and which will result in 7,000 deaths. Of course, the resurrection of the two prophets, their ascension into heaven, and the great earthquake will be a great conversion experience for many Jews, some of whom will finally give glory to God in heaven:

> And the same hour was there a great earthquake, and the tenth part of the city fell, and in the earthquake were slain of men seven thousand: and the remnant were affrighted, and gave glory to the God of heaven. (Revelation 11:13)

A second event that will take place has come to be known in Christianity as "the rapture," a time when, according to Christian tradition, the righteous who are still upon the earth will be taken to heaven to join Jesus at his Second Coming. In actuality, this event will constitute the first resurrection:

> For the Lord himself shall descend from heaven with a shout, with the voice of the archangel, and with the trump of God: and the dead in Christ shall rise first: Then we which are alive and remain shall be caught up together with them in the clouds, to meet the Lord in the air. (1 Thessalonians 4:16–17; see also D&C 88:96–98)

This great happening, however, will be only the beginning of the First Resurrection, for according to Bruce R. McConkie, a second portion of this resurrection, known as the "afternoon" of the First Resurrection will take place "after our Lord has ushered in the Millennium."[14]

Immediately thereafter, great tribulation and calamities will ensue, perhaps those described previously in this chapter, preparing humanity for the return of the Savior. It will also signal the end of the anti-Christ's reign, the siege of Jerusalem, and evil in the earth:

> The Lord shall cause his glorious voice to be heard, and shall shew the lighting down of his arm, with the indignation of his anger, and with the flame of a devouring fire, with scattering, and tempest, and hailstones. For through the voice of the Lord shall the Assyrian be beaten down, which smote with a rod. (Isaiah 30:30–31)

As discussed previously, only the righteous in the Church—those in the New Jerusalem in particular—will be protected during these three and a half years of turmoil upon the earth:

> Come, my people, enter thou into thy chambers, and shut thy doors about thee: hide thyself as it were for a little moment, until the indignation be overpast. For, behold, the Lord cometh out of his place to punish

> the inhabitants of the earth for their iniquity. (Isaiah 26:20–21; see also D&C 115:6; Revelation 18:4)

> Can you tell me where the people are who will be shielded and protected from these calamities and judgments which are even now at our doors? I'll tell you. The Priesthood of God who honor their priesthood, and who are worthy of their blessings are the only ones who shall have this safety and protection. No other people have a right to be shielded from these judgments. They are at our very doors; not even this people will escape them entirely. They will come down like the judgments of Sodom and Gomorrah. And none but the priesthood will be safe from their fury.[15]

> The redemption of Zion is the first step preparatory to the two last-named events. Just as soon as the Latter-day Saints are ready and prepared to return to Independence, Jackson County, Missouri, North America, just so soon will the voice of the Lord be heard, "Arise now, Israel, and make your way to the centre stake of Zion."[16]

Throughout our own country, one must simply try to visualize what conditions will be like prior to and during the battle of Armageddon. Joseph Smith clearly foresaw the degradation of humanity as this great conflict would get under way:

> The time is soon coming, when no man will have any peace, but in Zion and her stakes. I saw men hunting the lives of their own sons, and brother murdering brother, women killing their own daughters, and daughters seeking the lives of their mothers. I saw armies arrayed against armies. I saw blood, desolation, fires. The Son of Man has said that the mother shall be against the daughter, and the daughter against the mother. These things are at our doors.[17]

Drawing on past history, Orson Pratt similarly gave us a detailed glimpse of what we can expect:

> What then will be the condition of [the American] people, when this great and terrible war shall come? It will be very different from the war between the North and the South. Do you wish me to describe it? I will do so. It will be a war of neighborhood against neighborhood, city against city, town against town, county against county, state against state, and they will go forth destroying and being destroyed and manufacturing will, in a great measure, cease, for a time, among the American nation. Why? Because in these terrible wars, they will not be privileged to manufacture, there will be too much bloodshed—too much mobocracy—too much going forth in bands and destroying and pillaging the land to suffer people to pursue any local vocation with any degree of safety. What will become of millions of the farmers upon that land? They will leave their farms and they will remain uncultivated, and they will flee before the ravaging armies from place to place; and thus they will go forth burning and pillaging the whole country; and that great and powerful nation, now consisting of some forty millions of people, will be wasted away, unless they repent. . . .
>
> The Lord our God has already destroyed two great and powerful nations that once occupied the western hemisphere, because they fell into wickedness and would not repent. We have a record of this. The first nation he brought upon that hemisphere, were a people from the Tower of Babel. But the Lord made a decree, when he first led them forth to that land, that if they and their descendants should fall into wickedness, and would not repent, that he would visit them with utter destruction. He did so. About 600 years before Christ, that great nation was entirely swept off by the judgments of Almighty God, and their bones were

left bleaching upon the plains and mountains of that land—left unburied by the numerous armies that went forth slaying and being slain, and another colony was brought from Jerusalem in their stead, being a remnant of the tribe of Joseph.

The same decree was passed respecting one branch of that colony, that was made regarding the first nation. Said the Lord to them, "Inasmuch as you keep my commandments, you shall prosper in the land; but inasmuch as you keep not my commandments in the land, you shall be destroyed from the face thereof." That was literally fulfilled. After living upon that land till nearly the close of the fourth century of the Christian era, they fell into wickedness and were destroyed, with the exceptions of a few who went over to the opposite army.

And the Lord also made a similar decree, recorded, too, in the same book, in regard to the present great populous nation called the people of the United States. They must perish, unless they repent. They will be wasted away, and the fullness of the wrath of Almighty God will be poured out upon them, unless they repent. Their cities will be left desolate. A time is coming when the great and populous city of New York—the greatest city of the American republic, will be left without inhabitants. The houses will stand, some of them, not all. They will stand there, but unoccupied, no people to inherit them.

It will be the same in regard to numerous other cities, or, in the words of the Lord, "I will throw down all your strongholds, and I will execute vengeance and fury upon them, even as upon the heathen, such as they have not heard." It will all be fulfilled. But there will be a remnant who will be spared. It will be those who will repent of their sins; it will be those who believe in the Lord Jesus Christ and are willing to obey his commandments, willing to hearken to his voice, willing to be baptized for the remission of

> their sins, willing to be born of the spirit, or receive the Holy Ghost, by the laying on of hands, willing to walk uprightly and honestly with all men, and justly with one another.
>
> These and these only will be spared, for it is the decree of Jehovah, and this is not all. We have thus far, only told you that which will take place . . . upon the people of the United States. But great tribulations will also be among all the nations of the earth, who will not repent. They will be wasted with various judgments; but the heathen will be spared longer than these gentile nations who have had the scriptures in their midst, but would not obey them.[18]

Throughout the three-and-a-half-year period leading up to the battle of Armageddon, two things will undoubtedly occur that it will be well to keep in mind. We have alluded to both, but they bear repeating in order to obtain a true sense of what will happen on a personal level. The first—as with nearly all wars and periods of massive disaster—will be refugee migrations, people fleeing from the fighting. This means that as conditions in urban areas deteriorate, with mobs roaming about looting and killing, and law and order breaking down, literally tens of millions will leave the cities and seek safety elsewhere.

This will be the case throughout the world, including in the United States. The heavily populated coastal masses of people in this country will move in huge waves inland, away from urban turmoil. People on the West Coast will drive eastward to Idaho, Utah, Wyoming, Arizona, and New Mexico. A mass displacement of people will occur—of families seeking refuge and safety—descending by the thousands into the less populated western states.

At the same time, the millions living in the densely populated eastern portion of the country will push westward into the Midwest, to the Dakotas and the Great Plains states, as far southward as Texas and Oklahoma. Residents of these inland states will find themselves surrounded by great encampments of fearful and desperate refugees. How inland dwellers will cope with this influx and what conditions they will create remains to be seen.

An unfortunate dilemma of these mass movements, however, will be the fact that the degradation and predatory nature of much of our society will follow them. Mobs, pillagers, and gangs will move inland as well, victimizing anyone they can for food, spoils, rape, or the sheer fun of it.

The second certain occurrence will be a similar mass migration of Latter-day Saints seeking refuge and safety for themselves and their families in Jackson County, Missouri, the New Jerusalem and new headquarters of the Church. They may do so possibly in spite of counsel from the General Authorities of the Church that Latter-day Saints are to remain in their wards and stakes and that they will have safety there. Not all will be allowed into the New Jerusalem, but it is assured that tens of thousands will nevertheless crowd as near as they can to the prophet and General Authorities. Jackson County's population will quickly swell to hundreds of thousands of Latter-day Saints who hope somehow to find shelter from the increasing evil in the world around them.

The same may well happen to Salt Lake City, the traditional headquarters of the Church. The relative isolation and perceived security of the Salt Lake Valley will have the same magnetic attraction for many as a place away from the turmoil and ugliness of the rest of the world when society falls apart and war looms. However, they will encounter tens of thousands of Californians who will also see the Salt Lake Valley as a refuge from the violence and lawlessness of San Francisco and Los Angeles.

What we will have, then, will be a nation and a world of turmoil and violence as millions mill about seeking safety from the other millions who, under the influence of Satan and the anti-Christ, will seek to wantonly destroy what little good there is left in the world. At that point, and as the great armies of the beast surround Jerusalem, the only thing that can bring an end to a world gone mad will be the Savior himself.

Notes

1. Brigham Young, in *Journal of Discourses,* 8:123–24.

2. *Wilford Woodruff: History of His Life and Labors as Recorded in His Daily Journals,* comp. Matthias F. Cowley (Salt Lake City: Deseret News, 1909), 511–12.

3. Orson Pratt, in *Journal of Discourses,* 18:65.

4. Orson Pratt, in *Journal of Discourses,* 7:188–89.

5. Orson Pratt, in *Journal of Discourses,* 15:337.

6. Hal Lindsey and C. C. Carlson, *The Late Great Planet Earth* (New York: Bantam Books, 1970), 64.

7. These ideas are based on Ezekiel 38 and *The Harper Bible Atlas,* 92–93. See also www.*ldslastdays.com.*

8. John prophesied of seven, then eight, then ten kings who will be allied with the beast in the great battle to come:

"And there are seven kings: five are fallen, and one is, and the other is not yet come; and when he cometh, he must continue a short space. And the beast that was, and is not, even he is the eighth, and is of the seven, and goeth into perdition. And the ten horns which thou sawest are ten kings, which have received no kingdom as yet; but receive power as kings one hour with the beast. These have one mind, and shall give their power and strength unto the beast. These shall make war with the Lamb" (Revelation 17:10–14).

9. Bruce R. McConkie, *Mormon Doctrine,* 2d ed. (Salt Lake City: Bookcraft, 1966), 827.

10. Bruce R. McConkie, *Doctrinal New Testament Commentary* (Salt Lake City: Bookcraft, 1965–73), 3:502–3.

11 . In addition, "forty and two months" is also the duration of the anti-Christ's reign.

12. Although these events may be called miracles at the hands of the two prophets, they could well fit the description of some of the natural calamities described in chapter 6.

13. The timing of earthquakes during this period is a good example of the obscurity inherent in John's writings. He mentions earthquakes and other calamities several times: at the end of the sixth seal (Revelation 6:12), at the beginning of the seventh seal (8:5), and at the second coming of Christ (16:18). But it is unclear whether these are separate earthquakes or if he is describing the same one more than once. An increase in such calamitous events during or near the days of the anti-Christ, however, seems plausible because this would dovetail well with signs of the times discussed in chapter 4.

14. McConkie, *Mormon Doctrine,* 640.

15. Wilford Woodruff, *The Young Woman's Journal,* 5:512–13.

16. Brigham Young, in *Journal of Discourses,* 9:136.

17. Joseph Smith, *Teachings of the Prophet Joseph Smith,* ed. Joseph Fielding Smith (Salt Lake City: Deseret Book, 1976), 160–61.

18. Orson Pratt, in *Journal of Discourses,* 20:151–53.

9

The Second Coming of the Messiah

This lengthy dissertation by Parley P. Pratt, which was approved by Joseph Smith Jr. and Joseph Fielding Smith, summarizes well the conclusion of the battle of Armageddon, the Savior's return to the earth, and the final acknowledgment of the Jews that he is, in fact, their long-awaited Messiah, the one whom their forefathers rejected long ago and watched die on the cross.

> While they [the armies of Gog] are at the point to swallow up the Jews, and lay waste their country, behold the Lord's fury comes up in his face, a mighty earthquake is the result, insomuch that the fishes of the sea, and the fowls of the air, and all the creeping things, and all men upon the face of the earth, shall shake at his presence, and every wall shall fall to the ground, and every man's sword shall be turned against his neighbour in this army, and the Lord shall rain upon him, and upon his bands, and upon the many people that are with him, an overflowing rain, great hailstones, fire, and brimstone. And thus he will magnify himself, and sanctify himself, in the eyes of many nations, and they shall know that he is the Lord; thus they shall fall upon the open field, upon the mountains of Israel, even Gog and all his army, horses and horsemen. . . .
>
> "And I will set my glory among the heathen, and all the heathen shall see my judgment that I have

executed, and my hand that I have laid upon them; so the House of Israel shall know that I am the Lord their God, from that day and forward. And the heathen shall know that the House of Israel went into captivity for their iniquity, because they trespassed against me; therefore I hid my face from them, and gave them into the hand of their enemies. . . . When I have brought them again from the people, and gathered them out of their enemy's lands, and am sanctified in them, in the eyes of many nations; then shall they know that I am the Lord their God, who caused them to be led into captivity among the heathen; but I have gathered them into their own land, and left none of them any more there; neither will I hide my face any more from them, for I have poured out my spirit upon the whole House of Israel, saith the Lord God." . . .

Whoever will look into this subject, will find that Ezekiel has here described scenes very nearly connected with the coming of Christ; indeed, Zechariah, in his fourteenth chapter, has told us much, concerning the same great battle and overthrow of Gog and his army, and he has said in plain words, that the Lord should come at the very time of the overthrow of that army; yes, in fact, while they are in the act of taking Jerusalem, and have already succeeded in taking one half of the city, and spoiling their houses, and ravishing their women. Then behold their long expected Messiah, suddenly standing his feet upon the Mount of Olives, a little east of Jerusalem, to fight against those nations and deliver the Jews in the midst of the great shaking, which Ezekiel describes, when everything should shake at his presence, Zechariah says, "the Mount of Olives shall cleave in twain, from east to west, and one-half of the mountain removes to the north, while the other half falls off to the south," suddenly forming a very great valley, into which the Jews shall flee for protection from their enemies. . . .

While the Lord cometh with all his saints with

> him; then will the Jews behold that long, long expected Messiah, coming in power to their deliverance, as they always looked for him. He destroys their enemies, and delivers them from trouble, at the very time they were in the utmost consternation, and about to be swallowed up by their enemies. But what is their astonishment, when as they are about to fall at the feet of their Deliverer, and acknowledge him their Messiah, they discover the wounds which once pierced his hands and feet and side, and on inquiry at once recognize Jesus of Nazareth, the King of the Jews, the man so long rejected.[1]

Preparation for the Second Coming

As the nation of Israel is on the verge of collapse and Jerusalem is surrounded—under siege by the massive heathen army bent on destroying it—and as the two prophets prophesy in the city, the climax of the ancient war between Satan and the Lord that began in the premortal existence will be at hand. But the outcome won't turn on the military might of either side but on the direct intervention of the Lord himself.

We would do well to remind ourselves, however, that it will be a predominantly wicked world, not a righteous one, that will exist before the return of Christ. Despite that fact, God will make one last effort to reach out to the kingdom of the anti-Christ to convince his followers of the divinity of the Savior: "And thou shalt come up against my people of Israel, as a cloud to cover the land; it shall be in the latter days, and I will bring thee against my land, that the heathen may know me, when I shall be sanctified in thee, O Gog, before their eyes" (Ezekiel 38:16).

In this last great effort—after the battle of Armageddon and the conversion of the Jews—those nations will be permitted to more fully recognize Christ as the true and only God:[2]

> It is because of this—the light the nations have in their midst, which they will not receive—that the Lord will visit them first; and when he has visited and

> overthrown them, he will lay his hand heavily upon the heathen nations in Asia, and also those who are in Africa, and they will be visited with severe judgment, but they will not be utterly destroyed. A portion of the heathen nations will be redeemed. Why? They will see the power and glory of God that will be manifested among the tribes of Israel, who will be gathered out from their midst and return to their own land.
>
> They will see the glory of God manifested as in ancient times and they will say, "Surely Jaggernaut is no longer my god." "Surely I will not worship crocodiles, nor serpents; neither will I worship the sun, or the moon, and there is a god manifested among that people, Israel, who is worthy of the natures and attributes of a god. I will cast my gods to the moles and bats, and I will worship the God of Israel."
>
> Then will be fulfilled that which was spoken by the prophet Ezekiel, "then shall the heathen know that I the Lord am God." And it will come to pass, after that period, when Jesus shall have raised all the righteous from their graves, that he will descend with all the hosts of heaven accompanying him, and will stand upon the Mount of Olives, and he will go out of Jerusalem, and the Jews will go out to the mount to meet him and will acknowledge him as their Messiah and King; and then it shall come to pass, that the heathen nations will also more fully recognize him as the true and only God.[3]

To end the great war, numerous events will take place, most of which are included, as far as can be determined from the scriptures, at the opening of the sixth and seventh seals of the book of Revelation and in many other prophetic pronouncements over the millennia. These events, or calamities and tribulations, may come at the hands of the two prophets in Jerusalem prior to their deaths or directly from the Lord himself. The scriptures aren't clear in this respect, but we know that they will take place.

It is inevitable, however, that most of those who experience them won't recognize or acknowledge from whence they come. Despite great suffering and death from the invading army—whose soldiers will also fight among themselves—and from afflictions endured throughout the world, people will continue to wreak havoc among themselves and blaspheme God even as they are being decimated. Satan, the anti-Christ, and the great and abominable church will have such a stranglehold on the world that the bulk of humanity would rather suffer and die than turn to God. Thus, the great winnowing process will sift throughout humanity, separating the wicked from the righteous.

The tribulations that will descend on humanity before Christ's Second Coming will be of many kinds and, on occasion, will be repeated as humanity continues to resist repentance and acknowledgment of the truth. Among them will be scourges, earthquakes, the darkening of the sun and other heavenly bodies, the disappearance of the rainbow—the sign given to Noah after the great flood—rainstorms, hailstorms, fire, brimstone, thunders, lightnings, plagues of flies, and so forth. The punishments that will befall the unrepentant are summarized in the Doctrine and Covenants:

> Behold, I say unto you that before this great day shall come the sun shall be darkened, and the moon shall be turned into blood, and the stars shall fall from heaven, and there shall be greater signs in heaven above and in the earth beneath;
>
> And there shall be weeping and wailing among the hosts of men; And there shall be a great hailstorm sent forth to destroy the crops of the earth.
>
> And it shall come to pass, because of the wickedness of the world, that I will take vengeance upon the wicked, for they will not repent; for the cup of mine indignation is full; for behold, my blood shall not cleanse them if they hear me not. Wherefore, I the Lord God will send forth flies upon the face of the earth, which shall take hold of the inhabitants thereof, and shall eat their flesh, and shall cause maggots to come in upon them; And their tongues shall be stayed that they shall not utter against me; and their flesh

> shall fall from off their bones, and their eyes from their sockets; And it shall come to pass that the beasts of the forest and the fowls of the air shall devour them up. (D&C 29:14–20)

It has been the propensity of man, ever since the time of Adam, to revile against God when man's affairs don't go as well as he thinks they should. We have noted that the history of the human race is one of ups and downs, human cycles from plateaus of righteousness and prosperity to increasing arrogance and unrighteousness, leading to the withdrawal of the Lord's Spirit and blessings, and thence to lowlands of chastisement and difficulties, to be again followed by periods of repentance leading back to plateaus of righteousness and prosperity. And so forth.

But during those times when man has declined and the Lord has wreaked punishment on him for his unrighteousness, man often fails to recognize that the reason for his problems lies with himself because of his falling out of favor with God.

Throughout history, whenever nations or peoples have experienced hard times, they fail to recognize the hand of God and his punishment in their travails, but instead look for any number of other reasons why things don't go well for them. Certainly, those few who survived the destruction of Sodom and Gomorrah looked to aberrations in the natural world in which they were living as reasons for their suffering. Likewise, for many who looked back on the Flood at the time of Noah. They too certainly attributed the forty days of rain to a freak occurrence of nature.

It is certain that, although they may have regarded God as the source of their bad fortune, they didn't look to themselves as the reason why God did what he did. Even today, we look at calamities as the result of natural causes—Hurricane Katrina or Hurricane Rita—not God. The destruction of Sodom and Gomorrah may well have resulted from volcanism, earthquakes, or other similar natural events. The great Flood was perhaps the result of shifts in weather patterns that temporarily moved unusually rainy weather into an otherwise arid portion of the world. We can't ignore, however, that such natural disasters may well have occurred at the hand of God. He understands the natural systems that make our world work, and he can tweak them at any time and in any way he wishes.

The likelihood exists, therefore, that when men suffer and die during the calamities prior to the coming of the Savior—from flies, plagues, floods, earthquakes, fire, and the like—they will still fail or be unwilling to recognize the hand of God in what is happening to them and their world. Even more so, they will be blind to the fact that it is their own wickedness and unrighteousness that is to blame for their suffering. They will be so bound, as many are today, by the irrational workings of Satan that they will undoubtedly attribute their tribulations and misfortune to bad luck, nature running amok, or whatever.

Combine this with the fact that when men encounter misfortune, they often become defensive and rail against whatever has caused their problems. This will surely be the case with the tens of millions who will suffer and die in the calamities of the last days, as was so long ago foretold in the scriptures. Men will be in pain, suffer, and die, all the while looking desperately about for whatever they can find to blame for their misfortunes. If they do finally see the hand of God as the cause, they will turn even more against him, blaspheming and cursing him for their pain. Few will realize that if they would only humble themselves, repent, and turn against the evil surrounding them they might be spared.

By and large, however, that won't be the case, and the vast majority of humanity will die. The abomination of desolation will run its course. One calamity after another will descend on the earth until, together with the toll taken by the battle of Armageddon and other raging conflicts, wickedness is finally eradicated from the face of the earth:

> I do think that one form or another of chastisement will follow, with its seasons for repentance, for the preaching of the gospel, and crying to the nations of the earth: "Will you now listen to the Lord?" And if they shall not listen, then another affliction will come, until men shall either repent, or they shall perish. For these are the last days, the days preceding the coming of the Redeemer, and he will not come when the wicked stand and flourish.[4]

> For a desolating scourge shall go forth among the inhabitants of the earth, and shall continue to be poured out from time to time, if they repent not, until the earth is empty, and the inhabitants thereof are consumed away and utterly destroyed by the brightness of my coming. (D&C 5:19)

In summary, the world will be in absolute chaos during the forty-two months of the anti-Christ's reign, during which time the two prophets will preach repentance in Jerusalem. Conflicts will rage everywhere, anarchy will prevail, and any semblance of law and order will be an artifact of the past. As a result, billions throughout the world will suffer and lose their lives to war, famine, disease, and other natural causes. The battle of Armageddon will provoke further insanity and global turmoil, and millions will suffer and die. At the same time, the Lord will rebuke the unrepentant on the earth with repeated plagues and calamities in which additional millions will perish.

Near the conclusion of the forty-two months, the two prophets in Jerusalem will be killed, preparing the way for the Savior himself to return to the earth and to deal a final fatal blow to evil—vanquishing Satan, the anti-Christ, and the great and abominable church.

But what about the righteous, the truly faithful members of the Church who will be living in a world gone mad, with destruction, carnage, and death occurring everywhere? Many of the world's great cities will be turned to rubble, turned into ghost cities ruled by the lawless, by gangs bent only on killing, looting, and keeping themselves alive. Any semblance of civilization will be gone. There will be no law, no newspapers or television, little food, no hospitals, no schools. "The devil will have power over his dominion" (D&C 1:35). For their own survival, those still alive will be forced to live in seclusion and hiding, barely able to exist.

Throughout all of this, however, we are promised that the righteous, or at least the body of the Church, will be protected in its stakes and wards as well as in the New Jerusalem: "Nevertheless, Zion shall escape, if she observe to do all things whatsoever I have commanded her" (D&C 99:25).

> A time will come in the midst of this people when a desolating scourge will pass through our ranks, and the destroying angel will be in our midst as he was in Egypt when he slew all the firstborn of the Egyptians. God says, "The destroying angel shall pass by" and shall not harm you if you will observe to do these things.[5]

Among all the calamities humanity will experience at this crucial point in time, and immediately prior to Christ's personal intervention at his Second Coming, two final events will take place, as foretold in the scriptures—the disappearance of the rainbow and the darkening of the sun. The first of these, the disappearance of the rainbow, although taking place prior to Christ's Second Coming, may well occur at any time during the forty-two months of the reign of the anti-Christ:

> I have asked the Lord concerning his coming; and while asking the Lord, he gave a sign and said, "In the days of Noah I set a bow in the heavens as a sign and token that in any year that the bow should be seen the Lord would not come; but there should be seed time and harvest during that year; but whenever you see the bow withdrawn, it shall be a token that there shall be famine, pestilence, and great distress among the nations, and that the coming of the Messiah is not far distant."[6]

The second sign—one that will happen immediately before the Second Coming—will be the darkening of the sun:[7] "No man will see the sign of the Son of Man until after the sun is darkened and the moon has turned to blood. The prophet on the earth at that time will identify the sign."[8]

President Smith cautioned that men, still unrepentant, will attribute this apparently obvious sign of the Second Coming to natural phenomena, such as a comet or meteor. As Joseph Fielding Smith observed, when commenting on the signs that would occur prior to the Second Coming, "The sun has not yet been darkened. We are informed that this will be one of the last acts preceding the coming of the Lord."[9]

At that point, the world will experience the end of the battle of Armageddon and the war between good and evil on the earth concurrent with the Second Coming of the Messiah: "After the abomination of desolation is again fulfilled and the powers of heaven have shaken, then shall appear the sign of the Son of Man in heaven and then Christ's coming in glory" (JS–Matthew 1:32–36).

The Second Coming

> After your testimony cometh the testimony of earthquakes, that shall cause groanings in the midst of her, and men shall fall upon the ground and shall not be able to stand. And also cometh the testimony of the voice of thunderings, and the voice of lightnings, and the voice of tempests, and the voice of the waves of the sea heaving themselves beyond their bounds. And all things shall be in commotion; and surely, men's hearts shall fail them; for fear shall come upon all people.
>
> And angels shall fly through the midst of heaven, crying with a loud voice, sounding the trump of God, saying: Prepare ye, prepare ye, O inhabitants of the earth; for the judgment of our God is come. Behold, and lo, the Bridegroom cometh; go ye out to meet him. And immediately there shall appear a great sign in heaven, and all people shall see it together.
>
> And another angel shall sound his trump, saying: That great church, the mother of abominations, that made all nations drink of the wine of the wrath of her fornication, that persecuteth the saints of God, that shed their blood—she who sitteth upon many waters, and upon the islands of the sea—behold, she is the tares of the earth; she is bound in bundles; her bands are made strong, no man loose them; therefore, she is ready to be burned. And he shall sound his trump both long and loud, and all nations shall hear it.
>
> And there shall be silence in heaven for the space of half an hour; and immediately after shall the curtain

> of heaven be unfolded, as a scroll is unfolded after it is rolled up, and the face of the Lord shall be unveiled. (D&C 88:89–95)

When the city of Jerusalem is under siege, surrounded by an overwhelming army of evil but yet unconquered, when men throughout the world have suffered and died under endless plagues and calamities, when the sun will be darkened and the moon turned to blood, at that point will occur the greatest event in the history of humanity—the Second Coming of the Messiah.

His coming will determine not only the outcome of the war of Armageddon but the ultimate destiny of good and evil throughout the earth. But there is a great deal more to the Second Coming of the Savior than traditional Christianity has been led to believe. His arrival, as described in the verses above, will be only one of several appearances he will make preparatory to beginning his millennial reign on the earth.

It has been revealed through modern prophets that besides his coming in the Holy Land, which is the traditional Christian belief, he will appear in at least several places more—in the New Jerusalem, Missouri, and at Adam-ondi-Ahman.[10] This latter appearance will occur prior to his appearance in the Holy Land: "Jesus is coming here as well as to many other places. When the New Jerusalem is built on this land, Jesus will visit that city. . . . Zion will be favored with the presence of the Lord before the Jews are permitted to behold him. The Lord will come to the temple of Zion before he comes to the temple at Jerusalem."[11]

This first appearance at Adam-ondi-Ahman will also feature an appearance by Adam (see Daniel 7:21; D&C 116:1) and will occur at a great council of the then-existing Church authorities with the Savior and with Father Adam as well as with many heavenly beings. It will be unknown, however, to the rest of humanity. As Charles W. Penrose said, "[The people of the New Jerusalem will receive from the Savior] further instructions for the development and beautifying of Zion and for the extension and sure stability of his kingdom."[12]

Robert L. Millett, Dean Emeritus of Religious Education at Brigham Young University, has provided remarkably more details into this historic event, which will be one of the greatest meetings to be held in humanity's history:

> The Lord will make an appearance at Adam-ondi-Ahman, "the place where Adam shall come to visit his people, or the Ancient of Days shall sit" (see D&C 116). This grand council will be a large sacrament meeting, a time when the Son of Man will partake of the fruit of the vine once more with his earthly friends. And who will be in attendance? The revelations specify Moroni, Elias, John the Baptist, Elijah, Abraham, Isaac, Jacob, Joseph, Adam, Peter, James, and John, "and also," the Savior clarifies, "all those whom my father hath given me out of the world" (see D&C 27:5–14), multitudes of faithful saints from the beginning of time to the end.
>
> This will be a private appearance in that it will be unknown to the world. It will be a leadership meeting, a time of accounting, an accounting for priesthood stewardships. The prophet Joseph Smith explained that Adam, the Ancient of Days, "will call his children together and hold a council with them to prepare them for the coming of the Son of Man. He (Adam) is the father of the human family, and presides over the spirits of all men, and all that have had the keys must stand before him in this grand council. . . . The Son of Man stands before him, and there is given him [Christ] glory and dominion. Adam delivers up his stewardship to Christ, that which was delivered to him as holding the keys of the universe, but retains his standing as head of the human family."
>
> President Joseph Fielding Smith observed: "This gathering of the children of Adam, where the thousands, and the tens of thousands, are assembled in the judgment, will be one of the greatest events this troubled earth has ever seen. At this conference, or council, all who have held keys of dispensations will render a report of their stewardship. . . . We do

> not know how long a time this gathering will be in session, or how many sessions will be held at this grand council. It is sufficient to know that it is a gathering of the priesthood of God from the beginning of this earth down to the present, in which reports will be made and all who have been given dispensations (talents) will declare their keys and ministry and make a report of their stewardship . . . Judgment will be rendered unto them for this is a gathering of the righteous. . . . It is not to be a judgment of the wicked. . . . This will precede the great day of destruction of the wicked and will be the preparation for the millennial reign."
>
> Elder Bruce R. McConkie has likewise written: "Every prophet, apostle, president, bishop, elder, or Church officer of whatever degree—all who have held keys shall stand before him who holds all the keys. They will then be called upon to give an account of their stewardships and to report how and in what manner they have used their priesthood and their keys for the salvation of men within the sphere of their appointments. . . . There will be a great hierarchy of judges in that great day, of whom Adam, under Christ, will be the chief of all. Those judges will judge the righteous ones under their jurisdiction, but Christ himself, he alone, will judge the wicked."[13]

Shortly after his appearance at this council and in the New Jerusalem, the Savior will make his long awaited Second Coming in the Holy Land. Christianity has looked forward to this event for centuries, and it will take place much as described in the Bible:

> His next appearance will be among the distressed and nearly vanquished sons of Judah. At the crisis of their fate, when the hostile troops of several nations are ravaging the city and all the horrors of war are overwhelming the people of Jerusalem, he will set his feet upon the Mount of Olives, which will cleave and part asunder at his touch. Attended by a host from

> heaven, he will overthrow and destroy the combined armies of the Gentiles, and appear to the worshipping Jews as the mighty deliverer and conqueror so long expected by their race.[14]

The coming of the Lord to old Jerusalem, although ultimately glorious, will apparently begin obscurely but will increase in crescendo until it will be unmistakable to the righteous of the world:

> He [the Apostle Matthew] says then shall they see the sign of the coming of the Son of Man in the clouds of heaven. How are we to see it? As lighting up of the morning or the dawning of the morning cometh from the east and shineth unto the west—So also is the coming of the Son of Man. The dawning of the morning makes its appearance in the east and moves along gradually, so also will the coming of the Son of Man be. It will be small at its first appearance and gradually becomes larger until every eye can see it. Shall the saints understand it? Oh yes. Shall the wicked understand? Oh no. They attribute it to a natural cause. . . . It will be small at first and will grow larger and larger until it will be in a blaze so that every eye can see it.[15]

It would appear, then, that instead of somehow appearing to the entire earth at one time, the Lord's coming will occur at a fixed point in space and will appear beginning in the east, moving and becoming clearer and more glorious toward the west as the earth rotates—the same as the rising of the sun in the east and its setting in the west that we are accustomed to. If this is the case, Jesus' Second Coming may take twenty-four hours before it is seen around the entire earth.

Regardless of how the event unfolds, however, it will be unmistakable to those who recognize it for what it is. But for much of the world, still embroiled in evil and turmoil, it may be difficult to perceive the enormous heavenly event that is unfolding.

Nevertheless, as Jesus himself proclaimed, "They shall see

the Son of man coming in the clouds of heaven with power and great glory. And he shall send his angels with a great sound of a trumpet" (Matthew 24:30–31). Furthermore, as the Apostle Paul declared, "The Lord Jesus shall be revealed from heaven with his mighty angels, in flaming fire taking vengeance on them that know not God, and that obey not the gospel of our Lord Jesus Christ" (2 Thessalonians 1:7–8).

Ultimately, for those who continue to refuse or can't recognize the returning Christ for who he is, his Second Coming will present an unwelcome scenario:

> He comes! The earth shakes, and the tall mountains tremble, the mighty deep rolls back to the north as in fear, and the rent skies glow like molten brass. He comes! The dead saints burst forth from their tombs, and "those who are alive and remain" are "caught up" with them to meet him. The ungodly rush to hide themselves from his presence, and call upon the quivering rocks to cover them. He comes! With all the hosts of the righteous glorified. The breath of his lips strikes death to the wicked. His glory is a consuming fire. The proud and rebellious are as stubble; they are burned and "left neither root nor branch." He sweeps the earth "as with the besom of destruction." He deluges the earth with the fiery floods of his wrath, and the filthiness and abominations of the world are consumed.[16]

Symbolizing victory, Jesus will arrive upon the earth this second time clothed in red:

> Red is symbolic of victory—victory over the devil, death, hell, and endless torment. It is the symbol of salvation, of being placed beyond the power of all one's enemies. Christ's red apparel will also symbolize both aspects of his ministry to fallen humanity—his mercy and his justice. . . . He has descended below all things and mercifully taken upon him our stains, our blood,

> our sins. In addition, he comes in "dyed garments" as the God of justice, even he who has trampled the wicked beneath his feet. "And the Lord shall be red in his apparel, and his garments like him that treadeth in the wine vat." (D&C 133:48)[17]

It would seem that the return of the Savior will be unmistakable because of the brightness and glory of his coming, accompanied, as he will be, by angels and resurrected beings. In addition, the scriptures are emphatic in declaring that his appearance will be heralded loudly and that all flesh will see or hear him: "And the glory of the Lord shall be revealed, and all flesh shall see it together: for the mouth of the Lord hath spoken it" (Isaiah 40:5; see also Isaiah 30:30; Matthew 24:30; JS–Matthew 1:36). "And it shall be a voice as the voice of many waters, and as the voice of a great thunder" (D&C 133:22). "The Lord also shall roar out of Zion, and utter his voice from Jerusalem" (Joel 3:16). "And his voice shall be heard" (D&C 133:50; see also D&C 45:49).

It is apparent that many of the scriptures, ancient and modern, which speak of the signs of the times, describe events that will happen immediately prior to and after the Second Coming of the Lord. Many, however, have traditionally been interpreted to mean that they will take place long before the Second Coming, but it is much more realistic to apply them to the great destructions that will occur as Jesus makes his arrival on the earth.

We do know from the scriptures that certain catastrophic events will take place as soon as the Lord sets his feet on the Mount of Olives. Among those events, which may also be termed "the wrath of God," will be a massive earthquake, phenomena in the heavens, a great hailstorm, thunders, lightnings, tempests, rainstorms, fire, plagues of flies, brimstone, and great disturbances of the seas. Also taking place at that great moment, or shortly thereafter, will be two other significant events, although they don't fall under the label "wrath of God." These will be the conversion of the Jews and water issuing from under the temple in Jerusalem.[18]

Truly calamitous events will mark the end of the battle of Armageddon and of evil upon the earth:

> The noise of a multitude in the mountains, like as of a great people; a tumultuous noise of the kingdoms of nations gathered together: the Lord of hosts mustereth the host of the battle. They come from a far country, from the end of heaven, even the Lord, and the weapons of his indignation, to destroy the whole land. Howl ye; for the day of the Lord is at hand; it shall come as a destruction from the Almighty.
>
> Therefore shall all hands be faint, and every man's heart shall melt: And they shall be afraid: pangs and sorrows shall take hold of them; they shall be in pain as a woman that travaileth: they shall be amazed one at another; their faces shall be as flames. Behold, the day of the Lord cometh, cruel both with wrath and fierce anger, to lay the land desolate: and he shall destroy the sinners thereof out of it. (Isaiah 13:4–9)

Israel will be saved from the invaders surrounding what is left of Jerusalem, for the massive army laying siege to the holy city will be destroyed. Likewise, all of Satan's followers—most of those then still alive in the world, the anti-Christ and his regimes, and the great and abominable church—will be destroyed: "Calamity shall cover the mocker, and the scorner shall be consumed; and they that have watched for iniquity shall be hewn down and cast into the fire" (D&C 45:50). "For by fire and by his sword will the Lord plead with all flesh: and the slain of the Lord shall be many" (Isaiah 66:16).

The first and most meaningful calamity that will take place will be a massive earthquake, the likes of which humanity has never experienced:

> Then shall the Lord go forth, and fight against those nations, as when he fought in the day of battle. And his feet shall stand in that day upon the mount of Olives, which is before Jerusalem on the east, and the mount of Olives shall cleave in the midst thereof toward the east and toward the west, and there shall be a very great valley; and half of the mountain shall

> remove toward the north, and half of it toward the south. (Zechariah 14:3–4)
>
> And there was a great earthquake, such as was not since men were upon the earth, so mighty an earthquake, and so great. And the great city was divided into three parts, and the cities of the nations fell: and great Babylon [the heathen world] came in remembrance before God, to give unto her the cup of the wine of the fierceness of his wrath. And every island fled away, and the mountains were not found. (Revelation 16:18–20; see also Ezekiel 38:18–20; D&C 45:47–50; 49:23; 88:87)

It is apparent that this earthquake, although centered in Jerusalem, will affect nearly the entire globe, or that it will spawn other widespread earthquakes, causing major changes in the earth's surface. For example, "Every island fled away, and the mountains were not found" (Revelation 16:20). The former of these two effects may be attributable to simultaneous great disturbances in the seas, such as tsunamis or tidal waves, but the end result will be the same. The surface of the earth will be greatly restructured from what we are now familiar with[19] and much of humanity will die.

As noted previously, much of man's civilization has historically been concentrated in coastal areas, precisely where tidal waves will strike, just as the great tsunami disaster around the Indian Ocean demonstrated in late 2004. That calamity, which resulted from shifting tectonic plates, caused an earthquake west of the island of Indonesia and spread devastation and loss of life a thousand miles in every direction, including as far away as the east coast of Africa.

Of course, besides earthquakes might well come renewed and accelerated volcanic activity throughout the world, particularly around the Pacific Rim and Southeast Asia, which are already active volcanic regions. These events alone would account for prophecies about fire and brimstone: "I will plead against him with pestilence and with blood; and I will rain upon him, and upon his bands, and upon the many people that are with him, an overflowing rain, and great hailstones, fire, and brimstone" (Ezekiel 38:22).[20]

These events will be unprecedented in earth's geologic history. If the words of John the Revelator can be taken literally, the earth's surface will ultimately be left flat with no mountains or islands to be found. In other words, the globe will be left with only the great oceans and seas we now have and flat continents. The long-term implications of these changes are enormous. They will mean worldwide shifts in climatic patterns, waterways, and sea levels, with subsequent changes in agriculture, ecological systems, and human habitation. And, of course, many of the world's great cities will be flattened, as "every wall shall fall to the ground" (Ezekiel 38:20) and become uninhabitable rubble.

Accompanying this earthquake, or shortly following it, there will occur a pestilence of flies and great storms, which will include thunders, lightnings, tempests (windstorms), rainstorms, and at least one particularly horrendous hailstorm:

> And also cometh the testimony of the voice of thunderings, and the voice of lightnings, and the voice of tempests, and the voice of the waves of the sea heaving themselves beyond their bounds. And all things shall be in commotion; and surely, men's hearts will fail them; for fear shall come upon all people. (D&C 88:90–91)

> And there fell upon men a great hail out of heaven, every stone about the weight of a talent [seventy-five pounds]: and men blasphemed God because of the plague of the hail; for the plague thereof was exceeding great. (Revelation 16:21; see also D&C 29:16)[21]

What little is left of civilization after the earthquakes will obviously be further decimated by these great storms. Millions will die as a result, and not only will seventy-five-pound hailstones destroy them but all agriculture will cease (D&C 29:16). These worldwide calamities will certainly include hurricanes, tornadoes, and destructive thunderstorms. Indeed, the wrath of God will be poured out upon the whole earth until only the righteous few remain alive.

Other phenomena associated with Jesus' descent to the earth

will also occur. The scriptures tell us that not only will the sun be dimmed and the moon turned to blood, but additional astronomical events will be seen in the heavens as well:

> For not many days hence and the earth shall tremble and reel to and fro as a drunken man; and the sun shall hide his face, and shall refuse to give light; and the moon shall be bathed in blood; and the stars shall become exceedingly angry, and shall cast themselves down as a fig that falleth from off a fig-tree. (D&C 88:87; see also Isaiah 24:18–20; Revelation 6:12–13; D&C 133:49; Matthew 24:29)

The prophecy that "the earth shall . . . reel to and fro" may simply be a reference to the great earthquake that will occur upon Christ's arrival on the earth. However, it could also mean, although this is doubtful, that the earth will wobble on its axis. This is not impossible, as it has occurred a number of times throughout the earth's long history.[22] However, this is usually a slow process, involving millions of years, and when it does occur, the entire geological structure and history of the planet changes, as do all living things along with it.

As far as the stars are concerned, reference to the fact that they "shall cast themselves down" could easily be references to meteor showers, frequent heavenly displays, which we have all seen on clear nights. Or they could be symbolic descriptions of asteroids approaching and impacting the earth with spectacular and widespread destruction, as discussed in chapter 6. If that turns out to be the case, they will also account for scriptural references to fire and brimstone and will further contribute to the destruction of humanity.

Regardless of how all these calamities fall into place, the fact remains that soon after Jesus' Second Coming, the earth will be an entirely different place than what we have known, and wickedness will be removed from the earth. Satan will be cast out for a thousand years and the anti-Christ and the great and abominable church will cease to exist:

> The beast was taken, and with him the false

> prophet that wrought miracles before him, with which he deceived them that had received the mark of the beast, and them that worshiped his image. And he laid hold on the dragon, that old serpent, which is the Devil, and Satan, and bound him a thousand years. (Revelation 19:20; 20:2)

> And after these things I heard a great voice of much people in heaven, saying, Alleluia; Salvation, and glory, and honour, and power, unto the Lord our God: For true and righteous are his judgments: for he hath judged the great whore [the great and abominable church], which did corrupt the earth with her fornication, and hath avenged the blood of his servants at her hand. And again they said, Alleluia. And her smoke rose up for ever and ever. (Revelation 19:1–3)

Finally, the earth will begin to resemble the prophecies that declare "a new heaven and a new earth" suitable for Christ's millennial reign and on into eternity.

The Conversion of the Jews

One of the greatest events that will take place at the Second Coming of the Messiah will be the Jews' acknowledgment of him as their Savior, the one who was rejected and crucified by their forefathers 2,000 years ago. Their rejection of him at his first ministry upon the earth was because he didn't fit their expectation of a savior coming to earth triumphant and powerful to save them from their Roman oppressors. Instead, he came in obscurity and humility and lived among them as a mortal man.

This second time, however, he *will* arrive in power and great glory, even more so than the Jews first expected of him. He will be heralded in brightness and will descend from heaven as their great King, a God accompanied by angels and resurrected beings. He will stand upon the historic Mount of Olives and will call on the elements—on earthquakes, storms, and plagues—to finally cleanse the earth of unrighteous humanity and remove evil from the earth.

Upon his arrival, those Jews still living in the besieged holy city of Jerusalem will flock to him as the great Savior they have long awaited. At that time, he will welcome them to him but with a powerful reminder of who he is. There are two accounts of this poignant moment that describe this historic day:

> His next appearance will be among the distressed and nearly vanquished sons of Judah. At the crisis of their fate, when the hostile troops of several nations are ravaging the city and all the horrors of war are overwhelming the people of Jerusalem, he will set his feet upon the Mount of Olives, which will cleave and part asunder at his touch.
>
> Attended by a host from heaven, he will overthrow and destroy the combined armies of the Gentiles, and appear to the worshiping Jews as the mighty Deliverer and Conqueror so long expected by their race; and while love, gratitude, awe, and admiration swell their bosoms, the Deliverer will show them the tokens of his crucifixion and disclose himself as Jesus of Nazareth, whom they had reviled and whom their fathers put to death.
>
> Then will unbelief depart from their souls, and "the blindness in part which has happened unto Israel" be removed. "A fountain for sin and uncleanness shall be opened to the house of David and the inhabitants of Jerusalem," and "a nation will be born unto God" in a day. They will be baptized for the remission of their sins, and will receive the gift of the Holy Ghost, and the government of God as established in Zion will be set up among them, no more to be thrown down forever.[23]

At about this time, the Savior will come to the rescue of his covenant people:

> Then [after the parting of the Mount of Olives] shall come to pass the conversion of a nation in a day,

> the acceptance of the Redeemer by the Jews. "And then shall the Jews look upon me and say: What are these wounds in thine hands and in thy feet? Then shall they know that I am the Lord; for I will say unto them: These wounds are the wounds with which I was wounded in the house of my friends. I am he who was lifted up. I am Jesus that was crucified. I am the Son of God. And then shall they weep because of their iniquities; then shall they lament because they persecuted their king." (D&C 45:51–53; see also Zechariah 12:10;13:6)[24]

It may be well to point out that among those Jews who are on hand at Jesus' Second Coming will be those now comprising the nation of Israel as well as the ten lost tribes. In chapter 4, it was pointed out that uncertainty exists as to precisely when the ten tribes will return during the chain of events leading up to Christ's coming. Some scriptures and statements by Church authorities indicate that those tribes will be instrumental, along with the descendants of the Lamanites, in the rebuilding of Jerusalem and its temple, which is prophesied to be completed before the Second Coming. On the other hand, other scriptures and statements by Church authorities indicate that the ten tribes will return *after* the Second Coming and the battle of Armageddon and that they will go to the new Jerusalem in America:[25]

> And they shall assist my people, the remnant of Jacob, and also as many of the house of Israel as shall come, that they may build a city, which shall be called the New Jerusalem. And then shall they assist my people that they may be gathered in, who are scattered upon all the face of the land, in unto the New Jerusalem. And then shall the power of heaven come down among them; and I also will be in the midst.
>
> And then shall the work of the Father commence at that day, even when this gospel shall be preached among the remnant of this people. Verily I say unto you, at that day shall the work of the Father commence among all the dispersed of my people, yea, even the

> tribes which have been lost, which the Father hath led away out of Jerusalem. (3 Nephi 21:23–26)

Regardless of when the ten tribes return, it is significant that the people of Israel, God's chosen people, will finally accept him as their Savior and King.

Aftermath of the War

The carnage and destruction that will result from the battle of Armageddon will be unimaginable. Tens of millions will have died, in the Holy Land and throughout the rest of the world, on a scale humanity has never experienced. John the Revelator gave us a symbolic yet vivid account of the beginning and end of that great war to come:

> I saw heaven opened, and behold a white horse; and he that sat upon him was called Faithful and True, and in righteousness he doth judge and make war.
>
> His eyes were as a flame of fire, and on his head were many crowns; and he had a name written, that no man knew, but he himself. And he was clothed with a vesture dipped in blood: and his name is called The Word of God.
>
> And the armies which were in heaven followed him upon white horses, clothed in fine linen, white and clean. And out of his mouth goeth a sharp sword, that with it he should smite the nations: and he shall rule them with a rod of iron: and he treadeth the winepress of the fierceness and wrath of Almighty God.
>
> And he hath on his vesture and on his thigh a name written, King of Kings, and Lord of Lords.
>
> And I saw an angel standing in the sun; and he cried with a loud voice, saying to all the fowls that fly in the midst of heaven, Come and gather yourselves together unto the supper of the great God; that ye may eat the flesh of kings, and the flesh of captains, and the flesh of mighty men, and the flesh of horses, and of them that sit on them, and the flesh of all men, both

> free and bond, both small and great.
>
> And I saw the beast, and the kings of the earth, and their armies, gathered together to make war against him that sat on the horse, and against his army.
>
> And the beast was taken, and with him the false prophet that wrought miracles before him, with which he deceived them that had received the mark of the beast, and them that worshiped his image. These both were cast alive into a lake of fire burning with brimstone. And the remnant were slain with the sword of him that sat upon the horse, which sword proceeded out of his mouth: and all the fowls were filled with their flesh. (Revelation 19:11–21)

It will serve little purpose to dwell on the state of the world after these cataclysmic events. One must simply visualize media coverage of bombed-out cities, reminiscent of defeated Germany at the conclusion of World War II and of the devastation wrought by the great Southeast Asian tsunami in Indonesia and Sri Lanka in late 2004. Humanity's population will have been reduced by billions and death will be everywhere. All commerce will be at a standstill, agriculture will be virtually nonexistent, and our comfortable homes and present way of life will be things of the past. Although having next to nothing, the righteous will remain alive under the leadership of Jesus to rebuild for the Millennium.

To begin this great reconstruction process, an enormous cleanup will first be required. An example of the magnitude of this task will be the cleanup needed following the battle of Armageddon:

> They [the invading heathen armies] shall fall upon the open field, upon the mountains of Israel, even Gog and all his army, horses and horsemen; and the Jews shall go forth and gather the weapons of war, such as hand staves, spears, shields, and bows and arrows; and these weapons shall last the cities of Israel seven years for fuel, so that they shall cut no wood out of the forest, for they shall burn the weapons with fire; and they shall spoil those that spoiled them, and rob

> those that robbed them, and they shall gather gold and silver, and apparel, in great abundance.
>
> At this time, the fowls of the air, and the beasts of the field, shall have a great feast; yea, they are to eat fat until they be full, and drink blood until they be drunken. They are to eat the flesh of captains and kings, and mighty men, and all men of war.
>
> But the Jews will have a very serious duty to perform, which will take no less than seven months; namely, the burying of their enemies. They shall select a place on the east side of the sea, called the Valley of the Passengers; and there shall they bury Gog and all his multitude, and they shall call it the valley of Hamon Gog. And the scent shall go forth, insomuch that it shall stop the noses of the passengers; thus shall they cleanse the land.[26]

One positive note regarding the rebuilding of civilization will be the fact that despite the great destruction, empty buildings will be available for occupancy. With the bulk of humanity gone, Jesus' followers will have shelter:

> Enlarge the place of thy tent, and let them stretch forth the curtains of thine habitations: spare not, lengthen thy cords, and strengthen thy stakes;
>
> For thou shalt break forth on the right hand and on the left; and thy seed shall inherit the Gentiles, and make the desolate cities to be inhabited. (Isaiah 54:2–3)

The Resurrection

As noted earlier, many of the righteous, as well as those who died for him formerly, will be caught up to be with Christ at his triumphal return. These latter will be part of the First Resurrection. But there is much more than this reuniting of body and spirit than many Latter-day Saints realize. For example, Church members have always been taught that there will be a first and second resurrection.

In reality, however, there will be three resurrections, each of which is divided into segments determined by how we have lived during mortality here on the earth, and each of which will determine which kingdom we will be a part of in the life hereafter.

To understand this, Elder Bruce R. McConkie provides a summary of the various resurrections and how they will affect each of us:

> Every living being will be resurrected. "As in Adam all die, even so in Christ shall all be made alive" (1 Corinthians 15:22). Those who live and die before the millennial era, all in their proper order, will have their bodies and spirits reunited in resurrected immortality. The righteous who live after the second coming shall be changed from mortality to immortality in the twinkling of an eye, their bodies and spirits being united inseparably.
>
> The righteous dead who lived from the day of Adam to the time when Christ broke the bands of death "were with Christ in his resurrection" (D&C 13:54–55). "And the graves were opened; and many bodies of the saints which slept arose, and came out of the graves after his resurrection, and went into the holy city, and appeared unto many" (Matthew 27:52–53; see also Helaman 14:25).
>
> To those who lived before the resurrection of Christ, the day of his coming forth from the dead was known as *the first resurrection*. . . . To those who have lived since that day, the first resurrection is yet future and will take place at the time of the second coming. Though all men are assured of a resurrection, all will not be resurrected at the same time . . .
>
> Two great resurrections await the inhabitants of the earth: one is *the first resurrection* . . . the other is *the second resurrection*. But even within these two separate resurrections, there is an order in which the dead shall come forth. Those being resurrected with celestial bodies, whose destiny is to inherit a celestial kingdom, will come forth in the *morning* of the first resurrection.

> Their graves shall be opened and they shall be caught up to meet the Lord at his second coming. . . .
>
> The *afternoon* of the first resurrection takes place after our Lord has ushered in the millennium. Those coming forth at that time do so with terrestrial bodies and are thus destined to inherit a terrestrial glory in eternity (see D&C 76:71–80).
>
> At the end of the millennium, the second resurrection begins. In the forepart of this resurrection of the unjust, those destined to come forth, will be "the spirits of men to be judged, and are found under condemnation; and these are the rest of the dead; and they live not again until the thousand years are ended, neither again, until the end of the earth" (D&C 88:100–01). These are the ones who have earned telestial bodies, who were wicked and carnal in mortality, and who have suffered the wrath of God in hell "until the last resurrection, until the Lord, even Christ the Lamb, shall have finished his work" (D&C 76:85). Their final destiny is to inherit a telestial glory (see D&C 76:81–112).[27]

A final note concerning resurrections seems appropriate at this point. The prophets have made it clear that not only man, but all life upon the earth as well, was created in the premortal existence. Likewise, all life will undergo resurrection, just as man will:

> The end shall come, and the heaven and the earth shall be consumed and pass away, and there shall be a new heaven and a new earth. For all old things shall pass away, and all things shall become new, even the heaven and the earth, and all the fulness thereof, both men and beasts, the fowls of the air, and the fishes of the sea; And not one hair, neither mote, shall be lost, for it is the workmanship of mine hand. (D&C 29:23–25)[28]

Notes

1. Parley P. Pratt, *A Voice of Warning* (New York: Eastern States Mission, 1837), 39–41.

2. The same heathen nations will also have part in the first resurrection (see D&C 45:54).

3. Orson Pratt, in *Journal of Discourses,* 20:154.

4. Melvin J. Ballard, in Conference Report, June 1919, 89.

5. Brigham Young, in *Journal of Discourses,* 15:194.

6. *Contributor* 6 (March 1885): 232.

7. As discussed in chapter 6, atmospheric conditions resulting from either an asteroid impact or a super-volcanic eruption could easily cause disappearance of the rainbow and darkening of the sun, as well as many other calamities and plagues that will occur during this period of time.

8. Joseph Smith, *Teachings of the Prophet Joseph Smith,* ed. Joseph Fielding Smith (Salt Lake City: Deseret Book, 1976), 80.

9. Joseph Fielding Smith, in Conference Report, April 1966, 13.

10. Joseph Fielding Smith provided us with a meaningful commentary on this remarkable place: "Not far from the town of Gallatin, in Daviess County, Missouri, there is a place known to the people as 'Spring Hill.' Here, a settlement of the Saints was started in 1838. This hill is on the north of the valley through which runs Grand River, described by the Prophet Joseph as a 'large, beautiful, and rapid stream, during the high waters of spring.' In the spring and summer the surrounding valley is most beautiful, with its scattered farms discernible as far as the eye can reach. The citizens here go about their daily tasks all unaware of the wondrous occurrences which have taken place in this beautiful valley and on this hill. They are equally oblivious to the momentous events soon to be staged there.

"When the Prophet first visited the hill he called it 'Tower Hill,' 'a name I gave the place in consequence of the remains of an old Nephite altar or tower that stood there,' he wrote in his journal. By the Lord, however, this place was named 'Adam-ondi-Ahman, because, said he, it is the place where Adam shall come to visit his people, or the Ancient of Days shall sit, as spoken of by Daniel the prophet'" (Joseph Fielding Smith, *The Way to Perfection* (Salt Lake City: Genealogical Society of Utah, 1945), 287.

11. Orson Pratt, in *Journal of Discourses,* 14:334; 15:338.

12. Charles W. Penrose, "The Second Advent," *Improvement Era,* March 1924, 405.

13. Robert Millet, "The Second Coming of Christ: Questions and Answers," *The Doctrine and Covenants: The 25th Annual Sidney B. Sperry Symposium,* ed. Leon R. Hartshorn, Dennis A. Wright, and Craig J. Ostler (Salt Lake City: Deseret Book, 1996), 209–10.

14. Penrose, "The Second Advent," 405.

15. Joseph Smith, *The Words of Joseph Smith: The Contemporary Accounts of the Nauvoo Discourses of the Prophet Joseph Smith,* comp. Andrew F. Ehat

and Lyndon W. Cook (Provo, Utah: BYU Religious Studies Center, 1980), 130–31.

16. Penrose, "The Second Advent," 406.

17. Millet, "The Second Coming of Christ: Questions and Answers," 214.

18. The scriptures appear contradictory regarding when the waters will flow from the temple and the Dead Sea will be healed. Ezekiel and Joseph Smith both imply that these events will occur prior to Jesus' second coming (Ezekiel 47:1–10; Joseph Smith, *History of the Church,* 5:336–37). On the other hand, Zechariah indicates that they will occur *at the time* of the Savior's second coming (Zechariah 14:8), while Joel implies that they will occur *after* the Second Coming and the battle of Armageddon (Joel 3:18).

19. This may well correspond to a revelation given to the Prophet Joseph Smith in 1831 that "the earth shall be like it was in the days before it was divided" (D&C 133:18–29).

20. All of these prophecies, including those relating to great signs in the heavens, could fit descriptions of the effects of the impact of asteroids or super-volcanic activity, as discussed in chapter 6.

21. Hailstones are formed through a process similar to rain, through condensation of water vapor in the atmosphere into droplets which, when they become heavy enough, fall to the ground. Hail, on the other hand, goes through a freezing process, forming balls of ice instead of drops of water. The size of a hailstone is directly related to that freezing process. As the bit of ice begins falling to the ground, it may be caught in an updraft (which is commonplace in a thunderstorm), be lifted upward, and go through the condensation and freezing process again, in which case it grows larger. If it then begins to fall and is lifted upward again by another updraft, it will in turn increase in size each time it goes through this process. Hailstones as large as golf balls or even baseballs, which are rare because of their sheer weight, and which are obviously damaging to anything on the ground when they fall to earth, have been recorded. The fact that the hailstones in this particular prophesied storm will exceed seventy-five pounds is a certain indication of the violence that will characterize storms during this time.

22. Wobbling of the earth on its axis means that the North Pole would no longer point toward the North Star and might tilt a few degrees away from it. Also, the equator would then no longer be the nearest portion of the earth toward the sun during the equinoxes. The climatological implications of such an axis shift are enormous because it would be to the very structure of the earth itself and the system of life around the globe.

23. Penrose, "The Second Advent," 405.

24. Millet, "The Second Coming of Christ: Questions and Answers," 212.

25. Charles W. Penrose contended that the Savior's coming in glory would be his *third* appearance on the earth, preceded by the grand council at Adam-ondi-Ahman and his personal appearance to the Jews.

26. Parley P. Pratt, *A Voice of Warning,* 38–39. Although Parley P. Pratt noted that "staves, spears, shields, and bows and arrows" littered the area

around Jerusalem following the defeat of their enemies, it is more likely that this great cleanup effort will entail cleaning up the remnants of modern armaments such as armor, vehicles, aircraft, artillery, and the like. Whichever is the case, cleansing such a huge battlefield could take considerable time, as he indicated.

27. Bruce R. McConkie, *Mormon Doctrine,* 2d ed. (Salt Lake City: Bookcraft, 1966), 638–40.

28. It is uncertain how literally we should understand these verses. Taken literally, we can expect that hordes of creatures, even undesirable ones, lived in the premortal existence and will be with us in the hereafter as resurrected life. Lots of mosquitoes, flies, fleas, cockroaches, rats, snakes, and maybe even dinosaurs? Nevertheless, it is solace to many that they will be reunited with their beloved family pets, which they may have lost over the years.

10

The Millennium of Christ's Reign

In contemplating the future state of the earth, Elder Bruce R. McConkie said:

> This earth, according to the divine plan, is passing through a mortal or temporal existence of seven millennia or 7000 years (D&C 77:6–7). During the first six of these (covering a total period of 6000 years from the time of the fall of Adam) conditions of carnality, corruption, evil, and wickedness of every sort have prevailed upon the earth. Wars, death, destruction, and everything incident to the present telestial state of existence have held sway over the earth and all life on its face.
>
> When the seventh thousand years commence, however, radical changes will take place both in the earth itself and in the nature and type of existence enjoyed by all forms of life on its face. This will be the long hoped for age of peace when Christ will reign personally upon the earth; when the earth will be renewed and receive its paradisiacal glory; when corruption, death, and disease will cease; and when the kingdom of God on earth will be fully established in all its glory, beauty, and perfection (tenth article of faith).[1]

The Millennium, during which Jesus will personally reign over the earth will, of course, commence with his Second Coming and the defeat of the unrighteous and Satan's evil influence over mankind. It will find man's once vaunted civilization in shambles but with two holy cities, the ancient city of Jerusalem in the Holy Land and the New Jerusalem in America, still intact from which to rebuild a thousand years of righteousness. From these two locations, Jesus will institute a system of government that will be unlike any previously known—a society dictated by love, cooperation, and respect. "Those only shall be able to abide that day [the second coming of the Savior] who are worthy to live on a paradisiacal or terrestrial sphere."[2]

Previously, all human governments have been founded on oppression, dictatorial rule, taxation, commerce, and force. Although our American system has historically been the most enlightened—based on freedom and equality—it too has suffered from reliance on worldly wealth (in other words, our capitalist system) and has become ever more alienated from the virtues of God. The government to be initiated by Jesus will have no basis whatsoever on worldly wealth and no economic system. It will rely entirely on true equality, love, and humility—men working together in a great system devoid of pride, status, and selfishness. If we seriously consider this prospect, it is the only system that will work to properly prepare mankind for an eternity in which there will be no worldly wealth or economic status.

At the conclusion of the battle of Armageddon and the cleansing of the earth by the great calamities that will accompany Jesus at his Second Coming, there will have been accomplished a complete separation of the righteous and the wicked: "And until that hour [the coming of the Son of Man] there will be foolish virgins among the wise; and at that hour cometh an entire separation of the righteous and the wicked; and in that day will I send mine angels to pluck out the wicked and cast them into unquenchable fire" (D&C 63:54). Only those will remain on earth who have lived their mortal lives on a celestial or terrestrial level.

Contrary to the idealistic and generalized understanding most Christians have of the forthcoming millennial era, specific things will happen during that thousand-year period, some of which are referred to in the scriptures either symbolically or in terms that are difficult for us to understand. Fortunately, we have the advantage of latter-day revelation, as well as the Book of Mormon, which shed a great deal more light on what will be happening during those ten centuries and how we and the earth will be changed. A good example is the traditional Christian belief in the Day of Judgment, which blandly states that we will all someday be required to stand before our Creator and receive judgment from him on how we have led our mortal lives. Further than that, Christian belief does not go. But there is much more to it than that.

The Day of Judgment

One of the great events at the beginning of the millennial era will be the great Day of Judgment. Of those people still upon the earth, the righteous will be rewarded with an inheritance in the Father's kingdom, and the wicked will be cursed with eternal punishment:

> When the Son of Man shall come in his glory, and all the holy angels with him, then shall he sit upon the throne of his glory: And before him shall be gathered all nations: and he shall separate them one from another, as a shepherd divideth his sheep from the goats: And he shall set the sheep on his right hand, but the goats on the left. Then shall the King say unto them on his right hand, Come, ye blessed of my Father, inherit the kingdom prepared for you from the foundation of the world:
>
> Then shall he say also unto them on the left hand, Depart from me, ye cursed, into everlasting fire, prepared for the devil and his angels. And these shall go away into everlasting punishment: but the righteous into life eternal. (Matthew 25:31–34, 41, 46)

Contrary to most traditional Christian belief, which contends that God will administer judgment upon all men, latter-day scriptures tell us that judgment will be administered by Jesus' original Twelve Apostles, who were with him throughout his New Testament ministry. They will be among the angels and other heavenly beings who will descend to earth with the Savior at his Second Coming:

> And again, verily, verily, I say unto you, and it hath gone forth in a firm decree, by the will of the Father, that mine apostles, the twelve which were with me in my ministry at Jerusalem, shall stand at my right hand at the day of my coming in a pillar of fire, being clothed with robes of righteousness, with crowns upon their heads, in glory even as I am, to judge the whole house of Israel, even as many as have loved me and kept my commandments, and none else. (D&C 29:12)

Traditional Christianity has adopted a lackadaisical attitude toward this great Day of Judgment despite the fact that it will be a time of great soul-searching and possibly anguish:

> I say unto you, can you imagine to yourselves that ye hear the voice of the Lord, saying unto you, in that day: Come unto me ye blessed, for behold, your works have been the works of righteousness upon the face of the earth? Or do ye imagine to yourselves that ye can lie unto the Lord in that day, and say—Lord, our works have been righteous works upon the face of the earth—and that he will save you?
>
> Or otherwise, can ye imagine yourselves brought before the tribunal of God with your souls filled with guilt and remorse, having a remembrance of your guilt, yea a perfect remembrance of all your wickedness, yea, a remembrance that ye have set at defiance the commandments of God?
>
> I say unto you, can ye look up to God at that day with a pure heart and clean hands? I say unto you, can you look up, having the image of God engraven upon your countenances?
>
> I say unto you, can ye think of being saved when you have yielded yourselves to become subjects to the devil? I say unto you, ye will know at that day that ye cannot be saved; . . . Behold, my brethren, do ye suppose that such an one can have a place to sit down in the kingdom of God, with Abraham, with Isaac,

> and with Jacob, and also all the holy prophets. . . ?
> (Alma 5:16–21, 24)

Millions who now claim to be Christians yet practice little of Christ's gospel in their daily lives will be in trouble. Lip service won't help. Fortunately, only God and his apostles will be able to truly judge us on how well we have done in mortality. It is fairly certain, however, that many of us now have a pretty good idea of how we should be individually judged. When we are confronted by the Savior, and our earthly possessions and cares are stripped away, our position in eternal progression will become fairly obvious. It is certain that many who thought their churches would place them in good position will find that those same churches have in fact impeded their progress (Matthew 7:21–23), while others who may not have considered themselves religious, but were moral and honorable will have done pretty well. Whichever the case, there will be many gray areas that we, with our current lack of knowledge and understanding, will have to leave to God to sort out. This is probably why Jesus said, "Judge not unrighteously, that ye be not judged" (JST, Matthew 7:1).

After the great Day of Judgment, those who have been found worthy and have been resurrected will remain upon the earth to live for the remainder of the Millennium.

A Paradisiacal Earth

According to the tenth article of faith, as the Millennium commences, the earth will be renewed and receive its paradisiacal glory. It was noted in the preceding chapter that among the great calamities that will accompany Jesus' second coming, the mountains will be brought low, and the islands will disappear:

> And it shall be a voice as the voice of many waters, and as the voice of a great thunder, which shall break down the mountains, and the valleys shall not be found. He shall command the great deep, and it shall be driven back into the north countries, and the islands shall become one land; and the land of Jerusalem and the land of Zion shall be turned back into their own

> place, and the earth shall be like it was in the days before it was divided. (D&C 133:22–24)[3]

This is to be only the beginning of the renewal of the earth. As a matter of fact, the entire globe will be returned to the terrestrial state, which existed in the Garden of Eden. In those original days of man upon the earth, he was surrounded by a pleasant, productive place in which to live. Thorns, weeds, deserts, mountains, and the like did not then exist. On the contrary, the entire earth was a lush place, probably similar to a tropical island, with no wintertime, ice, or snow.

The continents of the globe during the early days of Adam were a single landmass, and the seas were likewise continuous and connected around it.[4] Death too was unknown then because immortality extended to all living things. All of this, however, changed with the fall of Adam, and the world became much the same as it now is.

Sometime during the Millennium, the earth will be returned to its Edenic state, a thousand years of renewal and regeneration that will "create new heavens and a new earth" (Isaiah 65:17). In essence, this renewal of the earth will be a day of transfiguration for the planet, much the same as the transfiguration of Jesus described in the New Testament. The earth will be returned to its paradisiacal glory: "Nevertheless, he that endureth in faith and doeth my will, the same shall overcome, and shall receive an inheritance upon the earth when the day of transfiguration shall come; when the earth shall be transfigured, even according to the pattern which was shown unto mine apostles upon the mount; of which account the fulness ye have not yet received" (D&C 63:20–21).

Many scriptures speak exhaustively concerning heat and burning during the last days in the punishment of the wicked and the renewal of the earth. It is to be assumed that these terms are used symbolically, reflecting the eternal mental suffering of the wicked who realize too late that they could have attained exaltation but failed to do so, as well as the fact that the earth itself will be completely changed from what it is now—so much so that it will be as if it had been melted and molded into an entirely different (and much improved) planet. This seems to be the meaning when latter-day revelations speak of the transfiguration, or renewal, of the earth during the Millennium: "And every corruptible thing, both of man, or of the beasts of the field, or of the fowls of the heavens, or of the fish of the sea, that dwells upon all the face of the earth, shall be consumed; and also that of element shall melt with fervent heat; and all things shall become new, that my knowledge and glory may dwell upon all the earth" (D&C 101: 24–25).

Satan Will Be Bound

Christianity understands well from the ancient scriptures that Satan will be bound during the Millennium and that his influence will no longer be felt upon the earth. However, it should be emphasized that it will not only be mankind's turn to righteousness that will cause this to happen, although that will play a large role. Instead, it will be through the sheer force of the Lord at the time of his return that will destroy evil from the earth. He will not only destroy unrighteous mankind and bind Satan, but he will also institute a form of government that will be founded on righteousness: "For the Lord shall be in their midst, and his glory shall be upon them, and he will be their king and their lawgiver" (D&C 45:59).

The sheer power of his influence on mankind will ensure that this perfect system will remain in force for a thousand years, until Satan is finally released and allowed his last great effort prior to his final destruction. "For the great millennium, of which I have spoken by the mouth of my servants, shall come. For Satan shall be bound, and when he is loosed again he shall only reign for a little season, and then cometh the end of the earth" (D&C 43:30–31; see also D&C 45:55; 84:100; 88:110–11; Revelation 20:1–3, 7). "And in that day Satan shall not have power to tempt any man" (D&C 101:28).

Children born during that period too will live and grow up without Satan's influence: "And the earth shall be given unto them for an inheritance; and they shall multiply and wax strong, and their children shall grow up without sin unto salvation" (D&C 45:58). In addition, those children in the past who have died prior to the age of baptism will be returned to their mothers during the Millennium to be raised and cared for.[5]

At the end of Christ's millennial reign, Satan will have his last opportunity to turn mankind away from God:[6]

> And when the thousand years are expired, Satan shall be loosed out of his prison. And shall go out to deceive the nations which are in the four quarters of the earth, Gog and Magog, to gather them together to battle: the number of whom is as the sand of the sea. And they went up on the breadth of the earth, and compassed the camp of the saints about, and the beloved city: and fire came down from God out of heaven, and devoured them. And the devil that deceived them was cast into the lake of fire and brimstone, where the beast and the false prophet are, and shall be tormented day and night for ever and ever. (Revelation 20:7–10)

> And Satan shall be bound, that old serpent, who is called the devil, and shall not be loosed for the space of a thousand years. And then shall he be loosed for a little season, that he may gather together his armies. And Michael, the seventh angel, even the archangel, shall gather together his armies, even the hosts of heaven. And the devil shall gather together his armies; even the hosts of hell, and shall come up to battle against Michael and his armies. And then cometh the battle of the great God; and the devil and his armies shall be cast away into their own place, that they shall not have power over the saints any more at all. (D&C 88:110–14)

Peace on Earth

The history of mankind has been a long, unending, and sordid story of strife, conquest, and evil despite the efforts of the many prophets who have repeatedly come to mankind to preach repentance. We have already detailed man's propensity to destroy others through war and murder, a propensity that will not end until Christ's return to the earth, when the wicked will be destroyed as stubble.

Only then will war and evil cease:

> And he [the Lord] will teach us his ways, and we will walk in his paths: for out of Zion shall go forth the law, and the word of the Lord from Jerusalem. And he shall judge among the nations, and shall rebuke many people: and they shall beat their swords into plowshares, and their spears into pruninghooks: nation shall not lift up sword against nation, neither shall they learn war anymore. (Isaiah 2:3–4)

In the absence of the wicked who have thus far lived among us and the dedication of the remaining righteous to adhere to the laws of the Lord, throughout the Millennium earth will experience a peace and tranquility which it has never heretofore known.

Peace throughout the Animal Kingdom

The peace that mankind will enjoy through the Millennium of Christ's reign will also extend to the animals that inhabit the earth around us. That will be an interesting change indeed.

For the many millennia of earth's long history, carnivorous animals have preyed on other animals. Scientists have come up with such terms as *the food chain* to describe such feeding behavior and have built this into their theory of evolution (survival of the fittest). This means that, among other environmental influences, those animals that can avoid being eaten by other predators will have the best chance to survive and produce more offspring. Those that are easily caught and eaten will quickly become extinct. Through this simple winnowing mechanism, the earth's entire system of life, along with its myriad ecosystems, has continuously evolved through hundreds of stages into what it is now. And this is an ongoing process with species evolving and others becoming extinct even today.

The concept of a food chain means that those smaller animals that eat plants are eaten by larger, meat-eating animals, which in turn are eaten by even larger meat-eating animals, and so on. The only exceptions to this cold process are some of the largest animals, such as lions, elephants, rhinos, and whales. But even then, they might lose some of their baby offspring to other predators. The only other exception is man. In the case of man, we were also at one time a part of the food chain, just like smaller primates, such as chimpanzees, baboons, and monkeys, are today. However, due to the intellect of our ancestors, as well as other evolutionary enhancements (so anthropologists contend), we stepped out of the food chain with our weapons and organization.

The idea of a food chain, or predation of one animal on another, will cease as the new millennium commences. The prophets tell us that all animals, including mankind, will adapt to peace with one another, and predation will be a thing of the past: "And in that day the enmity of man, and the enmity of beasts, yea, the enmity of all flesh, shall cease from before my face" (D&C 101:26).

It is assumed from this that all humanity will quickly adapt to vegetarianism, which will be a new experience to many of us, especially for those who enjoy a hamburger or juicy steak from time to time. Nevertheless, an all-vegetable diet will certainly be healthier than the way we eat now, and many of the problems of obesity, strokes, heart disease, and the like will also disappear.

Not only will mankind be driven to vegetarianism but also those animals that have always been considered predators. This includes such notorious meat eaters as lions, tigers, dogs, wolves, and sharks. In fact, the scriptures tell us that enmity among animals will cease and that most animals will become accustomed to eating grass or straw: "The wolf shall also dwell with the lamb, and the leopard shall lie down with the kid; and the calf and the young lion and the fatling together: and a little child shall lead them. And the cow and the bear shall feed; their young ones shall lie down together: and the lion shall eat straw like the ox" (Isaiah 11:6–7).

Mortality to Continue

Despite the vast changes that will take place during the millennium of Christ's rule, many things will not change. In most ways, we will continue to live as we always have—growing up, working for a living (albeit probably without money as a medium of exchange), getting married, having children, and growing old. However, the currently dreaded experience of death will have changed. Many people now fear death so immensely simply because of ignorance. They fear the pain often associated with dying and furthermore are uncertain of what to expect in the hereafter. Many contend even that death is the end of it all—that there is no life after death.

During the Millennium, death will be no more than an instant transformation from mortal to eternal being—a resurrection, if you will.[7] No pain will be involved during this process, and it will no longer be feared: "And he that liveth when the Lord shall come, and hath kept the faith, blessed is he; nevertheless, it is appointed to him to die at the age of man. Wherefore, children shall grow up until they become old; old men shall die; but they shall not sleep in the dust, but they shall be changed in the twinkling of an eye" (D&C 63:50–51).

The unification of mankind under the sole leadership of the Son of God will be further facilitated by the fact that we will all return to a single common language (presumably the Adamic language, which was spoken before the construction of the Tower of Babel): "For then will I turn to the people a pure language, that they may all call upon the name of the Lord, to serve him with one consent" (Zephania 3:9).

This in and of itself will be a miraculous achievement since mankind has spoken hundreds of different languages for thousands of years. As a matter of fact, mankind's inability to communicate in a common language has been one of the most divisive factors in our history, an ages-old underlying cause of misunderstanding, prejudice, and often pure hatred.

Just how this unification of language will occur will be an interesting proposition. Will it simply occur with the return of Christ to the earth—as a miracle—or will it be something that we must be taught and learn? We don't know.

Because of the peace that will reign during the Millennium, mankind will quickly recover from the devastation of the anti-Christ's rule and the battle of Armageddon. Soon prosperity will spread, and mankind, working in love and cooperation instead of in jealousy and enmity, will build a great and peaceful civilization:

> And they shall build houses, and inhabit them; and they shall plant vineyards, and eat the fruit of them. They shall not build, and another inhabit; they shall not plant, and another eat: for as the days of a tree are

> the days of my people, and mine elect shall long enjoy the work of their hands. They shall not labour in vain, nor bring forth for trouble. (Isaiah 65:21–23)

It is also certainly to be considered that after the Savior's return to the earth, racial differences, which have so long separated and alienated us from one another, will also disappear.

Will we all be of a single race? Along with our resurrected bodies, which will lack blood, will we also eat as we always have done (as vegetarians, that is), shave (for men), and in what other everyday ways will our lives change from what they are now? These are not vital issues, but they are interesting for those inclined to speculate about such things.

The End of Death, Sorrow, and Disease

For millennia, mankind has suffered from injury, disease, and death. These things have always been an unwelcome yet accepted part of life. We all have been hurt from time to time with injuries such as scratches, cuts, bruises, broken bones, and illnesses of various sorts. Some of us have suffered life-threatening diseases (some of which have been due to our lifestyle or foolishness) such as cancer, influenza, heart disease, and kidney failure. And finally, we all have at one time or another had someone close to us die for any number of reasons—disease, accidents, or simply old age. These are difficult times that result in painful times of sorrow and anguish.

We are, however, promised that during the Millennium, with our resurrected bodies, the difficult and sorrowful times will be behind us. We will no longer be subject to disease, injury, or death. As a matter of fact, even those who live in mortality during the Millennium—those who have not yet experienced the change from mortality to immortality in the twinkling of an eye—will also enjoy a life of no pain, disease, injury, suffering, or sorrow until their own time comes to die and experience immortality.[8] Unlike us, they will have a great deal more to look forward to: "And I will rejoice in Jerusalem, and joy in my people: and the voice of weeping shall be no more heard in her, nor the voice of crying. There shall be no more thence an infant of days, nor an old man that hath not filled his days: for the child shall die an hundred years old" (Isaiah 65:19–20).

A Fullness of Knowledge and Truth

Although we enjoy the fulness of the gospel due to the restoration of the Church through Joseph Smith, we still lack a fullness of the truth or knowledge. Past dispensations of the Church had access to knowledge or truths that we do not now have, as was the case with the City of Enoch, the Jaredites, and the Nephites.

With the dawning of this great new millennium, however, "He shall send Jesus Christ, which before was preached unto you: Whom the heaven must receive until the times of restitution of all things, which God hath spoken by the mouth of all his holy prophets since the world began" (Acts 3:20–21).

> Wherefore, the things of all nations shall be made known; yea, all things shall be made known unto the children of men. There is nothing which is secret save it shall be revealed; there is no work of darkness save it shall be made manifest in the light; and there is nothing which is sealed upon the earth save it shall be loosed. Wherefore, all things which have been revealed unto the children of men shall at that day be revealed. (2 Nephi 30:16–18; see also D&C 121:26–32)

Even those scriptures that have been unknown or sealed to us (like the sealed portion of the Book of Mormon) will be made known:

> "Yea, verily I say unto you, in that day when the Lord shall come, he shall reveal all things—things which have passed, and hidden things which no man knew, things of the earth, by which it was made, and the purpose and the end thereof—things most precious, things that are above, and things that are beneath, things that are in the earth, and in heaven." (D&C 101:33–34)

This era in mankind's history will be truly remarkable, something to look forward to. This great mass of knowledge and truth to be revealed through Jesus Christ or his prophets will be almost overwhelming. For centuries, man has slowly accumulated knowledge through experience, research, and revelation—much of which has been meticulously recorded through oral traditions, then through written records, and most recently through electronic media. Today we pride ourselves on our vast knowledge and note that we have been undergoing a knowledge explosion during the past century, thanks to computers, the internet, and modern high-tech research techniques. We, as has been previously noted, have gained more knowledge in the past one hundred years than man gained cumulatively throughout all of his prior history.

We now understand a great deal about other planets and galaxies, physical laws that govern the universe, microscopic life, the smallest units of which matter is formed, heredity (DNA), and the like, but there remain great gaps in our vast store of knowledge. For example, how did life begin? Is evolution a fact instead of a theory? Are there other inhabited planets? Is there life after death? What is the true and complete history of God's works here on the earth? How can we cure stubborn diseases? Why can't we get along with others? Is there a Satan? Is there a God?

The great scientists and thinkers who will remain on the earth after the second coming of Jesus will undoubtedly be amazed, as we all will, to learn the answers to these and many other similar questions. This indicates that our education will not cease during the Millennium. We will spend a great part of that thousand years learning and gaining experiences from the greatest teacher of all, the Son of God.

Conversion of All to the Truth

Contrary to what many Latter-day Saints expect, many living during the Millennium will not accept Jesus as their Savior, the Son of God. The scriptures tell us, as we have previously discussed, that those who are living a terrestrial or celestial life will survive Jesus' coming and live among us afterward. As Elder Bruce R. McConkie, says, there will be those who have lived lives of "honesty, uprightness, and integrity." However, those living a telestial level, or evil, existence will not survive the Savior's coming and will not be a part of the Millennium (including the sons of perdition). As Elder McConkie puts it, "Honest and upright people who have been deceived by the false religions and philosophies of the world will not have their moral agency abridged. They will continue to believe their false doctrines until they voluntarily elect to receive gospel light."[9]

> If the Latter-day Saints think, when the kingdom of God is established on the earth, that all the inhabitants of the earth will join the church called Latter-day Saints, they are egregiously mistaken. I presume there will be as many sects and parties then as now.
>
> In the millennium men will have the privilege of being Presbyterians, Methodists, or infidels, but they will not have the privilege of treating the name and character of Deity as they have done heretofore. No, but every knee shall bow and every tongue confess to the glory of God the Father that Jesus is the Christ.
>
> There will be every sort of sect and party, and every individual following what he supposes to be the best in religion, and in everything else, similar to what it is now. Will there be wickedness then as now? No.
>
> When Jesus comes to rule and reign King of Nations as he now does King of Saints, the veil of the covering will be taken from all nations, that all flesh may see his glory together, but that will not make them all Saints.[10]

This will undoubtedly result in an interesting set of social circumstances. Mankind during the Millennium will be ruled (as we will be discussing shortly) by the Church with Jesus at its head, and we will probably be living the law of consecration.

To understand how this can be, this will perhaps be like the society that we now find in many predominantly Latter-day Saint communities in Utah. Many nonmembers who relocate to Utah from elsewhere come seeking an environment of peace and security. They will freely admit that they do so to escape the congestion, crime, and low standards that prevail in many other parts of the country. This is a major that why Utah continues to increase in population.

So for tens of millions of non-Church members, then, they will be willing to conform to the standards that will prevail under

Christ's rule but without necessarily accepting the Church. This is their moral agency. Because of the intense contact they will unavoidably have with the Church, however, many of them will eventually recognize the truth and seek baptism. Others will not.

Regarding those who continue to refuse Jesus or membership in his Church, we must simply recall that much of mankind will be destroyed at the Second Coming. This will have been done through earthquakes, storms, tidal waves, fire, and so forth—all by natural means. The scriptures indicate that later, during the Millennium, despite the peace and love that will prevail, the same fate awaits those who continue to reject the Christ. They will have exercised their moral agency, chosen to turn away, and will likewise be removed from the earth:

> And it shall come to pass, that every one that is left of all the nations which came up against Jerusalem shall even go up from year to year to worship the King, the Lord of Hosts, and to keep the feast of tabernacles. And it shall be, that whoso will not come up of all the families of the earth unto Jerusalem to worship the King, the Lord of Hosts, even upon them shall be no rain. And if the family of Egypt go not up, and come not, that have no rain, there shall be the plague, wherewith the Lord shall smite the heathen that come not up to keep the feast of tabernacles. This shall be the punishment of Egypt, and the punishment of all nations that come not up to keep the feast of tabernacles. (Zechariah 14:16–19)[11]

The heathen nations that will not come up to worship will be visited with the judgments of God and must eventually be destroyed from the earth.[12]

Again, many will accept the gospel and join the Church. After all, Satan and the great and abominable church will be absent during the Millennium. These have been the greatest obstacles throughout all of mankind's history that have prevented many from recognizing gospel truths and heeding the words of the prophets. Eventually, only those who accept these truths and Jesus as their Savior and leader will remain on the earth: "For the earth shall be full of the knowledge of the Lord, as the waters cover the sea" (Isaiah 11:9). "And they shall teach no more every man his neighbour, and every man his brother, saying, Know the Lord: for they shall all know me, from the least of them unto the greatest of them, saith the Lord" (Jeremiah 31:34).

At this point the great winnowing process will be nearly completed. There will exist on earth only a society of those who accept Christ and willingly live by his precepts. So harmonious will this be that there will exist a spiritual bond between man and his Savior: "And in that day whatsoever any man shall ask, it shall be given unto him" (D&C 101:27). "And it shall come to pass, that before they call, I will answer; and while they are yet speaking, I will hear" (Isaiah 65:24).

The Kingdom of God on Earth

The history of theocracies as governing agencies has been a sorry part of mankind's history here upon the earth. A theocracy is a political and ecclesiastical institution wherein religion governs the secular as well as the religious affairs of a nation under one head, the church. Examples can be found in many countries, particularly in European history. Catholicism has had such power (and still does) over Italy, Spain, and Portugal. Various Protestant denominations have likewise had such power over other countries such as Germany and Austria, while the Church of England has maintained its power over Great Britain.

In virtually every case, those countries have historically practiced repression of those who did not adhere to the governing religion. A good example of all these evils was the enforcement of Catholicism upon Jews and Muslims during the Spanish Inquisition.

The reason such theocratic governments have been such a blight on many nations of the world is that they attempt, through law, intimidation, and coercion, to usurp our God-given gift of agency.[13] In such governments, the people are not accorded the right to adopt or practice whichever religion they choose.[14] This is a direct reflection of the evil plan suggested by Satan during the premortal existence, that mankind be given no agency whatsoever and instead be forced to abide by the dictates of God:

> And I, the Lord God, spake unto Moses, saying: That Satan, whom thou hast commanded in the name of mine Only Begotten, is the same which was from the beginning, and he came before me, saying—Behold, here am I, send me, I will be thy son, and I will redeem all mankind, that one soul shall not be lost, and surely I will do it; wherefore give me thine honor.
>
> But, behold, my Beloved Son, which was my Beloved and Chosen from the beginning, said unto me—Father, thy will be done, and the glory be thine forever. Wherefore, because that Satan rebelled against me, and sought to destroy the agency of man, which I, the Lord God, had given him, and also, that I should give unto him mine own power; by the power of mine Only Begotten, I caused that he should be cast down;
>
> And he became Satan, yea, even the devil, the father of all lies, to deceive and to blind men, and to lead them captive at his will, even as many as would not hearken unto my voice. (Moses 4:1–4)

Man's agency is thus a fundamental part of the plan of salvation, the earthly test we must undergo to determine if we are worthy to gain exaltation and to be with him throughout eternity. Therefore, any church or system of government that does not protect this vital freedom cannot be of God. Instead, those theocracies that fall in this category become a part of the great and abominable church, Satan's historic tool to lure mankind away from the plan of salvation.

Here in the United States, our nation was founded in large part by the Puritans and others who were fleeing religious regimes in order to reclaim and enjoy religious freedom. For this reason alone, our guarantee of religious freedom, as provided by the First Amendment of the Constitution, is fundamentally vital to all of us.[15]

But we should not forget that even early Mormonism was in reality a theocracy under the leadership of Brigham Young. Many Latter-day Saints fail to realize that the great Salt Lake Valley of Utah was part of the nation of (Catholic) Mexico when the early Church migrants left Nauvoo and settled there in 1847. A year later, after the successful conclusion of the nation's war with Mexico, the

Utah Territory became an official part of the United States. During the interim decades from then until 1896, when Utah achieved statehood, the Utah Territory was administered by no civil authority of any consequence except that provided by the Church under the direction of Brigham Young.

Although Brigham Young's Latter-day Saint theocracy was the only governmental authority that wielded any power in early Utah, it proved successful. Under President Young's governance, order was maintained, prosperity took root, and Utah became a showplace of a well planned, vibrant society. Towns and cities soon appeared, land was apportioned, commerce began and flourished, and civil order was maintained—all in a part of the country that no one else wanted and where no other civil authority reached.

To the east, the United States was expanding, and the great plains were becoming successful agricultural regions in demand. To the west, California's gold fields and powerfully expanding economy made Utah a virtual vacuum ignored by the rest of the country. The inspiration of Brigham Young and his farsighted leadership, as well as the theocracy he directed, were vital ingredients in the eventual development of the Intermountain West's becoming the prosperous and desirable place it is now. Although the Church's theocracy eventually yielded to civil government in 1896, the framework it established and the continuing influence of the Church since then have established Utah and its surrounding states as a growing and important part of the United States today.

The Church today is an ecclesiastical entity only with no secular or civil authority. This is in conformity with United States law. Eventually, however, it is destined to be the ruling governmental authority over the entire earth: "And in the days of these kings shall the God of heaven set up a kingdom, which shall never be destroyed: and the kingdom shall not be left to other people, but it shall break in pieces and consume all these kingdoms, and it shall stand for ever" (Daniel 2:44).

With the return of Christ to the earth and the beginning of his millennial reign, this great theocracy and Jesus' dominion over all the earth will begin: "And the kingdom and dominion, and the greatness of the kingdom under the whole heaven, shall be given to the people of the saints of the most High, whose kingdom is an everlasting kingdom, and all dominions shall serve and obey him" (Daniel 7:27).

As noted earlier, with his appearance at Adam-ondi-Ahman, Jesus will be given "dominion, and glory, and a kingdom, that all people, nations, and languages, should serve him" (Daniel 7:14).

> Wherefore, hear my voice and follow me, and you shall be a free people, and ye shall have no laws but my laws when I come, for I am your lawgiver, and what can stay my hand? (D&C 38:22)

> For the Lord shall be in their midst, and his glory shall be upon them, and he will be their king and their lawgiver. (D&C 45:59)

This great new world government under Christ will be administered out of both old Jerusalem and the New Jerusalem: "For out of Zion shall go forth the law, and the word of the Lord from Jerusalem" (Isaiah 2:4).

And the subordinate administrators of this new government will be entirely different from any heretofore known upon the earth. They will consist of many who were present at the council of Adam-ondi-Ahman as well as by many living during the Millennium—all representatives of the ancient and modern priesthood of the Church: "Christ and the resurrected saints will reign over the earth during the thousand years. They will not probably dwell upon the earth, but will visit it when they please, or when it is necessary to govern it."[16]

This great global government will be characterized, as opposed to the sad theocracies of man's past, by complete righteousness, humility, cooperation, and love in absolute conformity with God's laws, which his prophets have been preaching for thousands of years.

Temple Work

For the first century after the Restoration, only twelve temples existed, mostly in the Intermountain West. Nevertheless, the importance of temple work has always been an integral part of Latter-day Saint belief and practice. Since those first one hundred years, we have seen a marked acceleration of temple building activity. There are now more than one hundred temples scattered throughout the world, with more under construction or on planning boards.

This increase will continue into and throughout the Millennium. Church members are repeatedly urged to accumulate their family history data and see to it that temple work is done for their ancestors, as well as for others perhaps not in their family tree. As a result, the Church's family history database is now the largest and most comprehensive in the world. Nevertheless, a vast amount of temple work remains to be done.

A major problem, however, exists in retrieving family history data for more than a few generations due to the unavailability of accurate records in many parts of the world. Many family records have been lost or destroyed, and many were not kept at all. For this reason, there are tens of millions of our ancestors who remain unaccounted for—our forefathers who may well be waiting for their temple work to be done.

The Millennium will, therefore, be the time set aside for their ordinances to take place. Temple construction will continue to accelerate, and we will have assistance in finding and organizing all the records that are now unavailable.

Resurrected beings will assist in finding and organizing missing records and seeing to it that proper temple work is done. Records will be made available back to the beginning of man's time on the earth. And finally, due to the ignorance and shortcomings of men over the centuries, errors made in genealogical records and in temple ordinances (which are unavoidable despite the Church's many safeguards in this respect) will be rectified with this heavenly assistance.[17]

A New, Different, and Better World

As described throughout this chapter, the scriptures, especially latter-day scriptures and commentary from Church authorities, have provided us with a great deal of information about what we can expect during the Millennium. However, there is a great paucity of information as well. To expand on our previous commentary, numerous things deserve further discussion—or speculation. In other words, what can we as individuals expect the millennial world around us to be like?

We have noted some of the physical changes that will take place in the earth itself, most of which will be dramatic and will entirely alter the way we will live. For example, the earth will no longer be a sphere of oceans interspersed with continents and islands. Instead, we will be living on a globe with a single massive continent surrounded by an even more massive ocean.

Scientists, geologists, and geographers have long brandished about the concept of continental drift—the contention (which is fairly well established) that earth's landmasses (continents) are slowly moving about on the earth's crust, propelled by shifts in the mantle beneath. This movement is very slow—only inches a year in most places—but over time—thousands and millions of years—great shifts in the earth's surface are the result. For example, continental movement of only three inches a year will mean movement of a continent over forty miles during a period of a million years.

As a result of this movement, continents understandably have a tendency to drift away from each other in some places (as is the case between Europe and America due to the widening of the mid-Atlantic ridge, which is spreading at substantially more than three inches a year). In other places, continents are bumping into each other, as is the case in south Asia where two great crustal plates, the African plate and the Austral-Indian plate, are pushing northward against India. When these ponderous collisions[18] occur, the result is the buckling of landmasses where they meet—causing mountains to be pushed upward (as is the case with the Himalayas in northern India and Tibet)—earthquakes, and volcanic activity. These "collisions" are also taking place around the Pacific rim as identified by the same signs in Japan, the Philippines, the Aleutian Islands, Alaska, the western United States, and the Andes of South America. It is well to underscore the fact that this process is so slow that mountains may be pushed upward at only fractions of an inch per year, and earthquakes (which occur at places of stress and distortion in the earth's crust) may occur only sporadically as the crustal forces slowly increase from the colliding plates or continents.

It is interesting to note in all this that scientists, when discussing continental drift, contend that at one time (250 million years ago) all the earth's continents were a single landmass, Pangaea, located on the equator. This idea is remarkably similar to the scriptures' contention that at the time of Adam and the Garden of Eden, all the continents were joined into one landmass but became separated as they are now after the fall of Adam.

As far as the Millennium is concerned, we are told that at the time of Jesus' second coming, or shortly thereafter, the continents will again be joined as they originally were. We are also told by the prophets that other massive changes in the earth will occur at the same time: the mountains and the islands of the seas will disappear, and the seas will heave themselves beyond their bounds (D&C 88:90) It could well be that all these things will be interrelated—a consequence of the great earthquake that will wreak havoc when Jesus sets his feet upon the Mount of Olives. It seems probable that that same earthquake will cause or accompany a radical acceleration in reverse continental drift, which could easily spawn great storms, tidal waves, and volcanoes[19]—all a part of the great destruction and calamities that will befall unrepentant mankind before Jesus' millennial reign.

Other noteworthy changes will also occur related to the joining of the continents. The scriptures tell us that the millennial earth will be as the Garden of Eden, with a pleasant climate—no deserts, no mountains, and no wintertime. Climatologists and meteorologists will confirm the fact that the weather, and climates, that we now find around us are a complex interaction between the earth's atmosphere, ocean currents, the landmasses, incoming sunlight, and our north-south location on the globe. The complexity of this interaction among so many variables is the reason that weather forecasts have historically been notoriously unreliable. The earth's atmosphere is constantly moving and churning about, much the same as eddies and currents in a stream. Warmth and moisture are picked up from the oceans and redistributed to the continents. At the same time, continents deflect the air movement in different directions (as does the rotation of the earth on its axis). These great deflections and atmospheric swirling movements are also affected by the seasons.

During the Millennium when the earth will consist of only a single landmass and a single great ocean, all of this will change. Surrounded by this great mass of water, with no mountains—and assuming that our single great continent will be equatorially located—the earth's climate will be predictably more stable, warm, and moist, just as we are told the Garden of Eden was. A familiar example might be the Hawaiian Islands, surrounded by the Pacific, which are notorious for their warm year-round climate and balmy moist weather.[20] Scientists contend that Pangaea was also warm, moist, and tropical.

Of course, it is difficult to accurately assess how all this will truly fall into place as the Millennium commences. Scientists can only speculate and theorize what will become of our climate and weather systems on a globe with a single continent surrounded by a huge ocean. But the idea that it will be a lush, tropical paradise sounds plausible indeed.

As a result of these changes in earth's geography and Christ's rule, large-scale changes in man's society can also be expected during the Millennium. These changes will affect all of us and will result in a society much different than the one in which we now live. Nevertheless, many things may not change.

One significant social—or economic—change will be the fact that money will no longer exist during the Millennium because we will be living the cooperative law of consecration. The elimination of money will mean the corresponding disappearance of many things that are now so much a part of our lives: no international currency, no stock markets, no bank accounts, no retirement plans, no insurance, and so on. Our needs will be met through our own work and the willing sharing of those around us. As a result, poverty will disappear, and we will no longer fear disabilities or old age. We will no longer worry about our checking accounts or living from payday to payday, and much of the incentive for crime (amassing wealth) will be nonexistent. There will be an elimination of greed, economic classes, pride, and prestige—all of which were the frequent targets of Jesus' preaching.

With a society of brotherhood and peace, other harmful (yet necessary) trappings of our present world will also go by the wayside. For example, many of the laws in this country, as well as in many other countries around the world, are directed entirely at controlling (or trying to eliminate) harmful elements in our society. We have, for example, hundreds of laws proscribing fraud, prostitution, counterfeiting, and murder. Even our traffic laws may well fall into this category. Many of these laws also have to do with misusing our monetary system, such as stock market fraud, embezzlement, tax fraud, racketeering, and the like. The need for these laws will disappear in a moneyless society.

Other similar laws exist to prevent us from physically harming one another, such as laws against murder, rape, battery, and destruction of property. These acts too will disappear in a society of brotherhood, peace, and love. In such a society, agencies like police departments, military establishments, and government investigative agencies (the FBI, the CIA, the FSA), and the like will prove unnecessary. It is a sad commentary that throughout man's history such law enforcement and military expenditures have drained away a massive amount of our time, energy, and worldly wealth at the expense of other urgent humane necessities just to keep us under control—albeit ineffectively.

Even taxation by government will be eliminated in a moneyless society, especially a society with Jesus at its head that practices brotherly consecration of all we have to one another in peace and cooperation.

The gigantic health care industry will be another casualty of the new Millennium. In a world of no illness and a peaceful transition from mortality to immortality, we will no longer be concerned with doctors, hospitals, medications, health insurance plans, and funerals. Accompanying their loss will be no more attorneys, funeral expenses, or estate planning, and no more invalids, nursing homes, or disability programs. Of course, we will no longer have to concern ourselves with acquiring an inheritance from our elders or passing an inheritance on to our offspring.

Will we continue to have sporting events? It is likely that professional sports will disappear with no money around, but amateur sports could easily continue as they do now with church leagues, community teams, and the like. However, forget about the Super Bowl, the World Series, professional golf tournaments, international soccer games, and other high profile professional competition. It is likely that in a society dedicated to temple work, learning, and preparation for eternal life, even amateur sporting activities may be low on our priority lists.

Political parties and campaigns will become meaningless, especially since throughout history they have been prone to corruption, deceit, and divisiveness. In this respect, a one-world government under the leadership of the Savior will be a distinct relief to many.

Much of what was once commerce will also change drastically during the Millennium. International trade will be no more, and our entire system of trade will, of necessity, be reconfigured to fit the new geography of a new world. Assuming that we will still rely on airplanes, roads, and rail, these modes of transportation will become increasingly important but may well become rapidly obsolete when we, with our expanding knowledge, find other, better ways to move things around.

Our education "industry" will change radically. The scriptures tell us that we will have access to amazing knowledge during the Millennium, so it can well be expected that our education will continue, but our educational institutions will change. No longer will there be need for law degrees, medical degrees, psychiatric degrees, and economics or business degrees. Instead, we will probably learn new ways to raise food and care for one another. Even geographers and geologists will have much to learn about their new world. For example, how will lakes and rivers be situated on a flat continent?

But what about the physical things of life, those worldly things that we now surround ourselves with and consider life's necessities? Many of life's present accouterments will still be around, but many others may be more questionable, such as large elaborate homes ("in the right neighborhood"), automobiles, computers, home entertainment systems, recreational "toys" (boats, snowmobiles, motor homes, jet skis, off-road vehicles, and the like), television, and on and on.

The scriptures and our latter-day prophets have made it clear that we will be resurrected with much the same personality and attributes that we now possess—the same talents, interests, and knowledge. We can then reasonably expect that we will follow many of the same pursuits and interests as we do now, but we will most assuredly find it necessary to make many adjustments in them to fit into our new world.

All these changes, plus many we cannot yet conceive of, will mean a drastic transformation in our world, ourselves, and our priorities. Instead of holding on to the trappings of the past thousands of years—earning money, prestige, and getting ahead—we will at last be able to focus exclusively on those things of eternal importance. And they are the same things that Jesus and the prophets taught: loving one another, gaining knowledge, and being with our loved ones forever.

The End of the Millennium

A thousand years seems like a long time from our mortal and earthly perspective. But in terms of the earth's history, and even more so in terms of eternity (which, by definition, is *infinity*), it will pass quickly. And it will be a period dedicated to temple work and the preparation of God's children for their place throughout the remainder of eternity.

Near the close of this great thousand-year period, Satan will have his last opportunity to lure mankind away from God and the plan of salvation. He will again be loosed upon the earth in his final rebellion against the Lord.

Why men may be tempted to turn away from God may be difficult to understand since mankind at that time will have just completed ten centuries of peace and brotherhood under Christ's rule. Great progress will have been made, and men will have lived without suffering, sorrow, pain, or fear of dying. It would then seem that without such worldly cares, which we all now must endure, that all men would realize their blessings and want that earthly paradise to continue.

However, with human nature being what it is and with the renewed stirrings of Satan and his hosts, many will apparently find the benevolent theocracy of Christ repressive and perhaps boring. Man will become restless and dissatisfied with the blessings he has. Prompted by Satan—assuredly with promises of better things, excitement, and a release from stifling religion—many will turn against their Savior. And once again, we find that history will repeat itself. The scriptures tell us that at the end of the Millennium,

> He [Satan] shall be loosed for a little season, that he may gather together his armies. And Michael, the seventh angel, even the archangel, shall gather together his armies, even the hosts of heaven. And the devil shall gather together his armies; even the hosts of hell,

> and shall come up to battle against Michael and his armies. And then cometh the battle of the great God; and the devil and his armies shall be cast away into their own place, that they shall not have power over the saints any more at all. (D&C 88:111–14)

Although the Lord and the righteous throughout history have long contended with Satan, this last war will apparently be even greater than the battle of Armageddon, including all the strife and conflicts leading up to it. As the scriptures above state, Satan "shall gather together his armies; even the hosts of hell." He will surely have a massive army—all those who joined him in the premortal existence (one-third of mankind), plus those who will join him during the Millennium (although those who have lead a telestial life will not yet have been resurrected).

Contending with him will be Michael joined by "the hosts of heaven."

How this great war will be fought we do not know because weapons during the Millennium will surely be nonexistent, artifacts of a sordid past—our time. The outcome, however, is clear:

> And when the thousand years are expired, Satan shall be loosed out of his prison, and shall go out to deceive the nations which are in the four quarters of the earth, Gog and Magog, to gather them together to battle: the number of whom is as the sand of the sea. And they went up on the breadth of the earth, and compassed the camp of the saints about, and the beloved city: and fire came down from God out of heaven, and devoured them. And the devil that deceived them was cast into the lake of fire and brimstone, where the beast and the false prophet are, and shall be tormented day and night for ever and ever." (Revelation 20:7–10)

Following this last, great battle, several final things will take place. One will be the final resurrection—that of the wicked who have led a telestial existence. Also, the earth as we know it, and as it will be during the Millennium, will end. As Elder McConkie says,

"It will attain its final destiny as a celestial sphere, and the meek shall inherit it forever."[21]

> It is decreed that the poor and the meek of the earth shall inherit it. Therefore, it must needs be sanctified from all unrighteousness that it may be prepared for the celestial glory; for after it hath filled the measure of its creation, it shall be crowned with glory, even with the presence of God the Father; that bodies who are of the celestial kingdom may possess it forever and ever; for, for this intent was it made and created, and for this intent are they sanctified. (D&C 88:17–20)

This sanctification of the earth at the end of the Millennium was well summarized by Parley P. Pratt: "Man is destined forever to inherit this self-same planet, upon which he was first created; which shall be redeemed, sanctified, renewed, purified, and prepared as an eternal inheritance for immortality and eternal life, with the holy city for its capital, the throne of God in the midst, for its seat of government."[22]

Apparently, as part of the process of sanctifying the earth, the New Jerusalem—as was the case with the City of Enoch in the Old Testament—will be taken up into heaven:

> It is intended that it [the New Jerusalem] will be taken up to heaven, when the earth passes away. It is intended to be one of those choice and holy places, where the Lord will dwell, when he shall visit from time to time, in the midst of the great latter-day Zion, after it shall be connected with the city of Enoch.[23]

Besides being "resurrected" to celestial glory as the eventual dwelling place for those who have lived a celestial mortal life, what then will become of the earth as we have known it? Brigham Young said:

> When the earth was framed and brought into existence and man was placed upon it, it was near the

> throne of our Father in Heaven. And when man fell . . . the earth fell into space, and took up its abode in this planetary system, and the sun became our light. . . . This is the glory the earth came from, and when it is glorified it will return again unto the presence of the Father.[24]

Notes

1. Bruce R. McConkie, *Mormon Doctrine,* 2d ed. (Salt Lake City: Bookcraft 1966), 492. Much of this chapter is based on Elder McConkie, who provides the most authoritative and comprehensive discussion of the Millennium available to Latter-day Saints.

2. Ibid., 494.

3. Two items in this wording are worthy of note: The first is that this reconfiguration of the earth accompanying the great earthquake upon the return of Christ will happen amidst great noise—"the voice of many waters" and "the voice of a great thunder." The second is that "the great deep" will be "driven back into the north countries." The bulk of the earth's oceans exist in the south seas, south of the equator: the South Pacific, the South Atlantic, and the Indian Ocean. Their movement northward, then, makes good sense.

4. When the landmasses of the globe are joined together into a single landmass, as the prophecies foretell, it could be speculated that this will mean a massive alteration of continental drift associated with the great earthquake that will occur upon Christ's return to the earth. We can also assume that great climate changes will occur, presumably turning into global temperate and tropical climatic regimes.

5. Joseph Fielding McConkie, *Straightforward Answers to Tough Gospel Questions* (Salt Lake City: Deseret Book, 1998), 125; see also Joseph Smith, *History of The Church of Jesus Christ of Latter-day Saints* (Salt Lake City: The Church of Jesus Christ of Latter-day Saints, 1932–1956), 4:553.

6. We may well ask why it will be necessary to release Satan again after he has been vanquished. The reason for this last great war has not been revealed to us.

7. Joseph Fielding Smith also referred to this as "a sort of translation."

8. For those who have ever wondered about it, those who remain in mortality during the Millennium will still undergo a probationary period during that time just as we do (although it seems that living in a peaceful, loving society without the influence of Satan, and under the rule of the Savior, will be much more conducive to a good probationary outcome than we who live now can expect).

9. McConkie, *Mormon Doctrine,* 499.

10. Brigham Young, in *Journal of Discourses* (London: Latter-day Saints' Book Depot, 1854–1886), 12:274; 2:316.

11. Speaking of the period after the return of Jesus, Zechariah couches his prophecies in symbolism and terminology familiar in Old Testament times (for example, "the feast of tabernacles"). And as did John the Revelator, who used the term Babylon to refer to the apostate world, Zechariah used the term Egypt for the same purpose.

12. Joseph Smith, *Teachings of the Prophet Joseph Smith* (Salt Lake City: Deseret Book, 1976), 268.

13. The repressive influence of theocracies was a major force behind Europe's Dark Ages (500–1000 A.D.).

14. Even to this day, most such governments levy a religion or church tax, payable to the governing religion, on their populace.

15. Freedom of religion, as mentioned in the First Amendment, provides for the establishment of religion in this country and the freedom to practice it, both without government interference ("Congress shall make no law respecting an establishment of religion, or prohibiting the free exercise thereof"). Of late, however, many extreme atheistic elements in our society have begun construing the simplicity of this statement to mean "freedom *from* religion," that religion should have no place whatsoever in our government at any level. This is far from the original intent of the framers of the Constitution, many of whom were devoutly religious. As a matter of fact, both George Washington and Abraham Lincoln, two of our greatest presidents, often invoked the name of God in the functions of their offices.

16. Joseph Smith, *Teachings,* 268; see also Revelation 5:10; 20:4.

17. Joseph Fielding Smith, *Doctrines of Salvation* (Salt Lake City: Bookcraft, 1954–1956), 2:251–52.

18. "Collision" is probably not the most apt word to describe this process since it implies rapidity. On the contrary, these plates are pushing and grinding against each other so slowly that it would take several human generations to clearly perceive what is going on.

19. How the flattening of the mountains could occur at the same time remains to be seen. Related to this will be the disappearance of islands that in most cases are simply mountaintops extending upward from the ocean floor to above the ocean surface. When the earth's mountains are "brought low," of course, islands too will disappear. Rapid reverse continental drift, which the scriptures imply, will be a truly remarkable event, although it will spell worldwide doom and disaster everywhere for mankind. How this will be done is beyond the wildest speculation of modern earth scientists, but it is certainly not beyond the Lord's capabilities.

20. Central heating and cooling, as well as expensive insulation and double-pane windows, are relatively unknown in Hawaii. Residents can simply step out onto their *lanai* (porch) to enjoy the warm tropical breezes.

21. McConkie, *Mormon Doctrine,* 501.

22. Parley P. Pratt, *A Voice of Warning* (New York: Eastern States Mission, 1890), 43.
23. Orson Pratt, in *Journal of Discourses,* 21:153.
24. Brigham Young, in *Journal of Discourses,* 17:143.

CONCLUSION

There is little doubt that many readers will find the preceding chapters both controversial and thought provoking. But, as the title of this book implies, the last days of man's mortality here on earth will be marked by gloom—a period of testing, death, and destruction—followed by a thousand years of peace, hope, and brotherly love.

From the days of Jesus to our own time, people have long speculated what these last times would truly be like. In the past, Bible scholars and laymen alike have had only the words of ancient prophets to guide them in this respect. But now we have latter-day scripture and the words of modern Church authorities, which have added great detail to biblical prophecies. In addition, we have a wealth of information from historians and scientists to fill in some of the gaps in the religious accounts, although scientific and religious accounts are occasionally difficult to reconcile with one another.

For these reasons, I have attempted to combine the two wherever possible and as completely as I could. Of course, there are many places where gaps and irreconcilable differences remain, but I hope that the end result will be a better understanding of the age-old question: What will it *really* be like during the last days?

Many Christians, as well as those of other religions, have had nebulous ideas of what the last days will entail. Questions have always outnumbered answers. I have attempted to provide some answers, although the fact remains that much of this book consists of speculation and educated guesses. Nevertheless, the speculation is based on the best scientific knowledge and religious sources available. That notwithstanding, some of the conclusions may be wrong, but they assuredly provide meaningful information.

It is human nature to want to know what will happen in the future. We are all concerned about where our lives are going, about our own mortality, and about what our personal eternity will be like.

Yes, there will be a battle of Armageddon, but it will be preceded by many of the signs of the times that Christianity has long postulated. Although some of these signs are already coming to pass (wars and rumors of wars, false prophets, the Apostasy, the establishment of the state of Israel, the restoration of the Church, and the spread of the gospel throughout the world), others are apparently still in our future. We have not yet seen a marked increase in the natural calamities that the scriptures give us dire warnings of, probably because they will occur closer to the Second Coming than has traditionally been believed. Great earthquakes, storms, tidal waves, pestilence, and starvation are still awaiting us as the end draws nearer. Whether some of these will be caused by asteroid impacts, super volcanos, or other similar natural disasters, as I have speculated, remains to be seen.

The few years preceding the great climax of Christ's appearance will be marked by several events, among them the building of the New Jerusalem in Missouri and the rebuilding of ancient Jerusalem and its historic temple in the Holy Land. The lost tribes too must make their return. And mankind will fall further into unrighteousness. Instability and turmoil throughout the world will increase.

Eventually, the great new leader of the world, the anti-Christ,[1] will appear on the scene, and under his leadership, the entire world will teeter on the edge of chaos. Hatred and strife will mark his regime; civil turmoil and increasing wars will be the result. Those who remain true to the Lord and refuse to worship the anti-Christ or accept his mark will suffer repression and persecution. Only those who remain close to the Church, especially those in the New Jerusalem, will enjoy divine protection, but even then many Church members can expect persecution, suffering, and even death.

During the anti-Christ's reign, the world, including the United States, will sink to a state of war and civil turmoil that only divine intervention can stop. Satan will have reached the climax of his power here on the earth and will appear on the verge of victory in his ancient war with God over the souls of men.

At that crucial time, the Middle East, which has been a festering trouble spot for centuries, will be the site of the greatest war the world has ever known—the battle of Armageddon. Massive armies under the command of Satan will descend upon the nation of Israel, intent on destroying it and its historic temple, finally and forever. Faced with such an obviously invincible army, Israel will mount any kind of adequate defense to prevent its annihilation. Perhaps the United States and other countries will be drawn into this battle, but it will be only the direct intervention of the Lord that will save the Jews.[2] During this pivotal time, when the forces of the Israelis are on the verge of defeat and Jerusalem itself is under siege, two prophets of God will minister to the Jews and unleash the wrath of God on the surrounding heathen armies. Nevertheless, even the two prophets will eventually be killed, their bodies left in the streets as symbols of the fate that awaits Jerusalem. However, they will arise after three days, just as the enemy prepares to launch its final assault.

This last great act of godlessness will, however, be prevented by Jesus himself returning to the earth as long promised, surrounded by the hosts of heaven, as well as by many who have been taken up or resurrected from their graves to accompany him. As the Savior's feet touch the Mount of Olives, the heathen armies will at last meet their match.

The scriptures are clear that Jesus' return will be accompanied by an earthquake greater than any the earth has ever known. The wrath of God will be unleashed not only upon the armies bent on destroying Jerusalem but also upon unrepentant mankind throughout the world. It is promised that at this time Babylon (the heathen nations) will be ravaged by tidal waves, fire, storms, pestilence, and more. When these great tribulations end, only those who accept Jesus as their Savior and divine king over the entire earth will remain alive.

Prior to Jesus' return, however, he will appear privately to the leadership of The Church of Jesus Christ of Latter-day Saints at Adam-ondi-Ahman in Missouri, accompanied by his resurrected prophets and apostles from all the centuries past. This great council will be a time of accounting and will be highlighted by Jesus assuming personal leadership of the Church and of all mankind on earth. Only after this historic meeting will he appear to the world on the Mount of Olives and through force proclaim his rule over the earth.

This is the time that Christianity has long awaited and will be greeted with joy and thanksgiving by those still upon the earth, who have lived lives worthy enough to meet him. Many more will be resurrected at this time in the morning of the first resurrection.

The government instituted by Jesus will be administered through many resurrected and mortal beings. It will be a government of peace and love, so much so that Satan will be bound—removed from the earth for the first time in man's existence. The earth, which will undergo great physical changes at the time of Jesus' coming or shortly thereafter, will again resemble the Garden of Eden, a paradise of warmth and tranquility. All life will live in peaceful coexistence. Illness, suffering, war, and sorrow will be unknown. Death will not be a time to be feared, but a quick, welcome transition into immortality. Man will be dedicated to a great expansion of the temple work that we see around us now with assistance from heavenly beings. Knowledge will be made available to us all, making the Millennium a time of great learning and preparation for our eternal lives.

This will be a thousand years of happiness and progress unthought of in human history. It will make the preceding millennia of man seem sordid and primitive. Except for the great winnowing (the refiner's fire) that the world will experience when the end comes, it will be a time to look forward to—a time foreseen by all of us in the premortal existence.

As the Millennium runs its course, however, Satan will eventually be given his freedom to again tempt mankind and will again win many converts. A last great battle will ensue with Satan and his forces from hell arrayed against Michael and the hosts of heaven. In that last great battle, Satan and his army will at last be vanquished forever, the resurrection of those who lived a telestial existence will take place, and the earth will be prepared for its own celestial existence.

The course of this is much the same as the course in many of our lives, except here it is a course that will determine our personal eternities. Just as it usually takes great effort and trials to gain something worthwhile in this world, in precisely the same manner will we all be tested to gain our own place in the Millennium. We won't necessarily be perfect when we get there, but under the personal administration of Jesus Christ during those thousand years, we will have the opportunity to learn, gain experience, and move ever closer to the perfection required of those aspiring to the celestial kingdom. The horrific years prior to and during the battle of Armageddon will be worse than any known throughout the history of mankind, but they will pass, and when Jesus gathers the great council at Adam-ondi-Ahman, we will all be able to cheer and give thanks that thereafter the earth will be a better place for us and our loved ones.

Only then will Jesus' message of love and peace become an eternal reality: "For behold, this is my work and my glory—to bring to pass the immortality and eternal life of man" (Moses 1:39).

Notes

1. He will most assuredly not call himself the anti-Christ and will probably be difficult to recognize for a time until his grip on the world is assured.

2. Whether nuclear weapons will be used during this great war is unclear. Certainly the scriptures give us no hint of them except perhaps indirectly when the prophets have spoken of fire and brimstone coming down from the heavens.

About the Author

Brent Davis, a lifelong Latter-day Saint, was born and raised in Idaho and Utah. He served a mission to Switzerland and has spent several years as a Gospel Doctrine teacher.

He graduated from the University of Utah with a bachelor's degree in physical geography. He also holds a master's degree in geography from Indiana University. As an adult, he has maintained an avid interest in earth sciences, particularly climatology, archaeology, ecology, and paleontology. Besides his continual studies in those areas, he can frequently be found in the backwoods of Utah digging fossils, camping, fishing, and collecting artifacts.

Over the years, Brent has worked as an accountant, office manager, and business owner in Spokane, Washington. In addition, he has traveled widely, visiting the Far East, Europe, and South Africa—all the while looking at rocks, artifacts, and flora and fauna. Currently, he manages a business newspaper in Logan, Utah.

Brent resides in southeastern Idaho with his wife, Inge. They have two grown children who have families of their own.

0 26575 77654 6

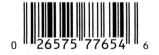